BLACK AMERICA SERIES

CHATTANOOGA

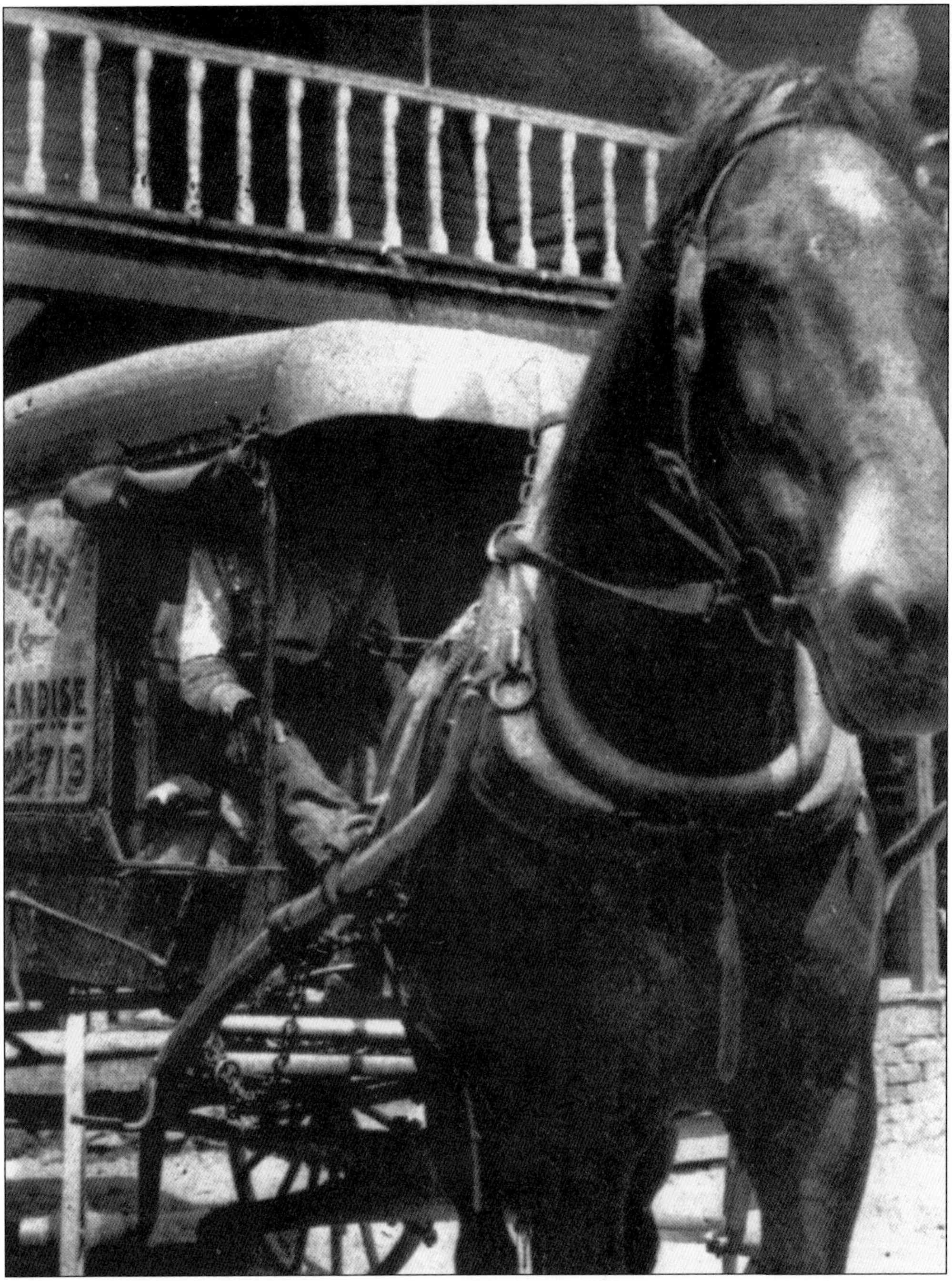

In the 1890s, the Speight family opened the first grocery store on Lookout Mountain, which was run out of their home on East and West Road. Mr. Speight delivered groceries up and down the mountain. Some of the land containing the Speights' home was later donated for the first black school.

BLACK AMERICA SERIES

CHATTANOOGA

The Chattanooga African American Museum

ARCADIA PUBLISHING

ISBN 978-0-7385-1843-5

Published by Arcadia Publishing
Charleston, South Carolina

Printed in the United States of America

Library of Congress Catalog Card Number: 2005928576

For all general information contact Arcadia Publishing at:
Telephone 843-853-2070
Fax 843-853-0044
E-mail sales@arcadiapublishing.com
For customer service and orders:
Toll-Free 1-888-313-2665

Visit us on the Internet at www.arcadiapublishing.com

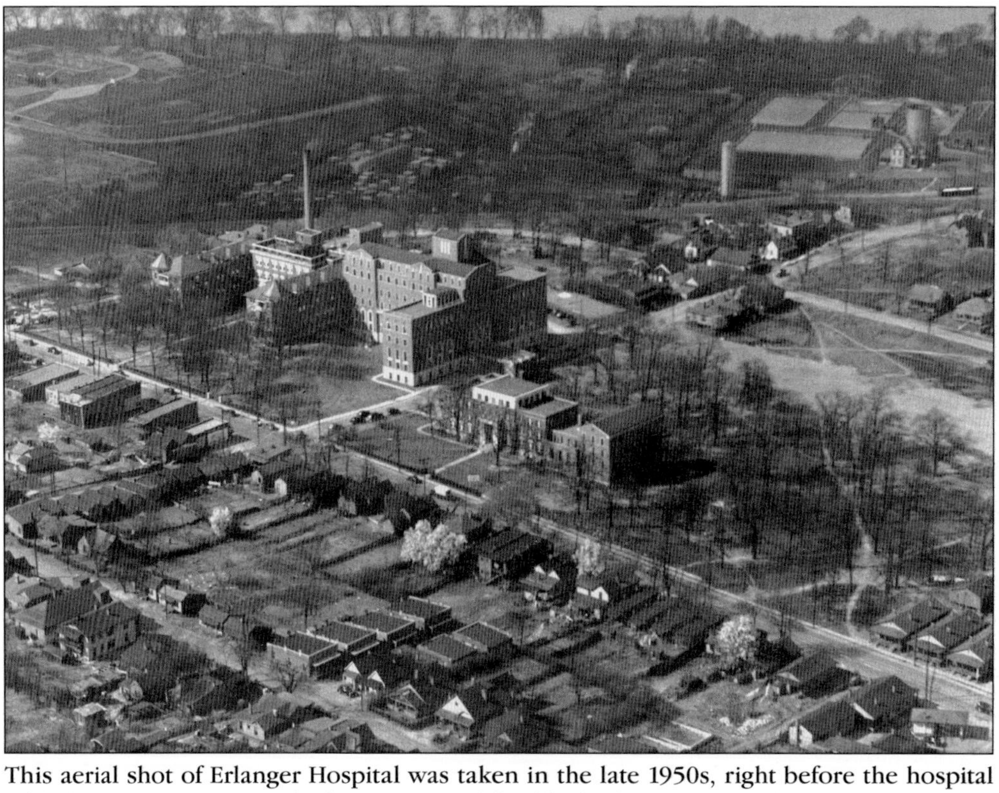

This aerial shot of Erlanger Hospital was taken in the late 1950s, right before the hospital added West Wing Four, which was created for black physicians to admit and treat their patients. In the late 1960s, the segregation of patients was discontinued. At that time, black doctors were able to practice and admit their patients to all floors at Erlanger.

Contents

ACKNOWLEDGMENTS

The Chattanooga African American Museum is grateful to the following agencies, individuals, institutions, and families for their assistance and cooperation in the compilation of this work:

Vilma Scruggs-Fields
Carmen Davis
Vivian Greene
Daphne Stargin
Danny Toney
Gerald Norwood
R. Bruce Wilkey
Raymond Evans
Gladys Paris
Henry Christian
David Allen for BJ Photography
C. William Payne
Marvin Cousin
Albert Fields
John Edwards for *Chattanooga Courier*
Adrian Edwards for *Chattanooga Courier*
Obie Dial
Herman Prater
Brazelton Studio
OK Studio
John Woods
James Photography
Chattanooga Times Free-Press
Warren Parker for Parker Unlimited

INTRODUCTION

African American heritage has a long history along the Tennessee River. In 1540, before any whites were in the area, there were some Africans with the Spanish expedition that passed a few miles to the east of present-day Chattanooga. More than 200 years later, when the Cherokee Indians moved into this area to support the British war effort during the American Revolution, they found some Africans already here. They had escaped from enslavement at the hands of whites. They were accepted into the Cherokee society.

The African American presence in Chattanooga has been felt and its contribution visibly noted for centuries. In what is now the Chattanooga area, a native community came into being called Ross's Landing. Pioneers crossed into Tennessee—then a part of North Carolina—in search of new land to call home, and they built many historical sites. By 1820, there were 821 people living here. Of these, 39 were enslaved Africans who belonged to the Cherokees, and 16 were free Africans, including wealthy doctors, lawyers, and businessmen. Some of the free Africans living among them went to Oklahoma during the removal of Native Americans.

In 1837, the Cherokees were forcibly displaced from Ross Landing, and the new settlers soon named the community Chattanooga. Unlike some other parts of the South, there were few plantations; most slaves were thought to be personal servants or laborers rather than field hands. Long gone were the contraband camps of tents and mud huts. No longer were blacks restricted and confined to riverbanks. Most were employed by the foundries and iron works. They became skilled as paddlers, straighteners, and molders. Some of the blacks started their own factories. The Rising Sun Manufacturing Company enjoyed a prosperous history, producing grates, fenders, and metal works.

By 1890, the African American population totaled 12,563. Chattanooga's African American families settled in all areas of the city, creating a community through the building of homes, schools, businesses, and churches.

After the Civil War, freedmen, churches, and associations raised thousands of dollars to build schools. The first free public school in Chattanooga was Howard High School for Blacks, founded by Rev. E. O. Tade in 1865. James A. Henry, an Atlanta University graduate, became the first black principal of Howard in 1884. Howard High School is now one of the historic sites of Chattanooga. Other schools were Chattanooga National Medical College, Zion College, National Business College, Strange Beauty College, and the Boone Higgins Trade School.

In the wake of the Civil War, the Chattanooga community experienced growth, development, and prosperity. New businesses were started and industries developed, and jobs were available. As a result, civic, social, fraternal, and business organizations were formed. Garden clubs, secret societies, youth organizations, and business groups gave proof that this was the beginning and the best was yet to come.

Chattanooga became the center of art and cultural development by using its churches, schools, and venues of entertainment to promote its social development. Local artists included such notables as the group Wings over Jordan, the Clevant Derrick Singers, Roland Hayes, Jimmy Blanton, the great queen of the Blues Bessie Smith, and many more.

From 1870 to 1910, blacks made up 40 percent of the population in Chattanooga. This created success in the political area. Hiram Tyree was one of the first to enter the political arena, serving as commissioner for 10 years. Others to gain political clout included Eugene Reid and Charles Grigsby. In 1886, William Hodge and Style L. Hutchins represented Hamilton County in the lower house of the general assembly.

The growth of social activities was highly visible in sports events from 1880 through 1930. The Black Choo Choos baseball team and the winning Howard High School football team of 1909 were the pride of the city.

More subtle and significant changes were taking place. Dr. Emma Wheeler and her husband opened the first black hospital. Fraternal societies such as the Masons and Shriners thrived with the active chapters. The first public high school in the city, Howard High School, was opened, and it was one of the most outstanding in the South.

African Americans have made their mark in the history of Chattanooga. At the present time, there are more than 10 historic sites in Chattanooga, including the home of Bessie Smith, Booker T. Washington Park, Wiley Memorial Church (the oldest African American church in the city), Wheeler Hospital (the first black hospital), Howard High School, and the Chattanooga African American Museum/Bessie Smith Hall (the first African American museum in the city).

History has been made, and the Chattanooga African American Museum's mission is to preserve it.

One

The Chattanooga African American Museum

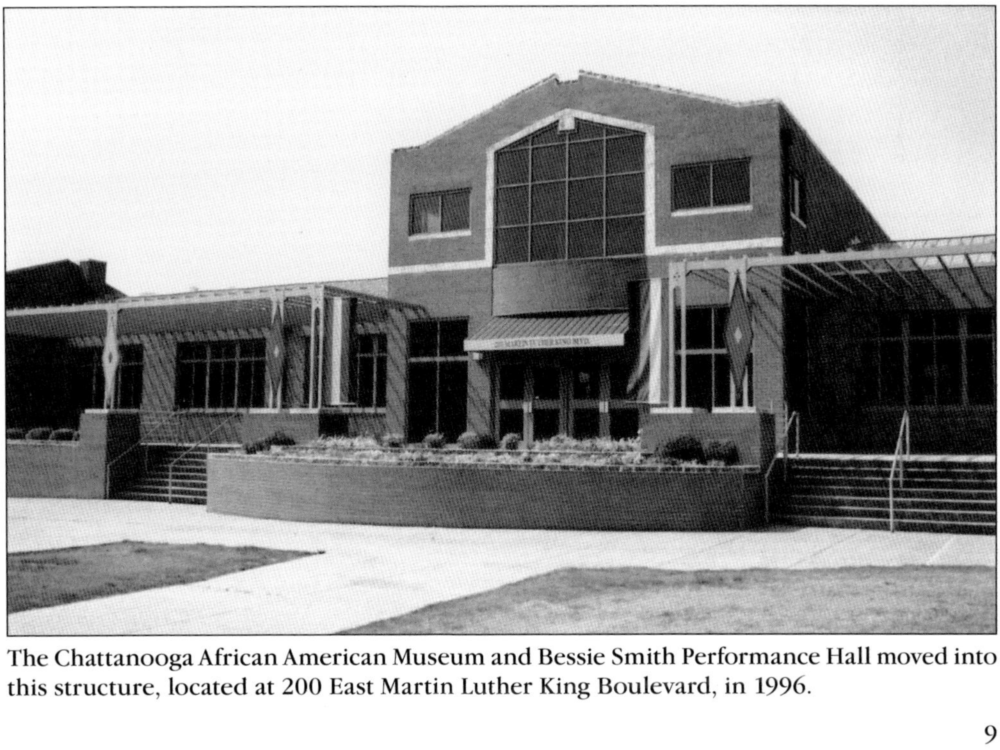

The Chattanooga African American Museum and Bessie Smith Performance Hall moved into this structure, located at 200 East Martin Luther King Boulevard, in 1996.

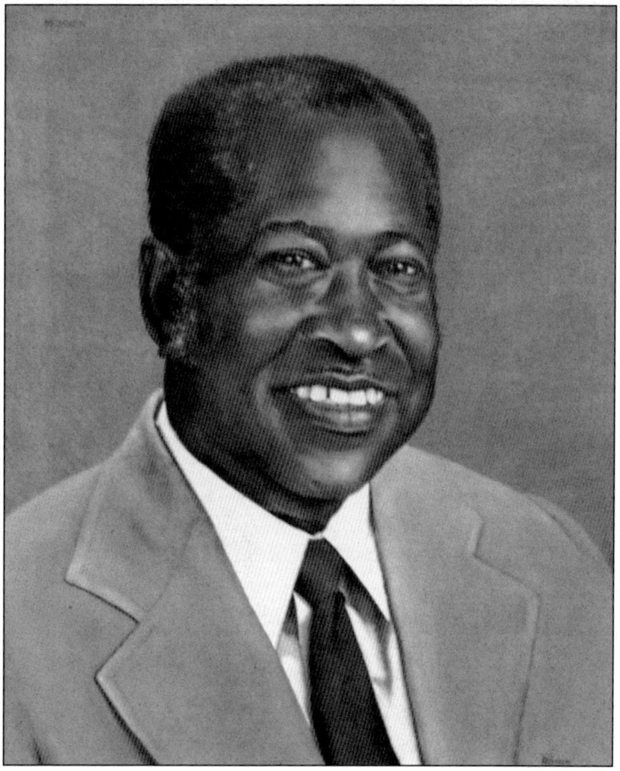

Roy C. Noel is the cofounder of the Chattanooga African American Museum (CAAM). Noel was a respected educator and businessman in the community. His business skills and community connections played a key role in putting together a committee of people to help form the museum.

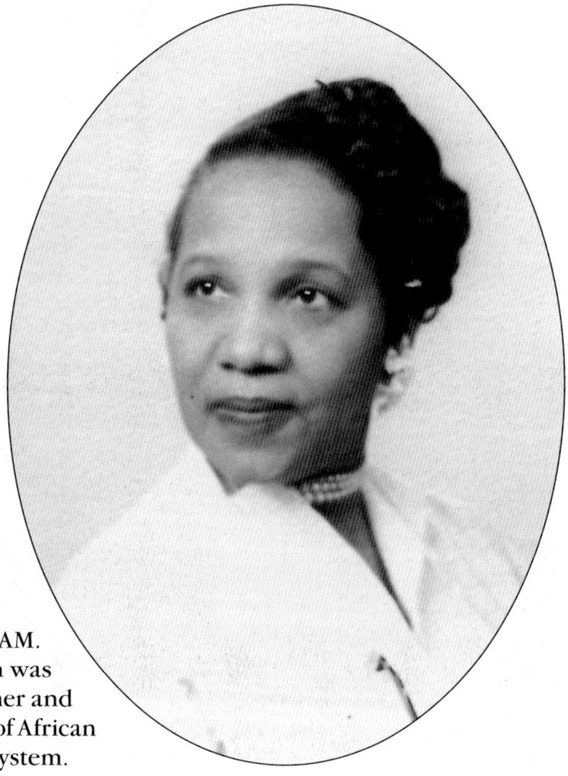

Jacola Goodwin is the cofounder of CAAM. CAAM was chartered in 1983. Goodwin was an outstanding elementary school teacher and an outspoken advocate for the teaching of African American history in the public school system.

In 1977, the Chattanooga African American Heritage Council was chartered by Roy C. Noel and Jacola Goodwin. This would mark the beginning of a quest to start the CAAM.

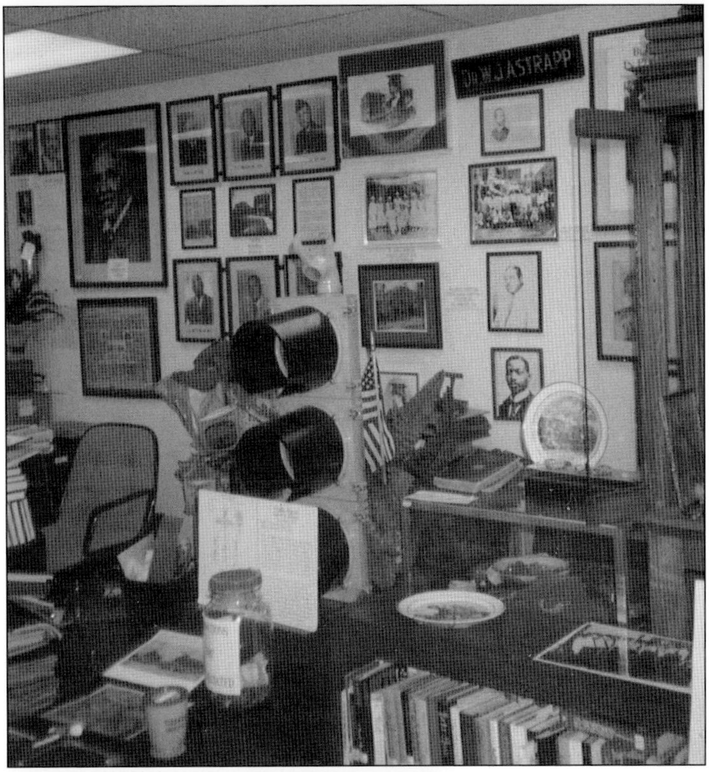

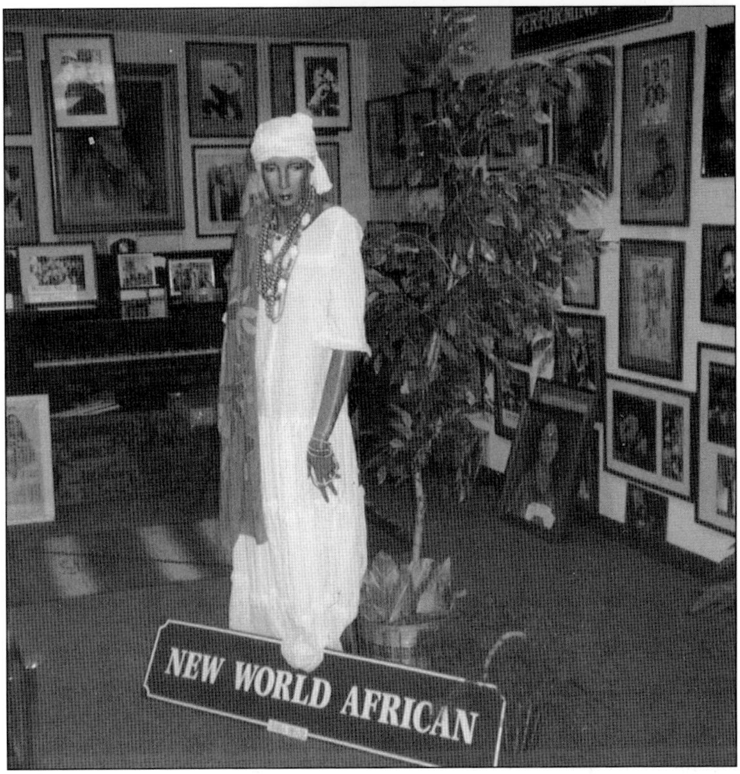

In 1983, the CAAM opened its doors. The original location was in the Central City Complex located on Martin Luther King Boulevard. The museum was located in one room of this building.

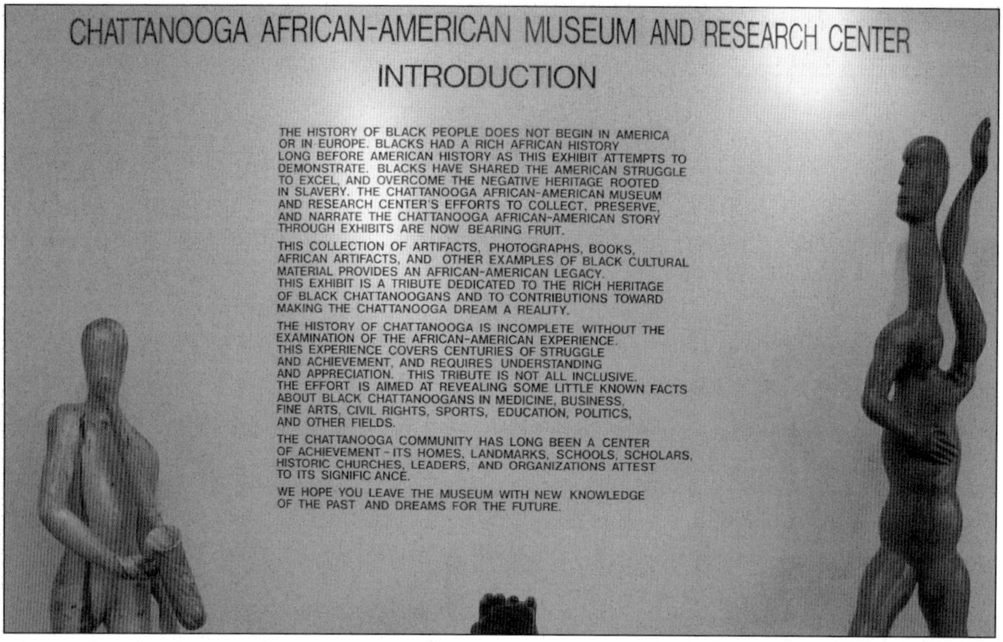

This is the entrance to the museum's current facility on East Martin Luther King Boulevard. The statues are by local sculptor Calvin Dennis. Dennis, a graduate of Howard High School, has been sculpting for over 20 years, and his works have been featured in the Hunter Museum of American Art, the Hamilton County Court House, and the office of the mayor of Chattanooga, Tennessee.

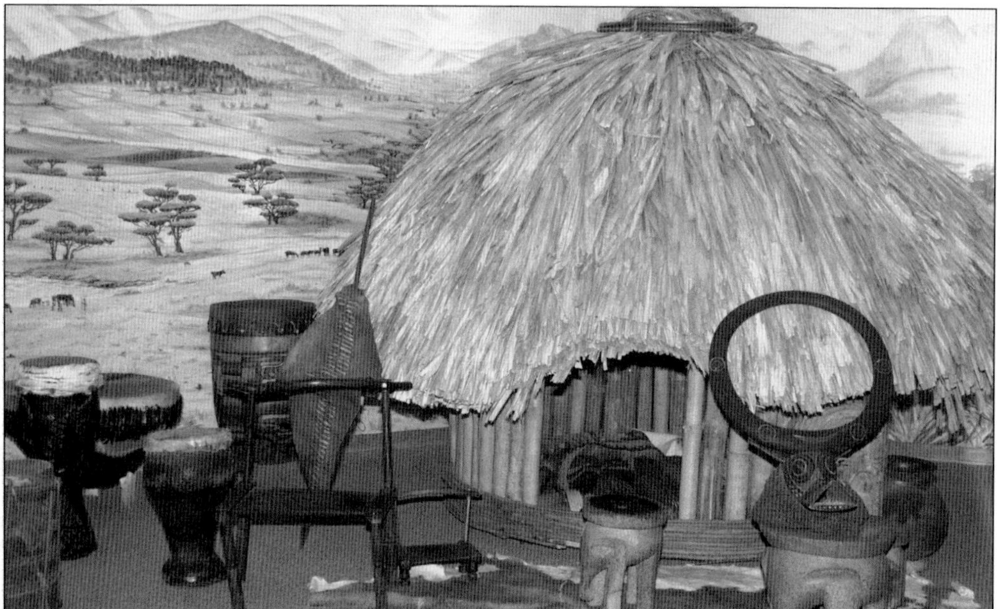

This replica of an African hut was constructed by Ormiston Edwards of Trinidad and is also located in the first part of the museum's current facility. The museum focuses on African and African American culture and history and specifically Chattanooga African American history and its contributions to the nation and community as a whole.

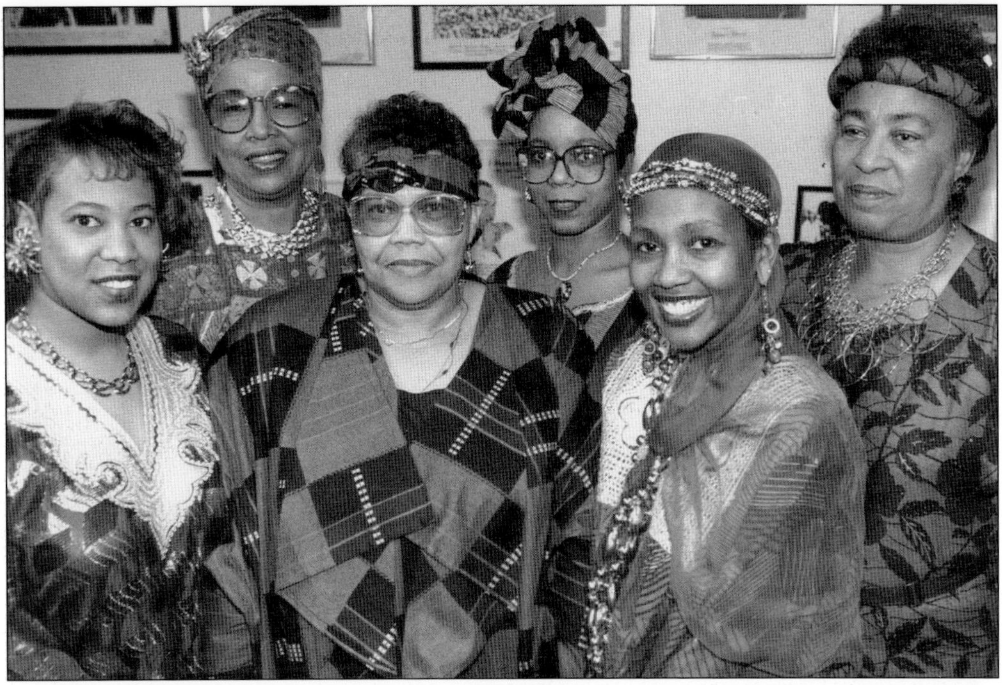

The Africana Ball was held annually from 1990 to 2001 in celebration of Black History Month. The ladies pictured from left to right are Nicelle Price-Gray, Tommie Bryson, Vivian Greene, Deidra Partridge, Debrah Carter, and Vilma Fields.

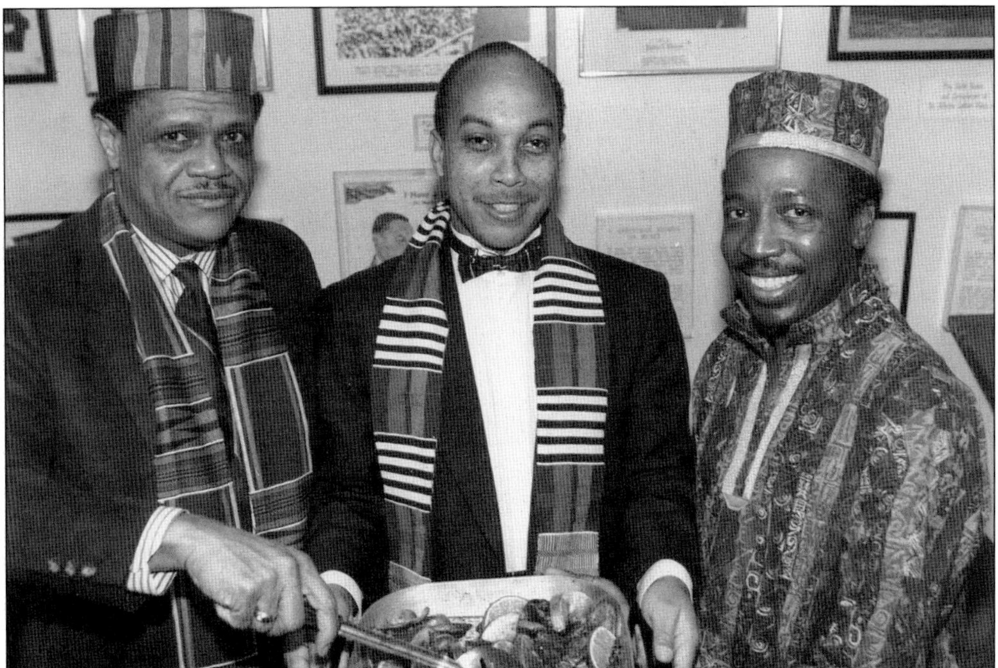

The Africana Ball food cook-off was held as part of the cultural history and traditions presentation at the event. Pictured above are, from left to right, Irvin Overton, Vincent Fields (cook-off winner), and George "Little-Man" Ricks.

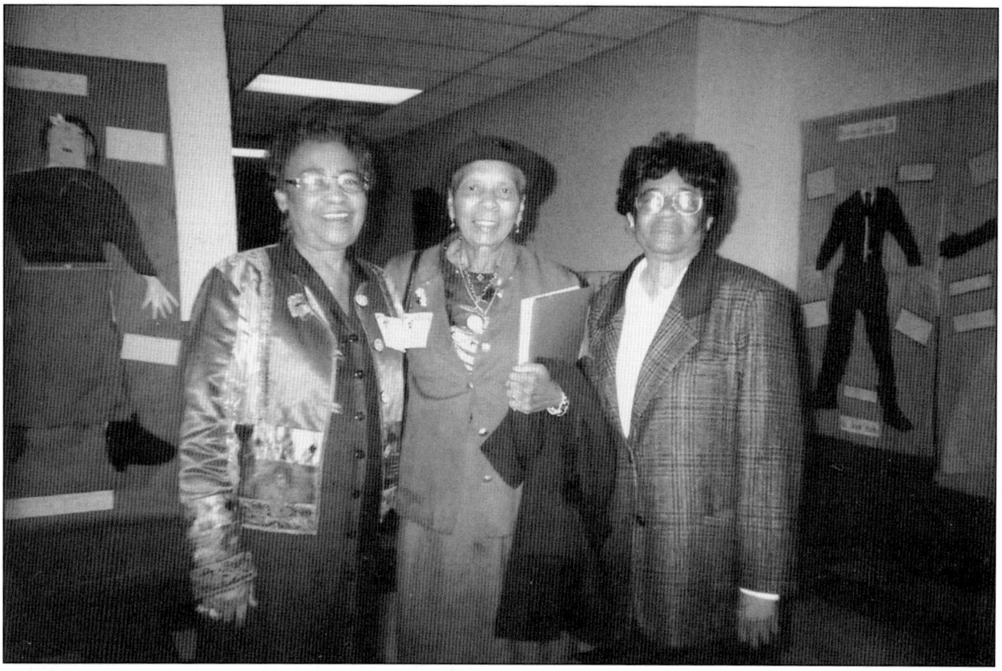

CAAM executive director Vilma Fields; Dr. Margaret Burroughs, cofounder of the DuSable Museum; and Tennessee state representative Tommie Brown visit Brown Academy are pictured from left to right during a museum outreach program. Tommie F. Brown Academy for Classical Studies opened in 2002 in honor of the state representative.

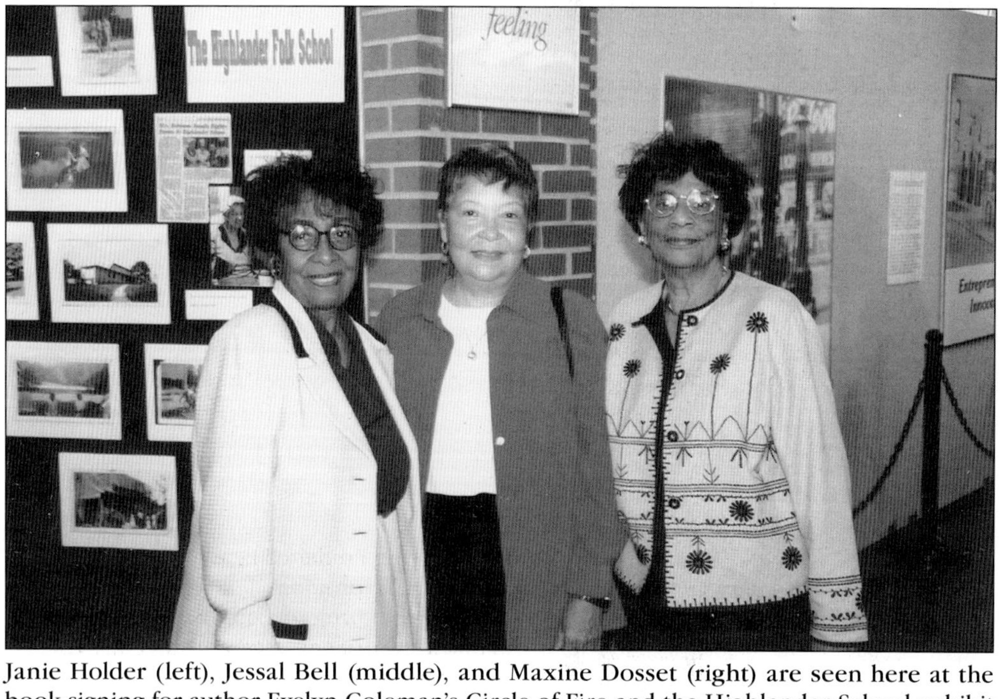

Janie Holder (left), Jessal Bell (middle), and Maxine Dosset (right) are seen here at the book signing for author Evelyn Coleman's Circle of Fire and the Highlander School exhibit opening at the museum.

Pictured from left to right are Susan Jones-Dorsanville and Tarsha Barnes at the book signing for Jones-Dorsanville's book *Silhouette* held at the museum. Jones-Dorsanville, a Chattanooga native, is now a publisher of *Black Hair Care* and *Teen* magazines in New York.

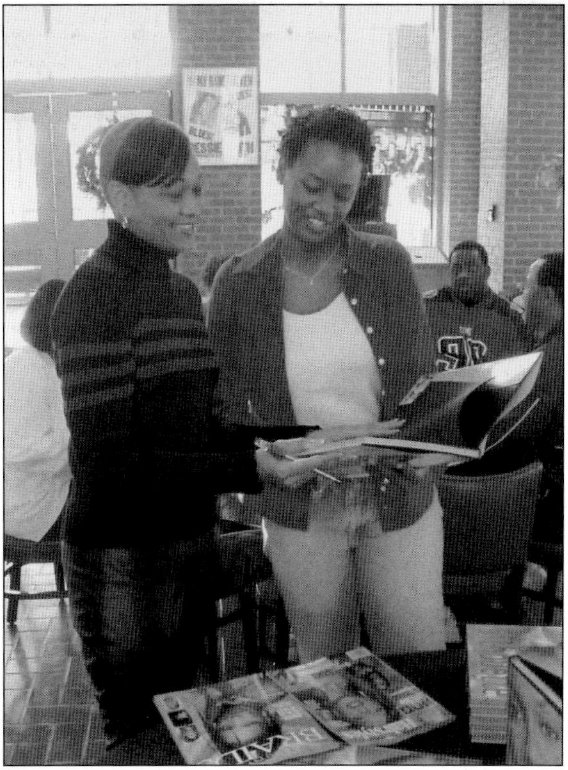

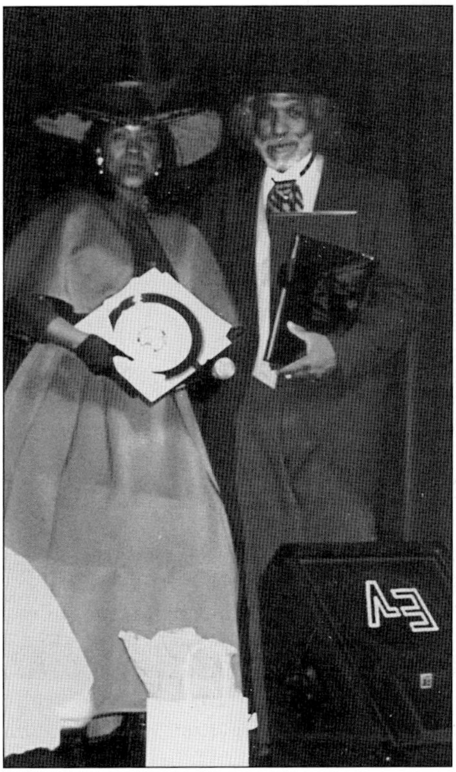

Mr. and Mrs. Frederick Douglass IV are at a Heritage Day program held at the museum. Heritage Day programs are held in celebration of black culture and accomplishments. These programs are offered by the museum during the months that Hamilton County schools are in session.

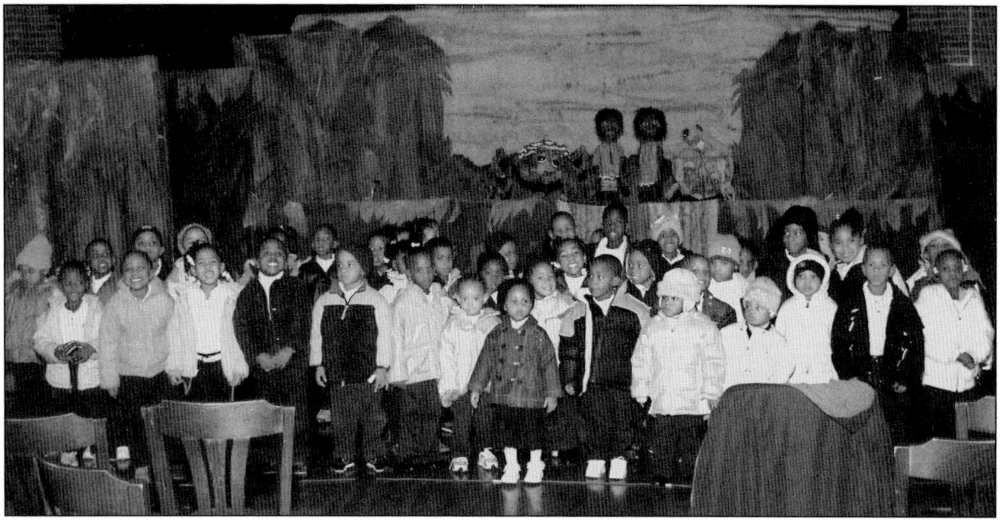

Rainbow Daycare students get caught in the act as they pose in front of the "Ananse! Early in the Day" set at a museum-sponsored Heritage Day program. Heritage Day programs are held once a month at the CAAM during both the fall and spring school semesters. Ananse is a puppet show based on West African folklore.

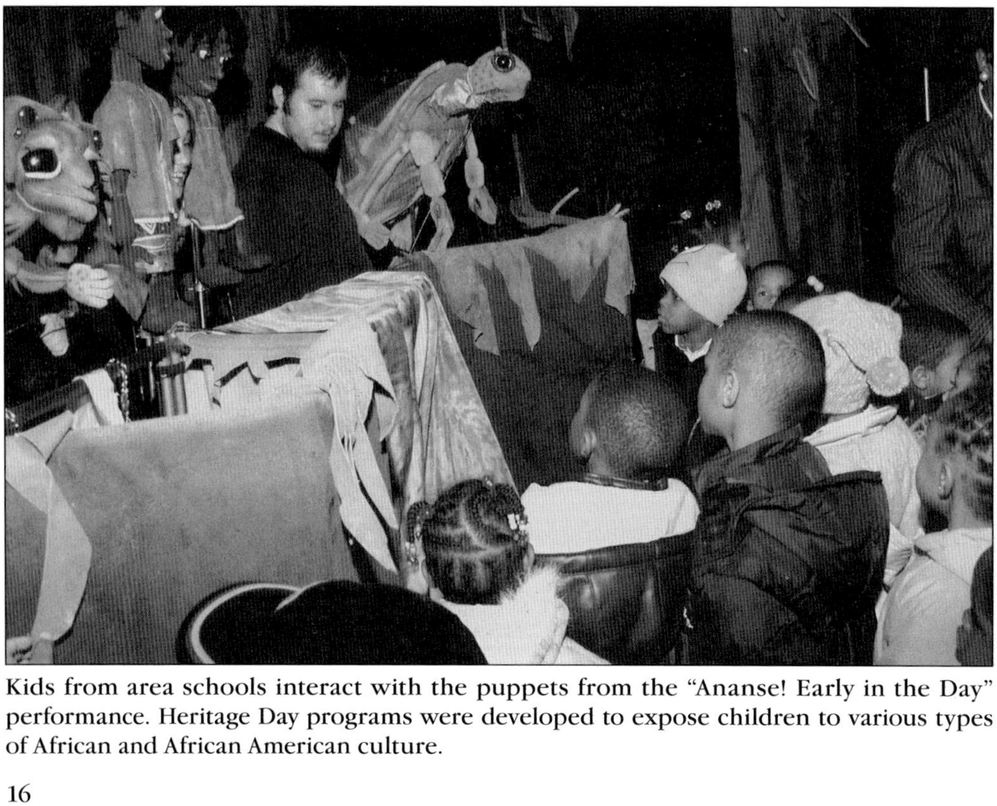

Kids from area schools interact with the puppets from the "Ananse! Early in the Day" performance. Heritage Day programs were developed to expose children to various types of African and African American culture.

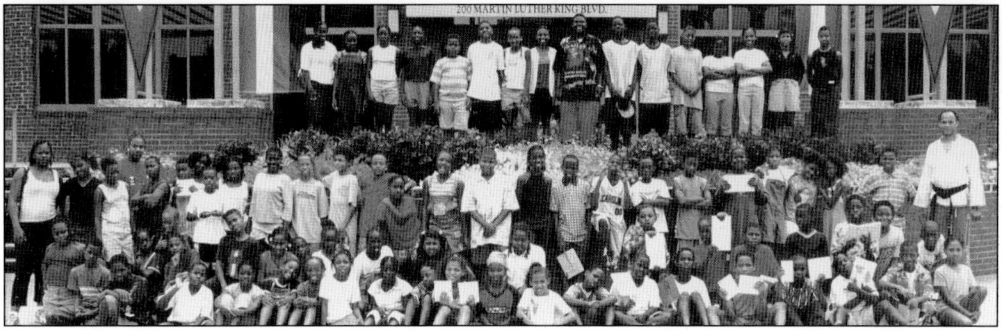

Students participating in the Art Fun Factory cultural program take a break and pose in front of the museum for a group photograph. The Art Fun Factory program is made possible with funds provided by Allied Arts of Chattanooga, Tennessee Arts Commission, Night to Remember, and ML King Weed and Seed.

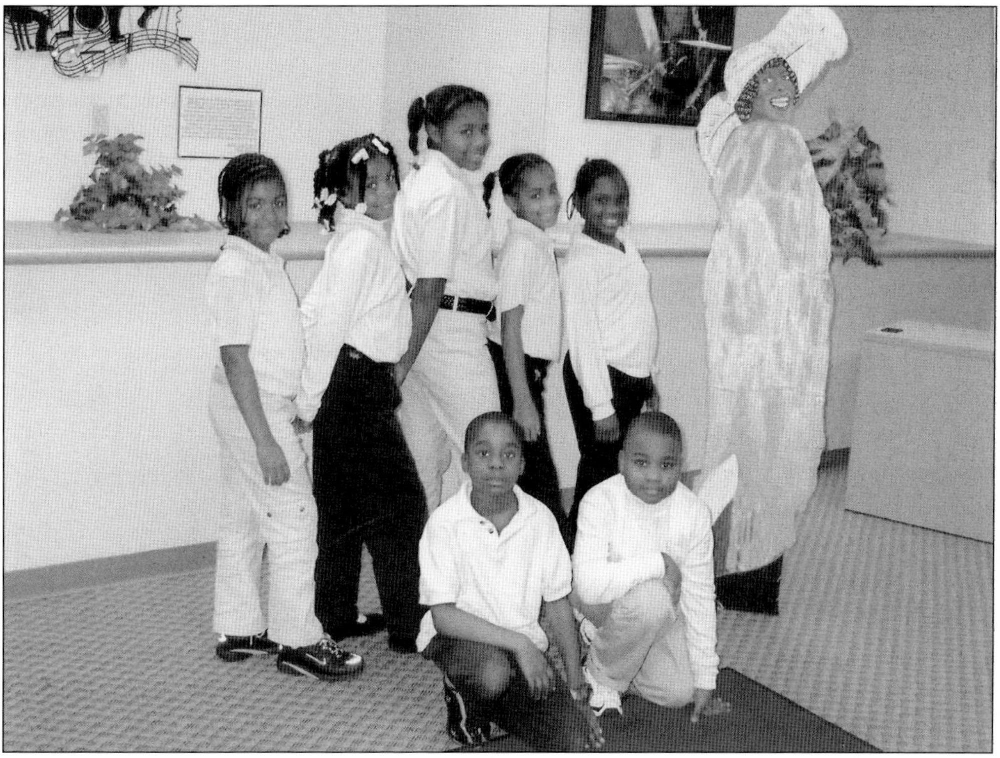

Art Fun Factory is a culturally enriching program that CAAM offers year-round to enrich the lives of children throughout the city. Classes offered include piano, tap/ballet, African dance/drums, karate, drama, creative art, survey of art, percussion, and guitar.

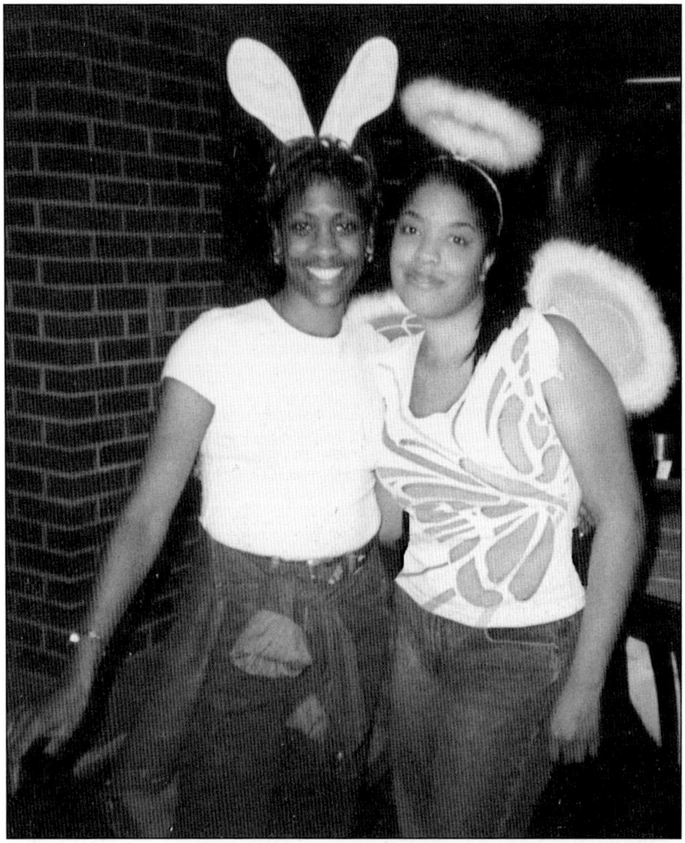

CAAM staff members Daphne Stargin (left) and Carmen Davis (right) are dressed up for Hoopin' Howlin' Halloween. This annual event is cosponsored by CAAM and Power94 to provide a safe alternative to trick-or-treating for local kids. Over 500 students participate annually.

An impromptu jazz ensemble played at the Southside Jazz Junction during the Chattanooga Homecoming Jazz and Scholarship Festival (CHJSF). This festival is held annually, and the proceeds benefit music-lesson scholarships for middle- and high-school students to encourage the preservation of jazz music.

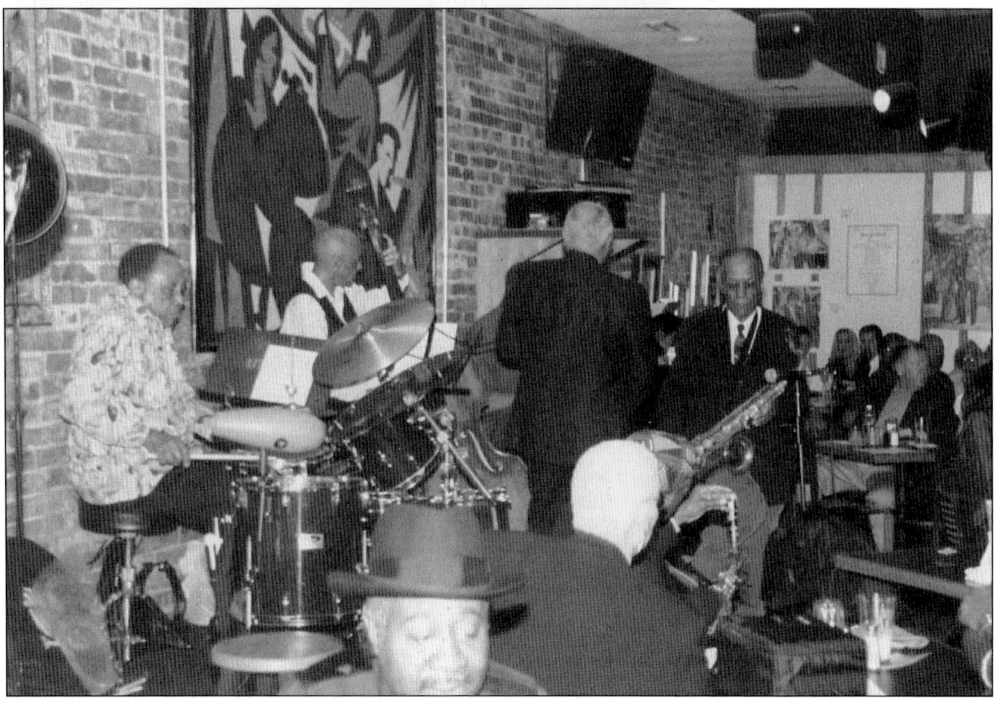

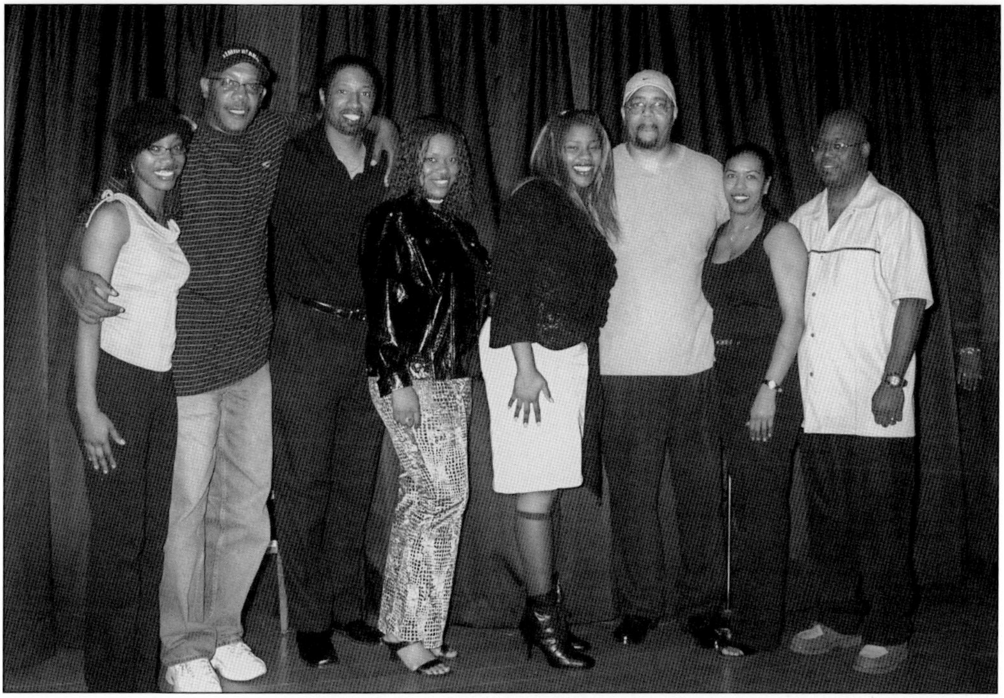

Kelly Price (fourth from left), along with Power 94 staff members, is seen at a meet-and-greet held in the Bessie Smith Performance Hall sponsored by CAAM and Brewer Broadcasting (CAAM's media partners).

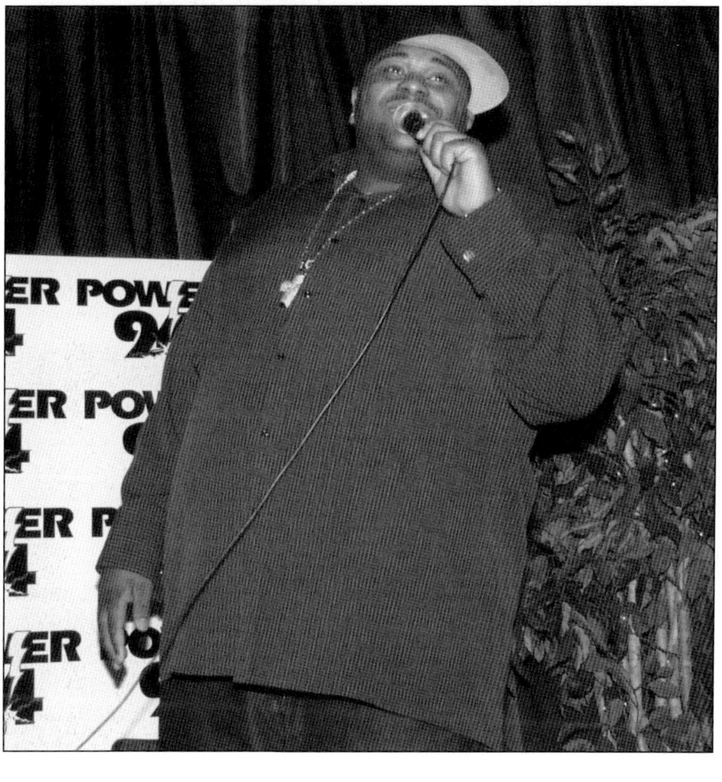

Reuben Studdard is shown here at a meet-and-greet held at the Bessie Smith Performance Hall sponsored by CAAM and Brewer Broadcasting (CAAM media partners).

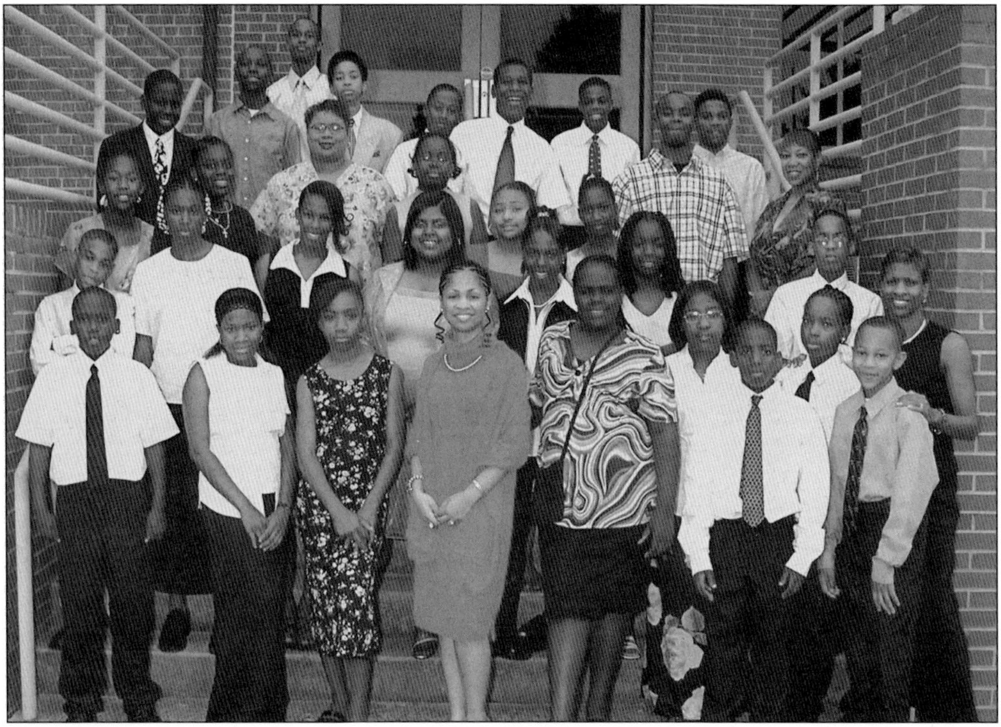

Inner City Ministries and CAAM cosponsored an etiquette program for inner-city pre-teens. These are the 2002 graduates along with their instructors.

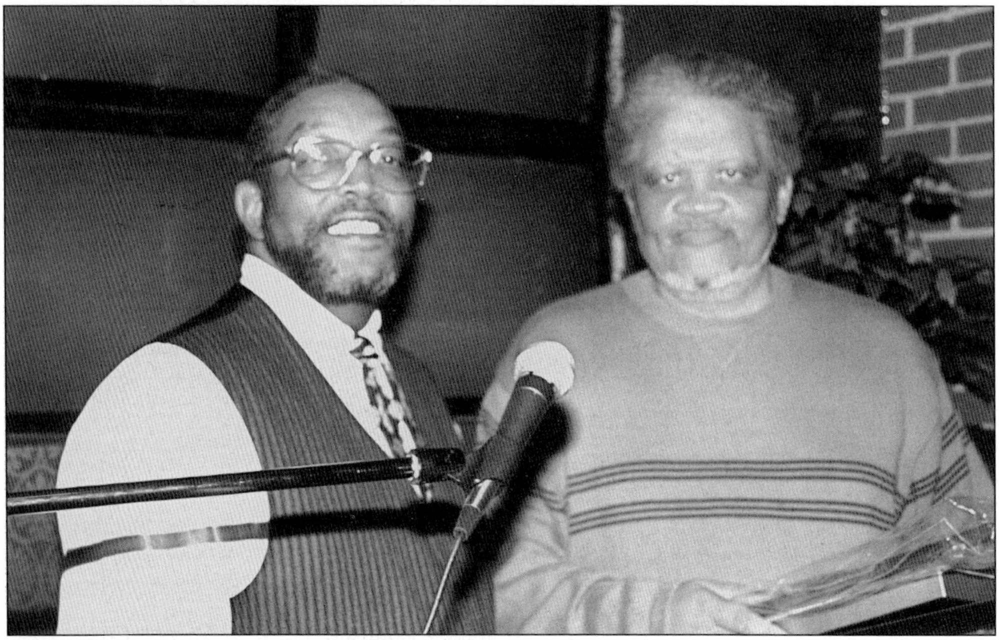

Former CAAM education director Lee Henderson is shown along with acclaimed novelist and Chattanooga native Ishmael Reed at a book reading and discussion held at CAAM. Reed has created a distinct niche in American letters with experimental works that often parody the white as well as the black establishment.

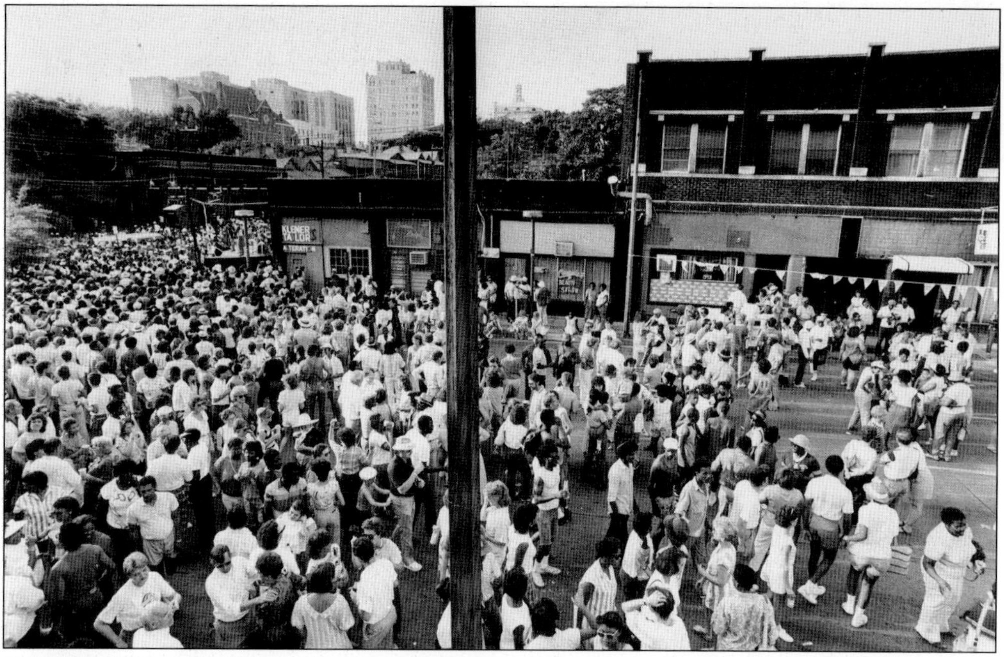

Held annually as a tribute to "the Empress of the Blues," the Bessie Smith Strut attracts more than 100,000 people to enjoy great food, music, and vendors. The strut is held on Martin Luther King Boulevard and is the only free night offered during the annual Riverbend Festival.

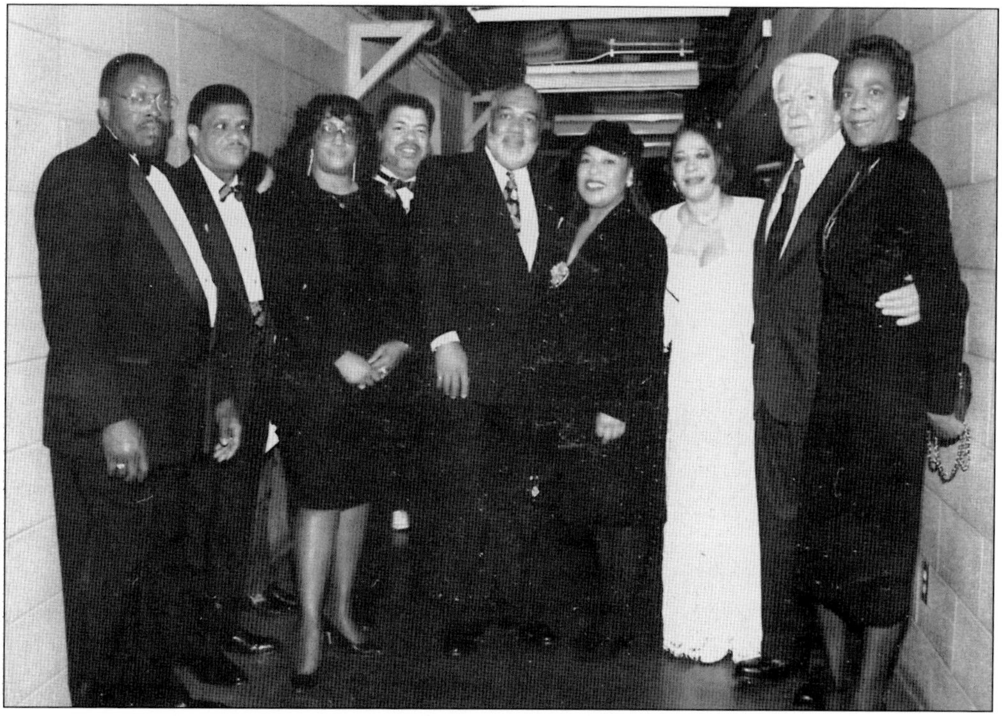

Past Night to Remember (NTR) performer Roberta Flack (in hat) is shown here with promoters and board members. NTR is a charitable event held annually to provide scholarships for local students and funding for cultural programs for kids.

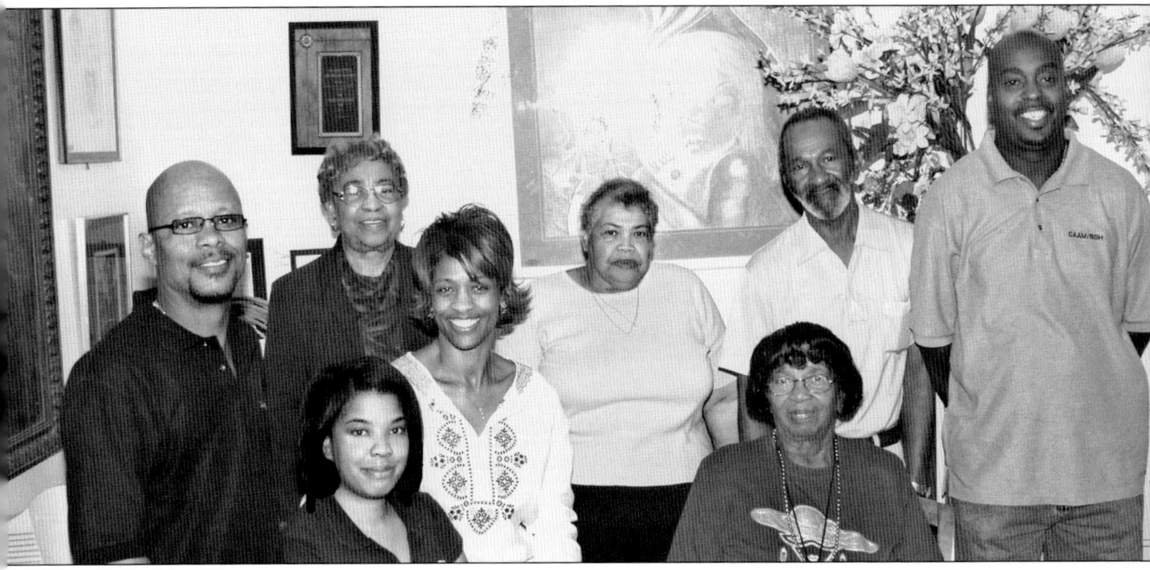

The CAAM staff is shown here from left to right: (standing) Danny Toney, Vilma Fields, Vivian Greene, Henry Christian, and Gerald Norwood; (seated) Carmen Davis, Daphne Stargin, and Gladys Paris. Not pictured is Bruce Wilkey.

Two

Family and Community

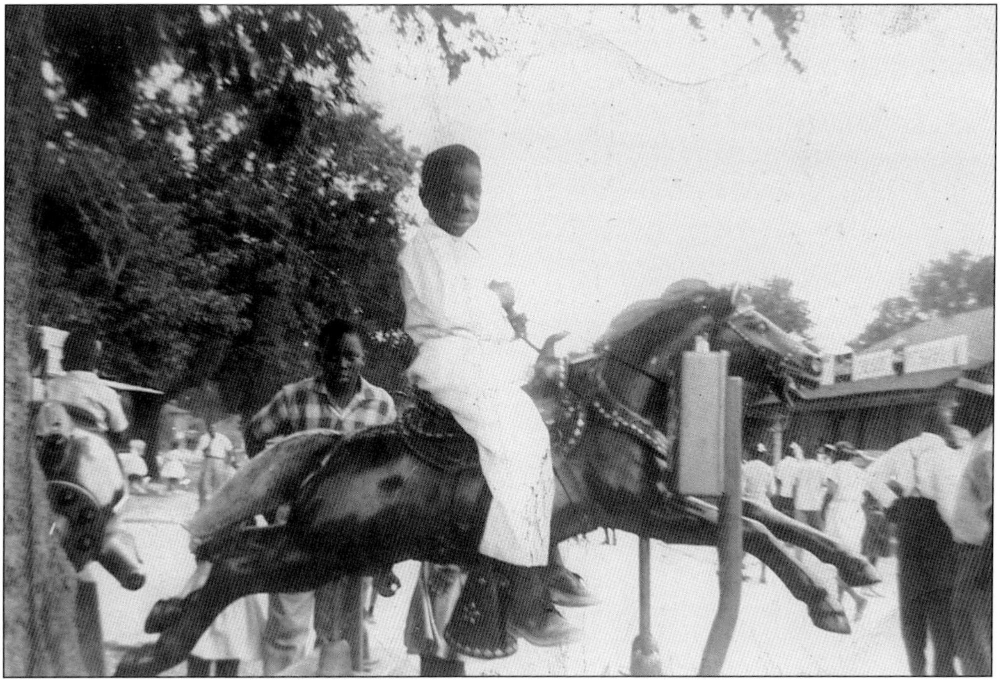

Ronnie Davis enjoys a ride at Lincoln Park around 1955. This was the only park available for use by African Americans during that time.

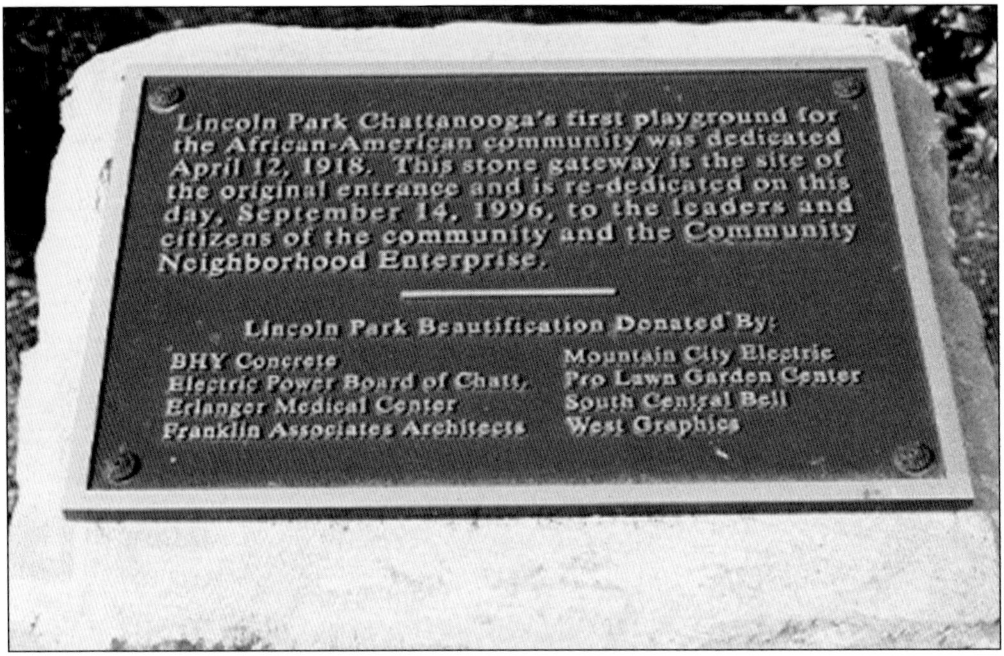

Lincoln Park was developed after World War I and was located on Central and Cleveland Avenue, serving as the African American community's first playground in Chattanooga. This cornerstone has been placed in the site where the entrance gate once stood.

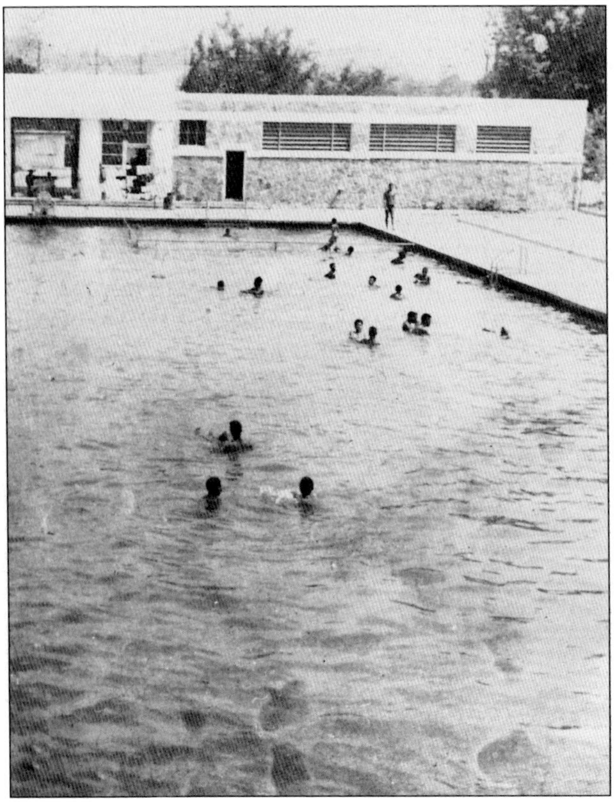

Lincoln Park housed the only public swimming pool for African Americans in Chattanooga for many years. It was the largest swimming pool for African Americans in the South.

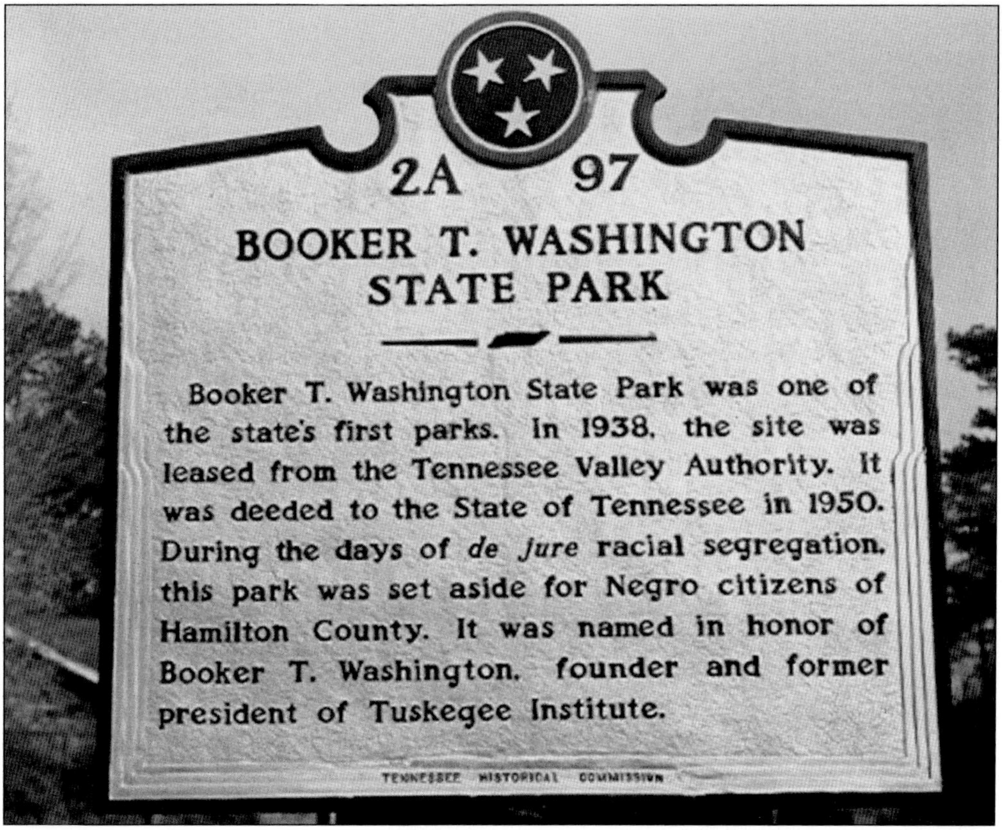

A historic marker is located at the entrance to Booker T. Washington State Park. The park is a state-owned facility.

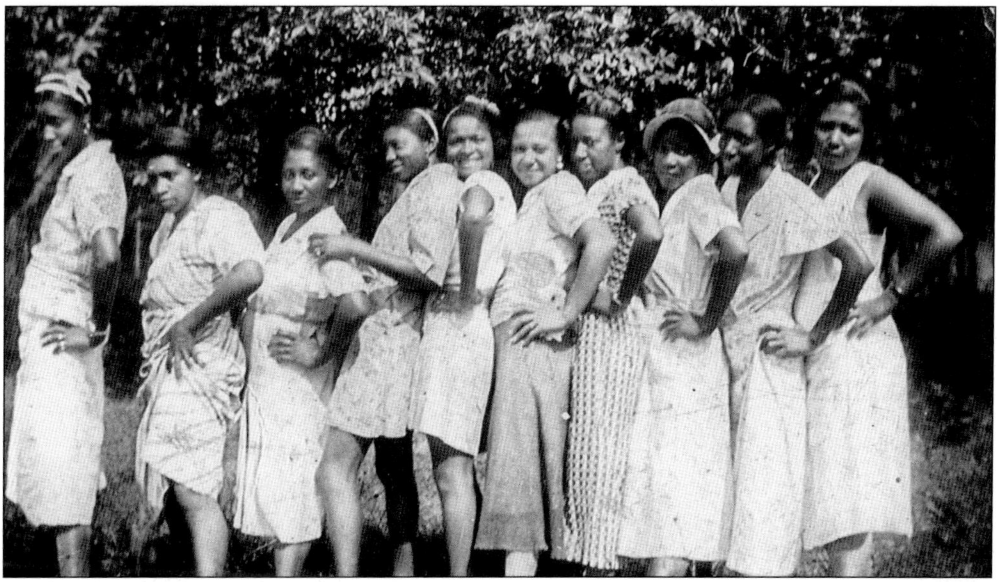

A group of unidentified Hill City ladies are shown at Booker T. Washington State Park in the early 20th century.

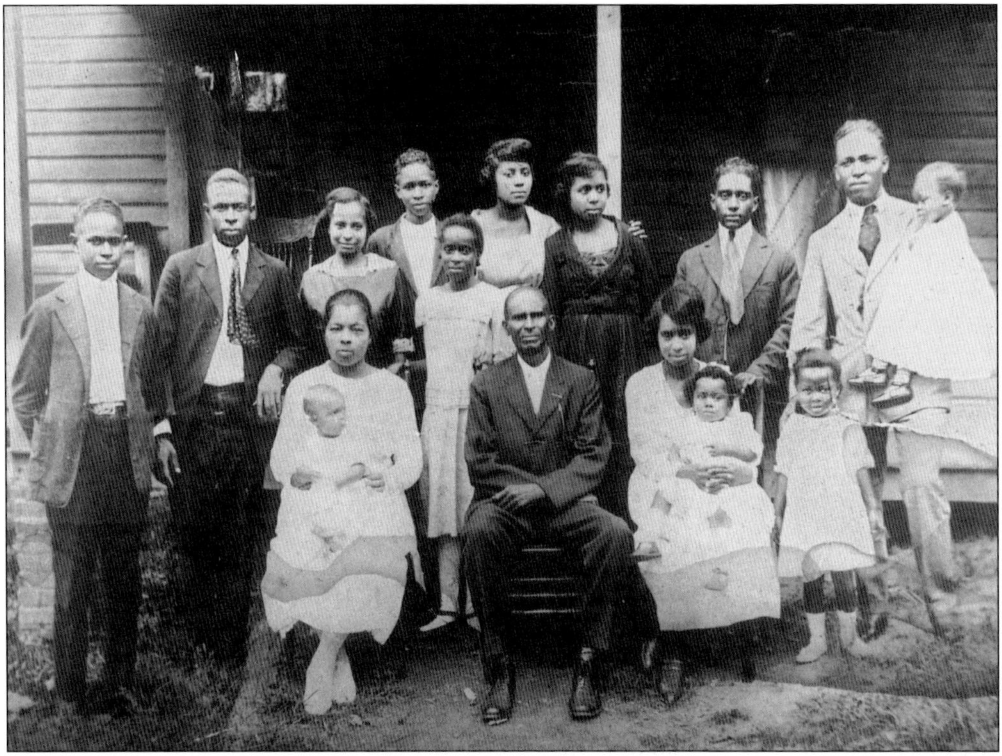

The Scruggs family, shown around 1895, of Hill City (now known as North Chattanooga), owned the property adjacent to the Pine Breeze Sanatorium.

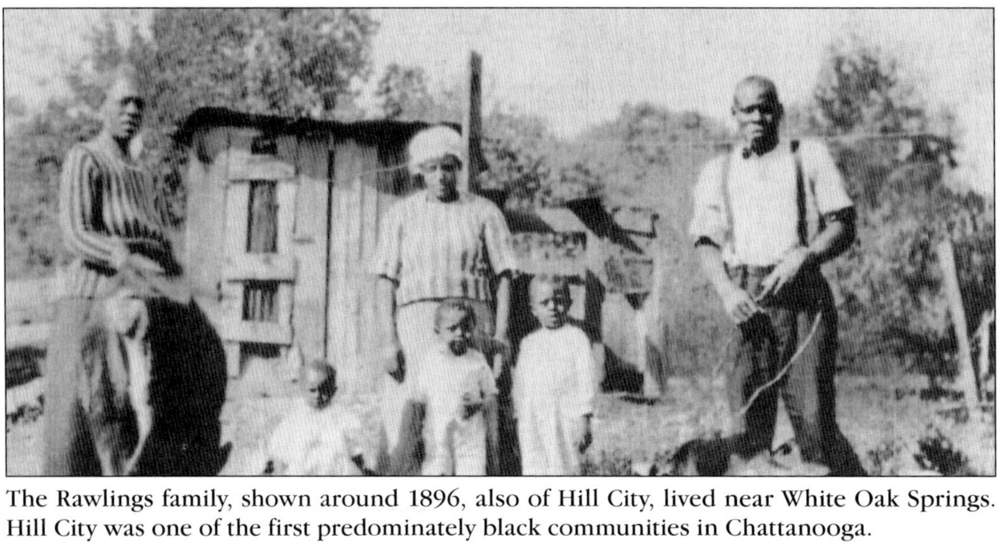

The Rawlings family, shown around 1896, also of Hill City, lived near White Oak Springs. Hill City was one of the first predominately black communities in Chattanooga.

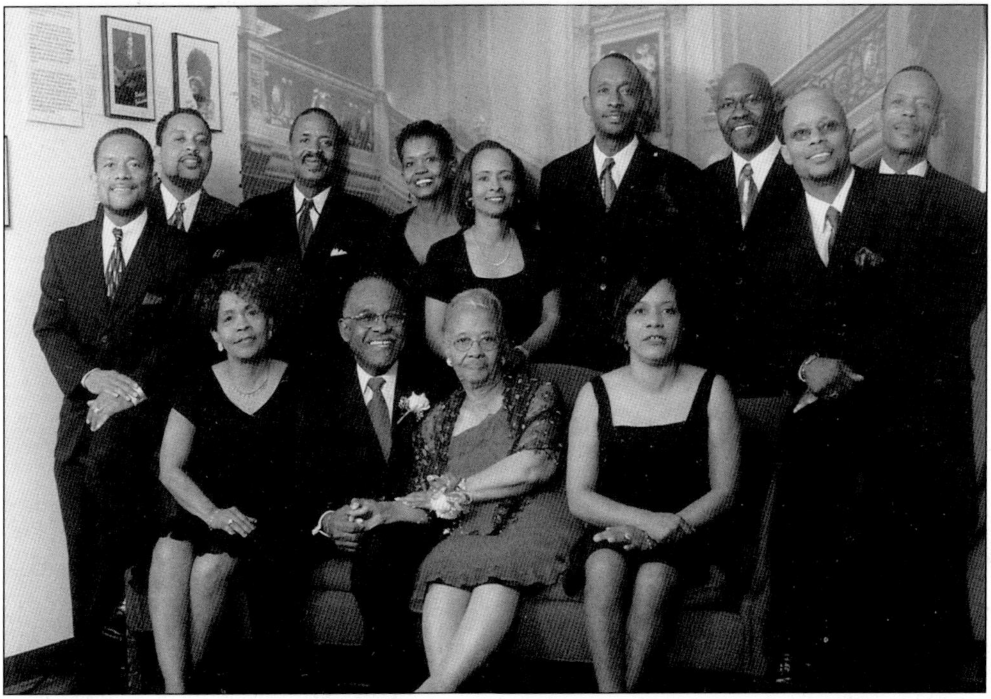

Rev. and Mrs. Harris Toney, longtime residents of the Washington Hills community, and their 11 children are pictured at a family celebration in June 2004.

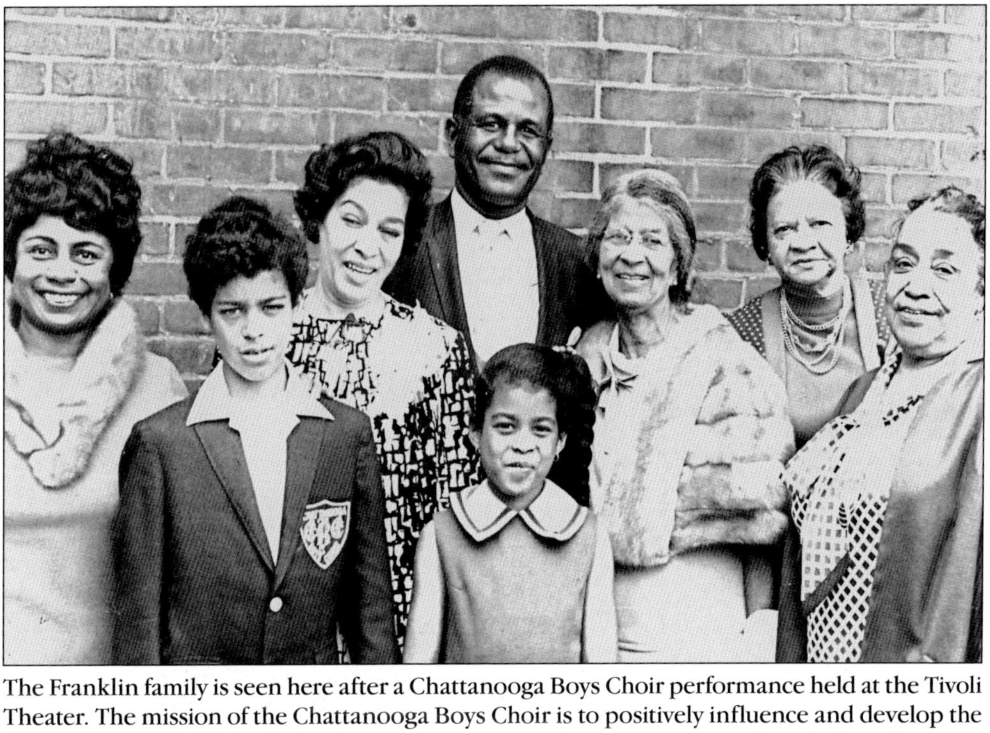

The Franklin family is seen here after a Chattanooga Boys Choir performance held at the Tivoli Theater. The mission of the Chattanooga Boys Choir is to positively influence and develop the lives of boys by providing a music program of the highest quality, which includes education, appreciation, and performance. The choir has been in existence for more than 50 years.

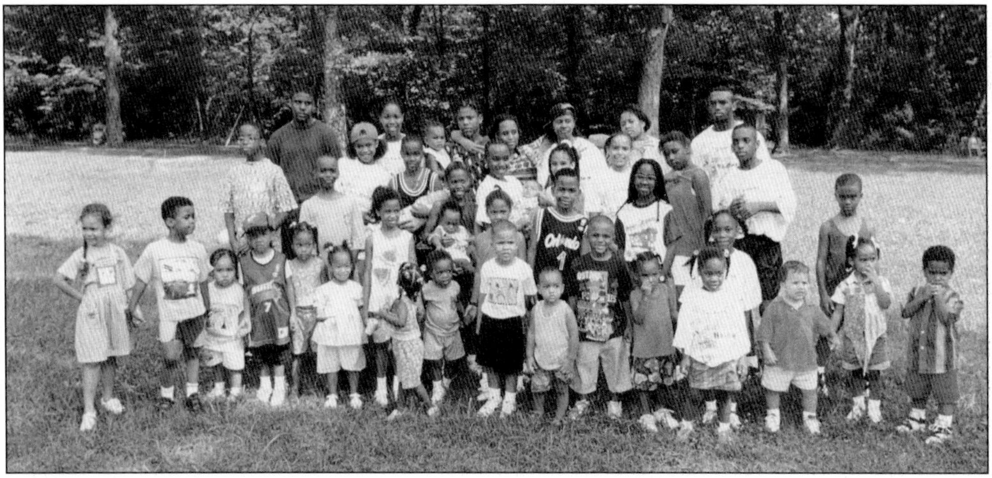

The success of African American families in Chattanooga attracted African American families from Georgia, Alabama, and East and West Tennessee. Here they found a city of beauty and the possibility of leadership roles in civic, social, economic, political, and cultural affairs. Over the years, these families expanded; some members stayed and some moved to other places, but they often come back for celebrations like family reunions. Pictured is the Scruggs family reunion held at Booker T. Washington State Park in 1996.

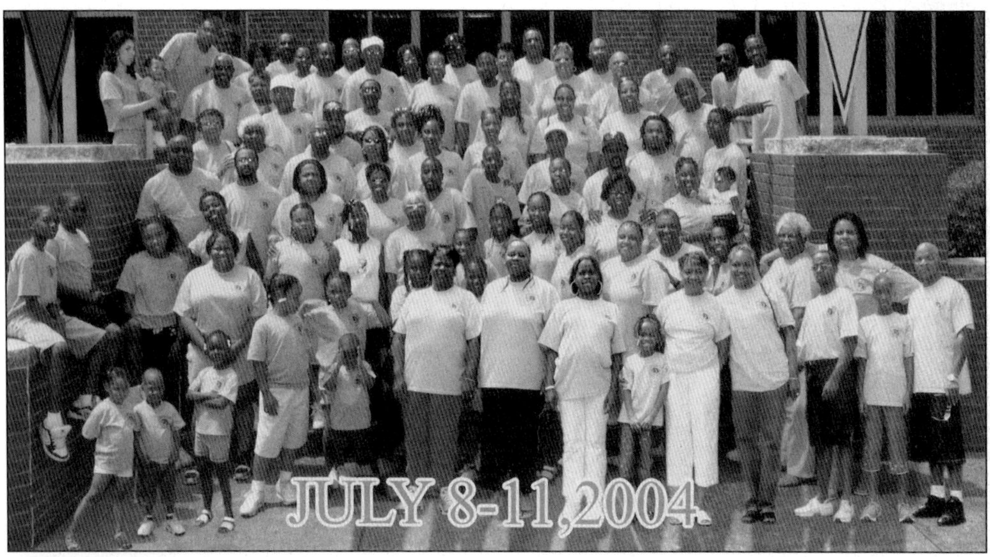

A close-knit family was as basic to African American families as it was to African tribal societies. The extended family was a strong family based on the African tribal societies. The extended family included aunts, uncles, grandparents, other relatives, neighbors, and friends in the community. This is the Player family reunion held at Bessie Smith Performance Hall.

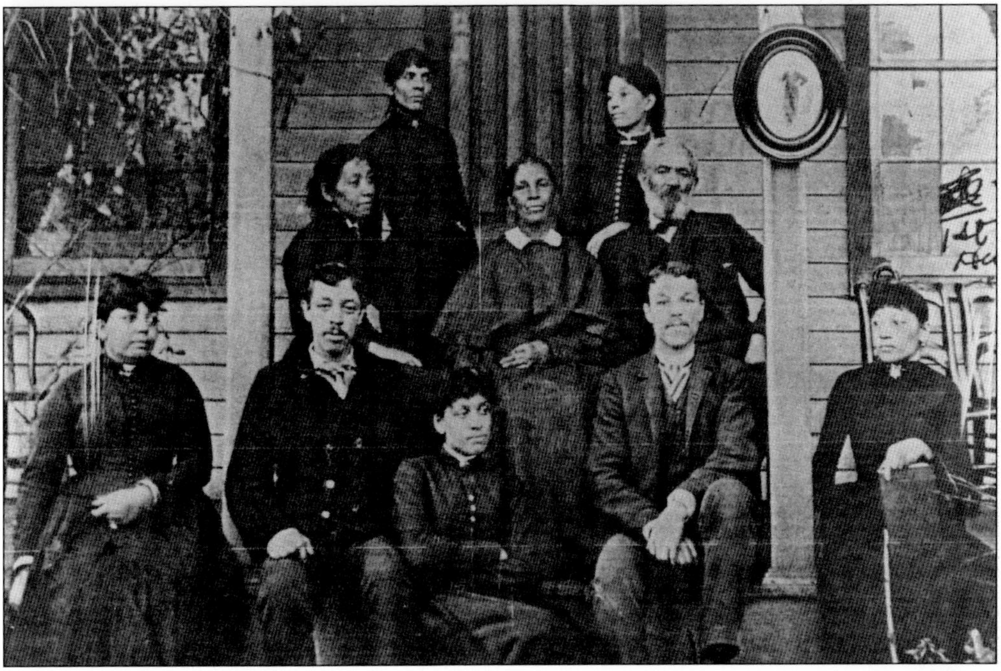

The Lewis family, early prominent citizens of Chattanooga, is pictured here *c.* 1889. William Lewis was the first African American blacksmith and wagon-maker of Chattanooga. There is a historic marker located at Seventh and Market Street, where his business once stood.

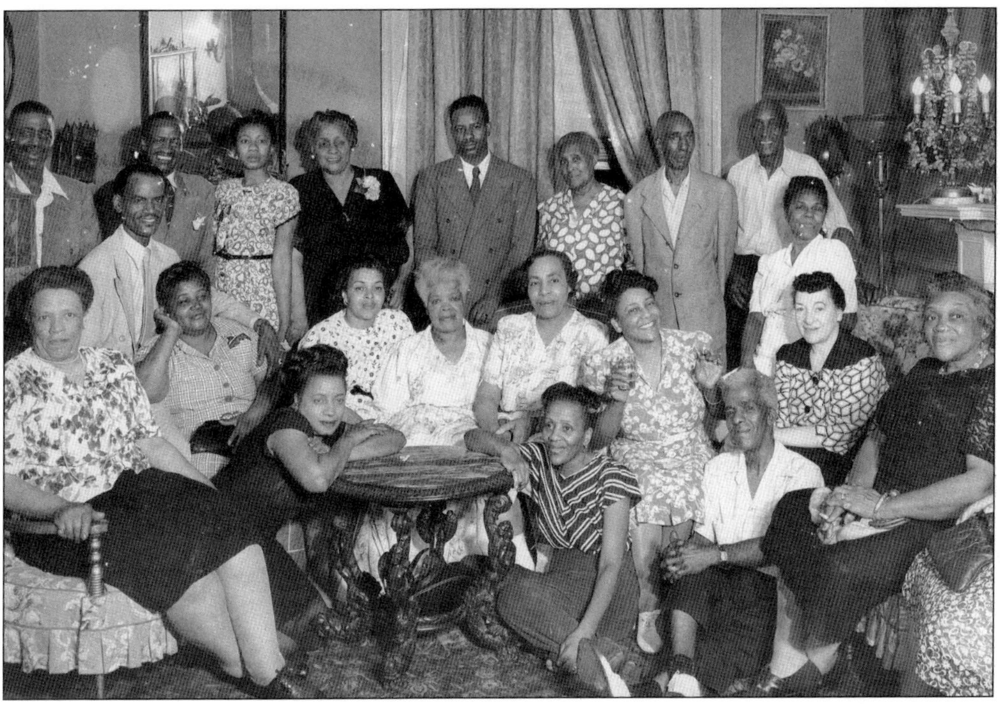

This Edwards family photograph was taken inside the South Chattanooga home of Mrs. Hines before one of the family's Sunday dinners around 1953. The Sunday dinner is a long-standing tradition in the Edwards family that still takes place today.

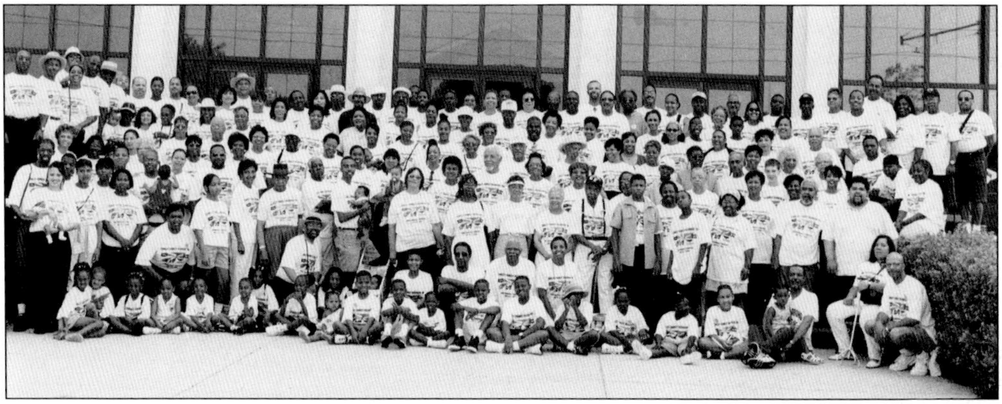

The 1999 Conley family reunion was held in Chattanooga. This is one of many families that gather to pass down their heritage to younger members and honor their elders.

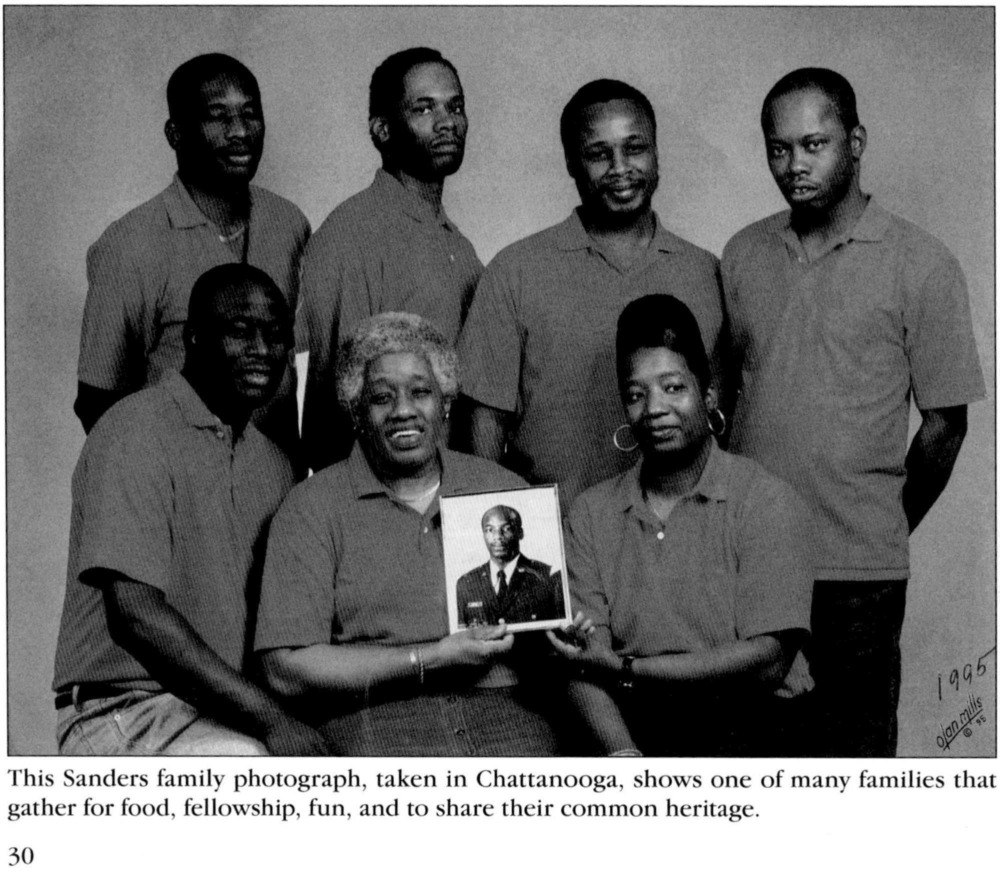

This Sanders family photograph, taken in Chattanooga, shows one of many families that gather for food, fellowship, fun, and to share their common heritage.

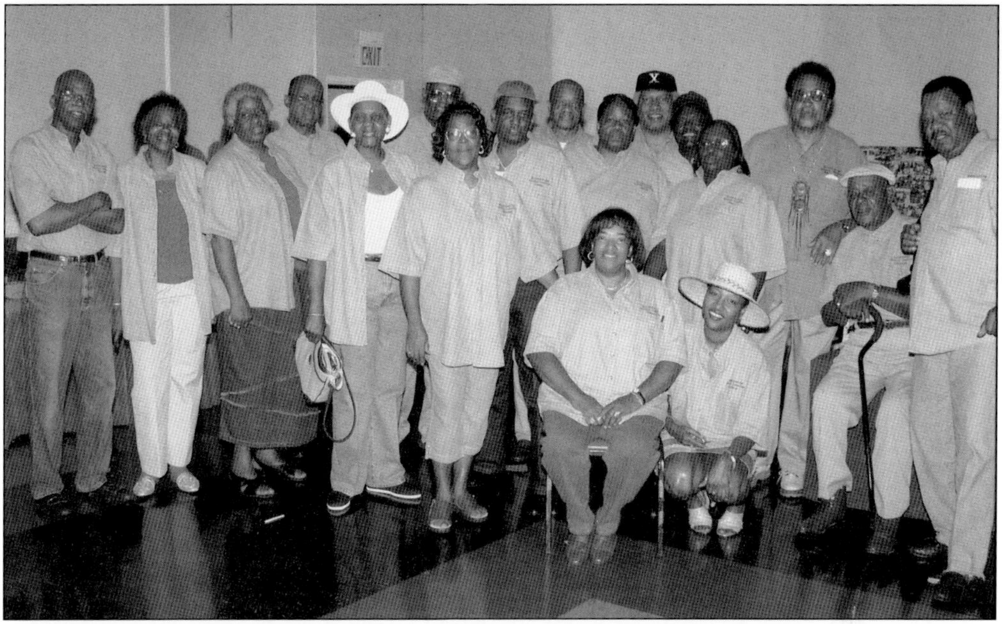

The Southside family reunion started in 1999 and is held annually. This event brings together former and current South Chattanooga residents for fun, food, and fellowship.

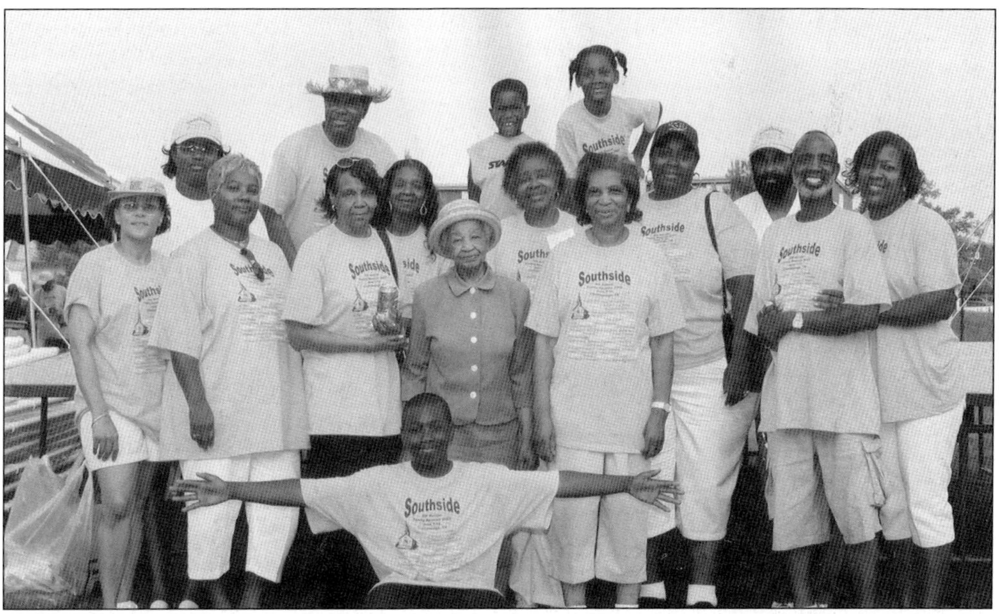

A family attending the 2002 Southside family reunion enjoys the festivities in souvenir t-shirts. This is a growing sign of the importance of these types of functions in African American communities.

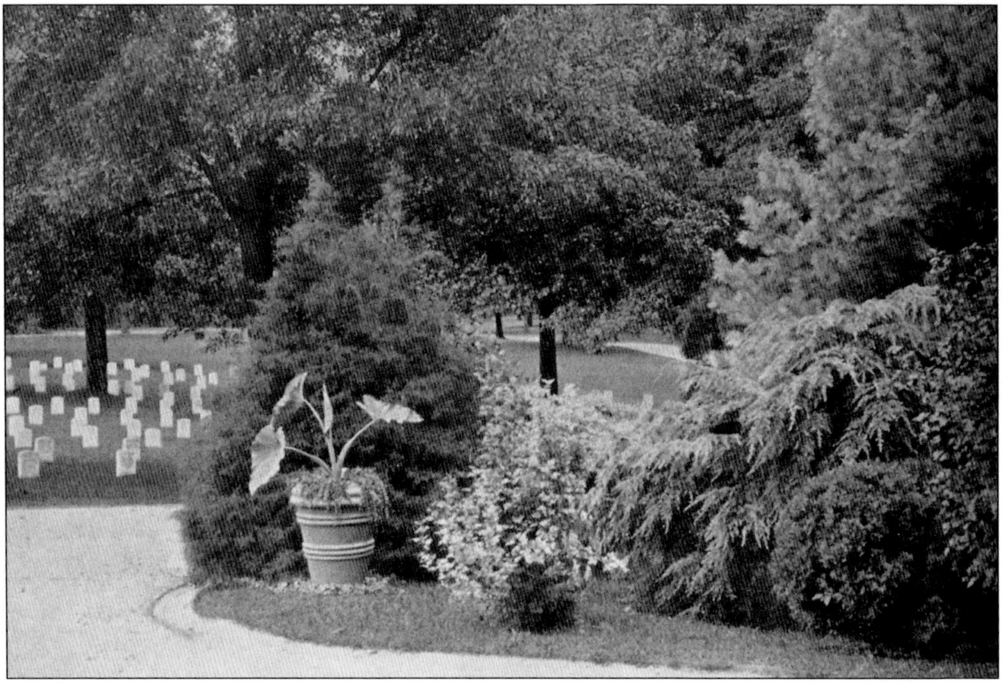

The 42nd regiment of the United States Colored Troops established Chattanooga's National Cemetery. From 1864 to 1865, these troops cleared land, did landscaping, and dug up the remains of buried soldiers within a 50-mile radius and brought them back to be buried in this cemetery.

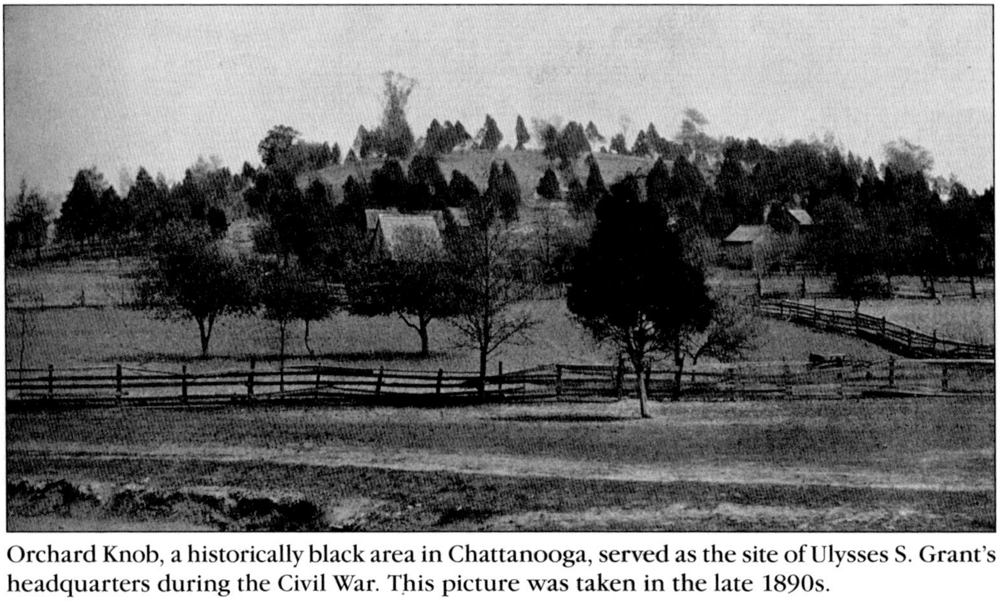

Orchard Knob, a historically black area in Chattanooga, served as the site of Ulysses S. Grant's headquarters during the Civil War. This picture was taken in the late 1890s.

Gwen Harris is seen in front of her grandparents' house in South Chattanooga on Long Street around 1957. Oftentimes grandparents play just as a significant role in raising their grandchildren as they played in raising their own children.

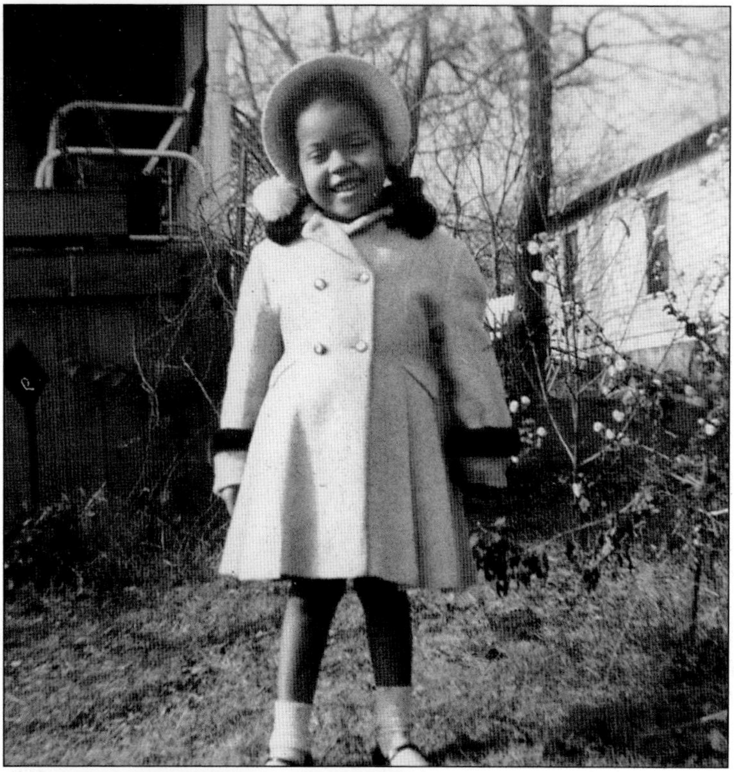

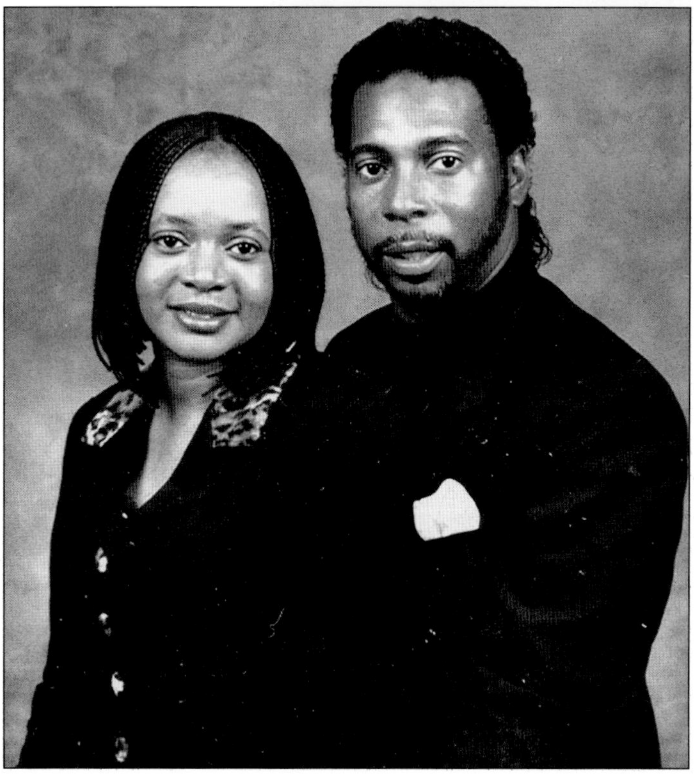

Shirley and Danny Gordon have two children and one grandchild. Mrs. Gordon has been in the cosmetology business for over 20 years. Mr. and Mrs. Gordon are co-owners of Hair Logic Beauty Salon.

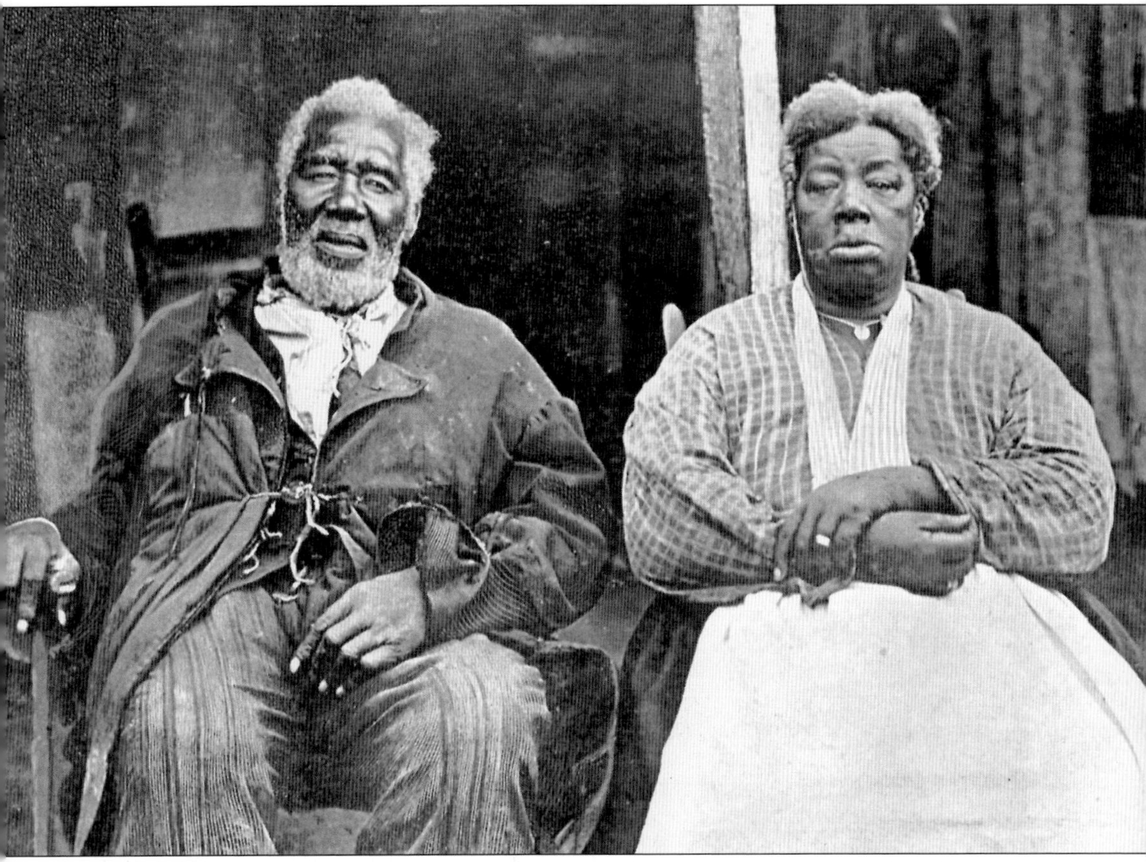

Uncle Ben, pictured here at 100 years old with his seventh wife, traveled the streets of Chattanooga with his donkey and cart full of rags for many years.

Three

ORGANIZATIONS

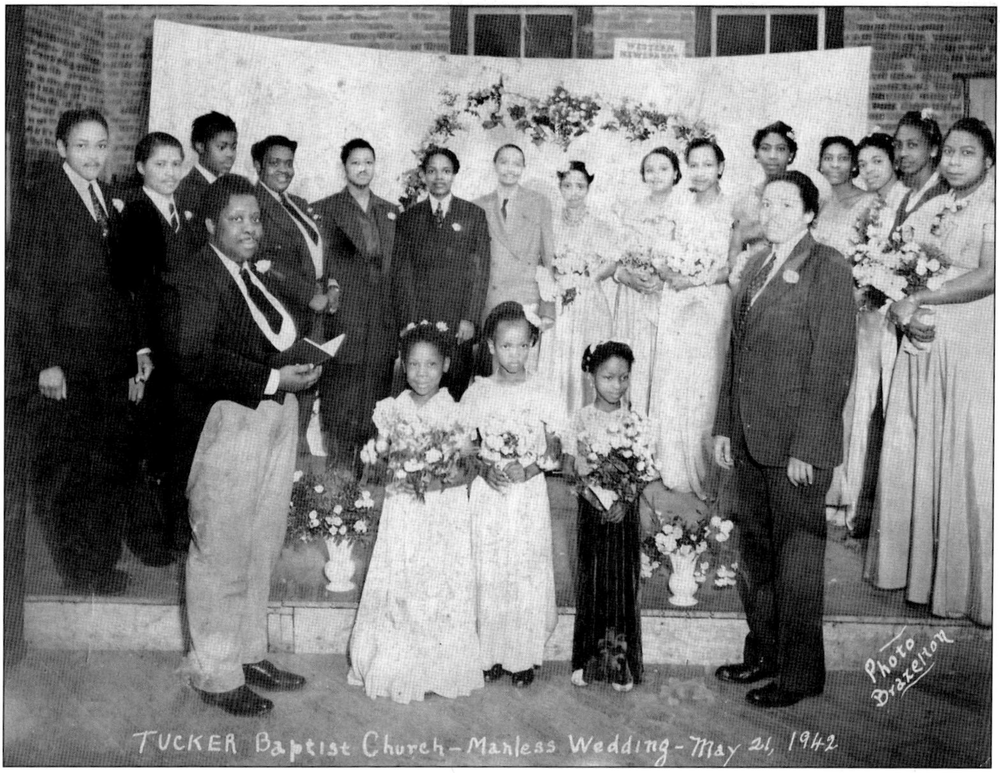

Pictured is a man-less wedding performed by the Pygmy Social Club in 1942. This social club was organized in 1934 to exchange ideas and activities with other social clubs and to help with charitable organizations.

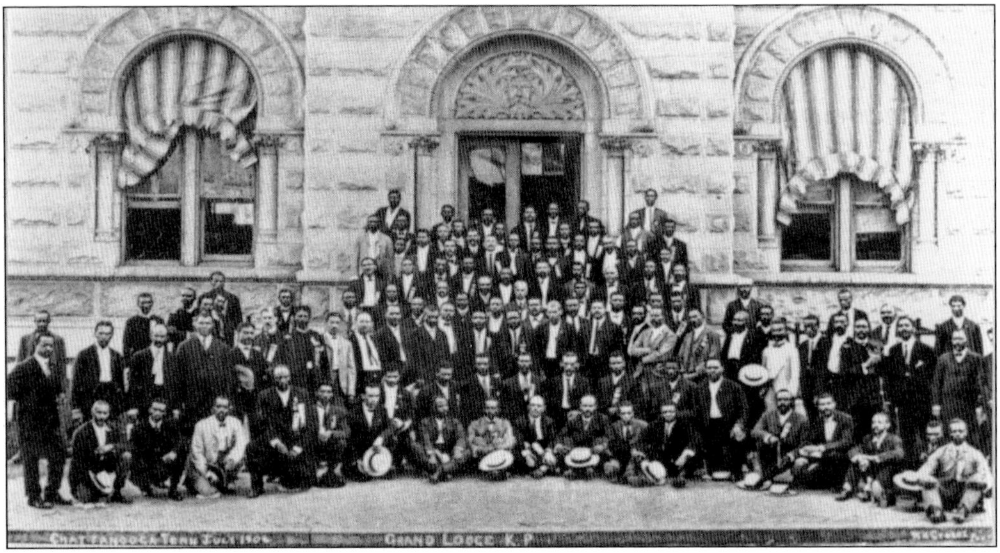

The Colored Lodge of Knights of Pythias is one of the nation's oldest fraternal orders. This picture was taken in 1904. The first Colored Lodge of Knights of Pythias, Lightfoot Lodge No. 1 of Mississippi, was founded on March 26, 1880.

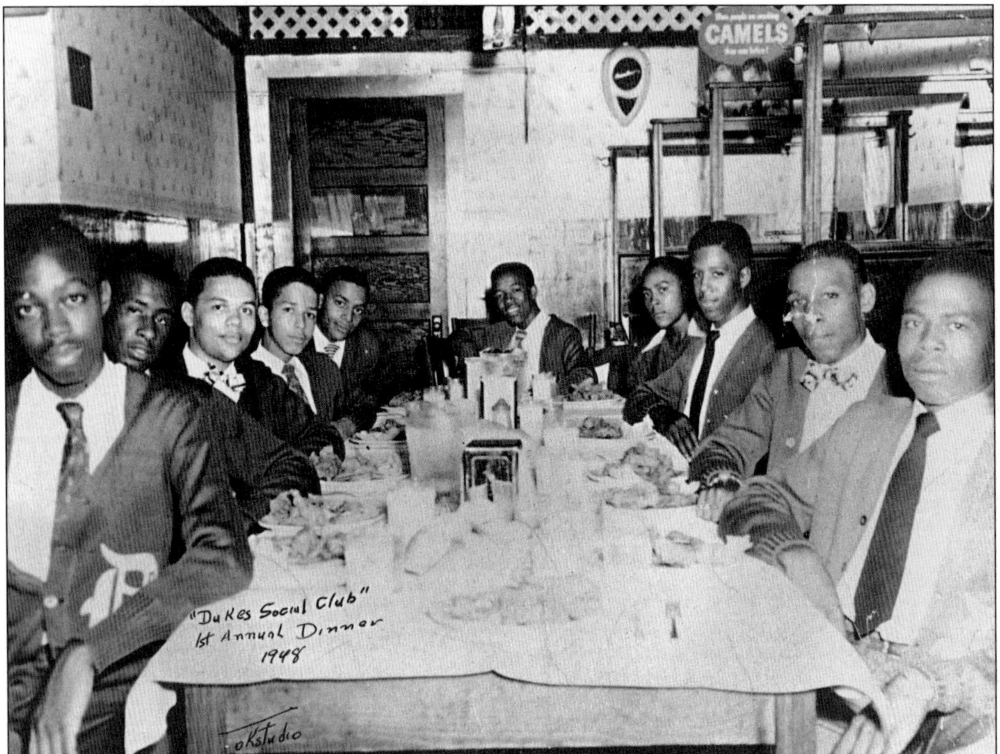

Many social clubs were formed in area high schools to encourage community service and positive social activities. Shown here is Duke Social Club of Howard High School in 1948 at their first annual holiday dinner.

A historic marker honors the National Alliance of Postal and Federal Employees and Women's Auxiliary. This organization had its beginnings in Chattanooga.

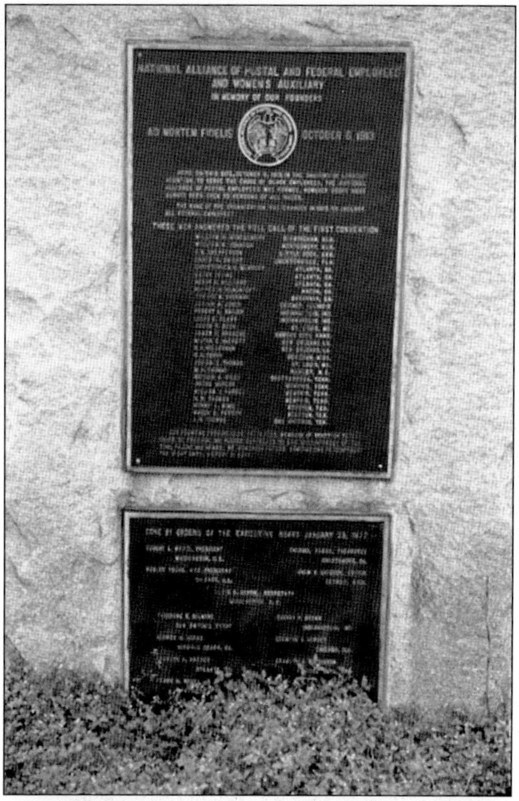

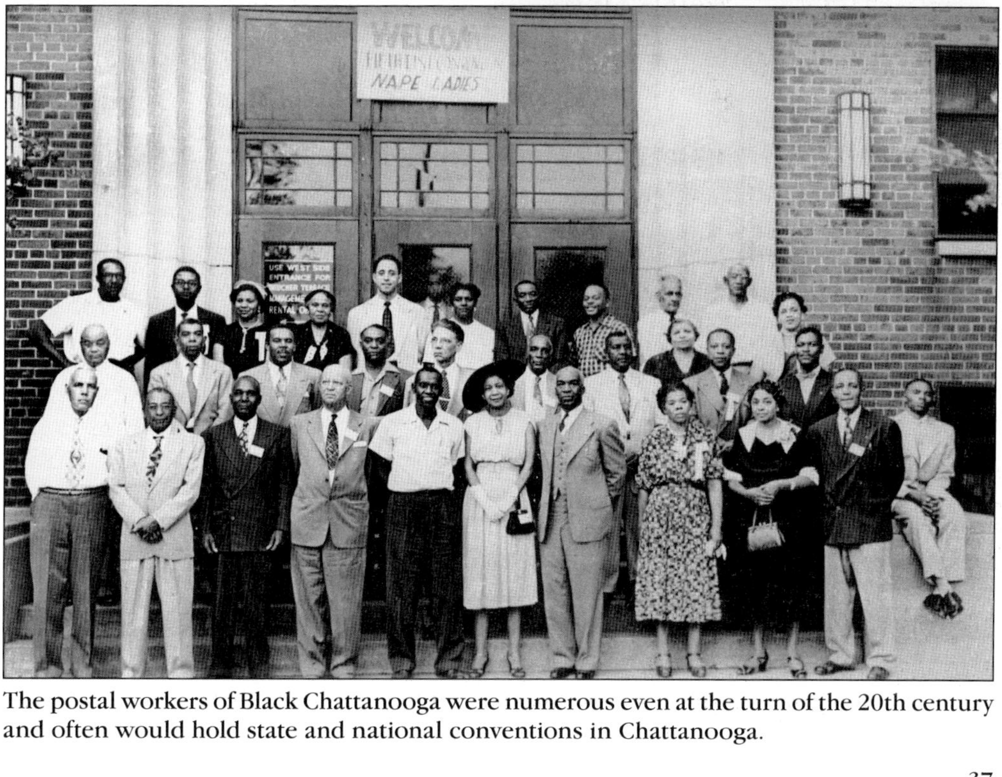

The postal workers of Black Chattanooga were numerous even at the turn of the 20th century and often would hold state and national conventions in Chattanooga.

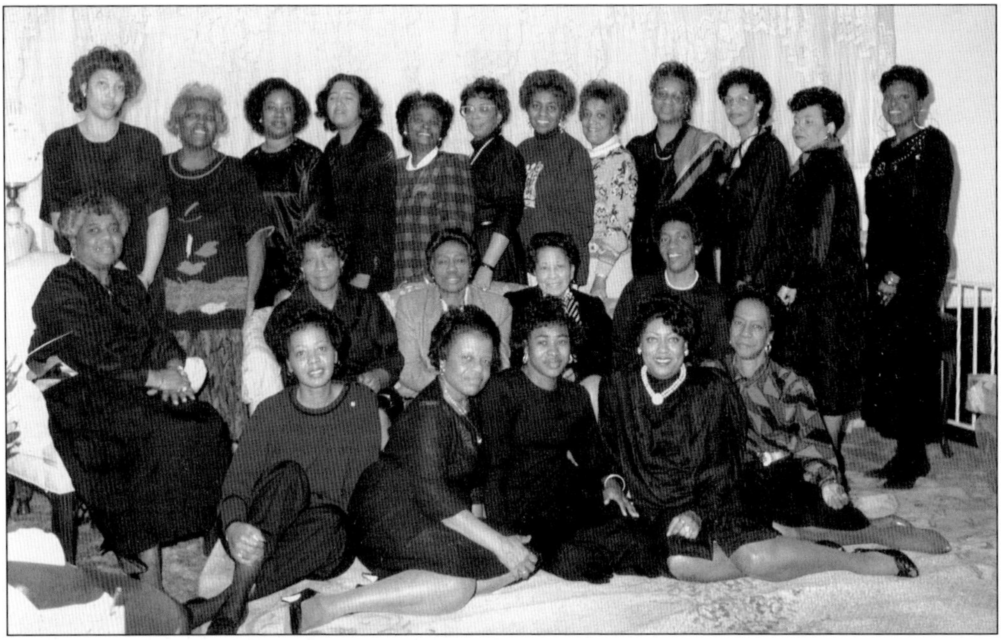

The Beta Pi chapter of the national sorority of Phi Delta Kappa, Inc., was founded in 1958. Phi Delta Kappa is an international association for professional educators. The organization focuses on providing innovative programs, relevant research, visionary leadership, and dedicated service to promote quality education.

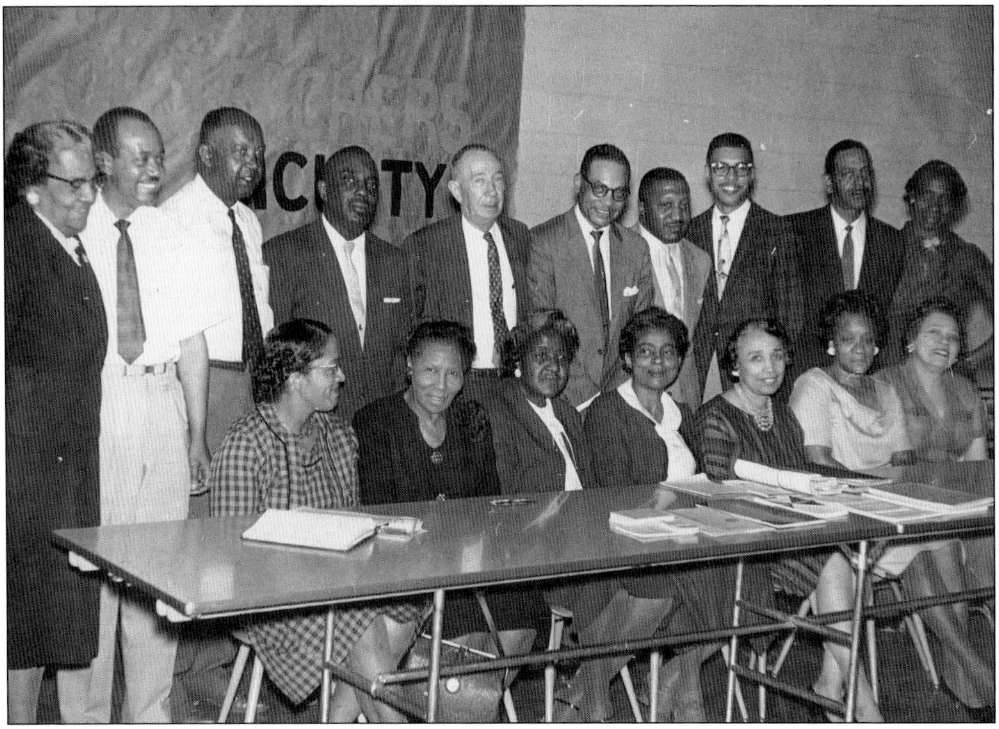

Mountain City Teachers Association was organized to give black teachers a place to voice concerns and share ideas.

Mountain City Medical Association was organized in the 1960s to create a platform from which black physicians could come together to form and express ideas and bargain collectively.

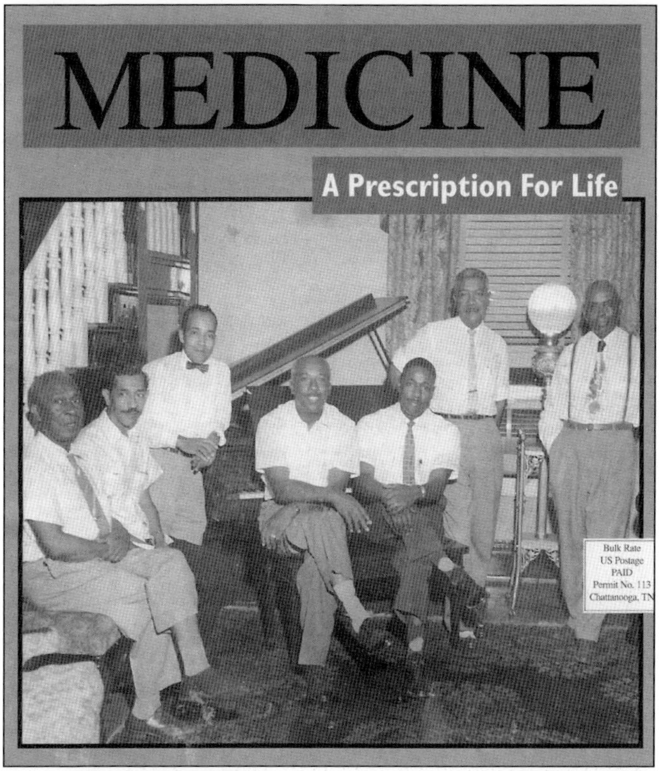

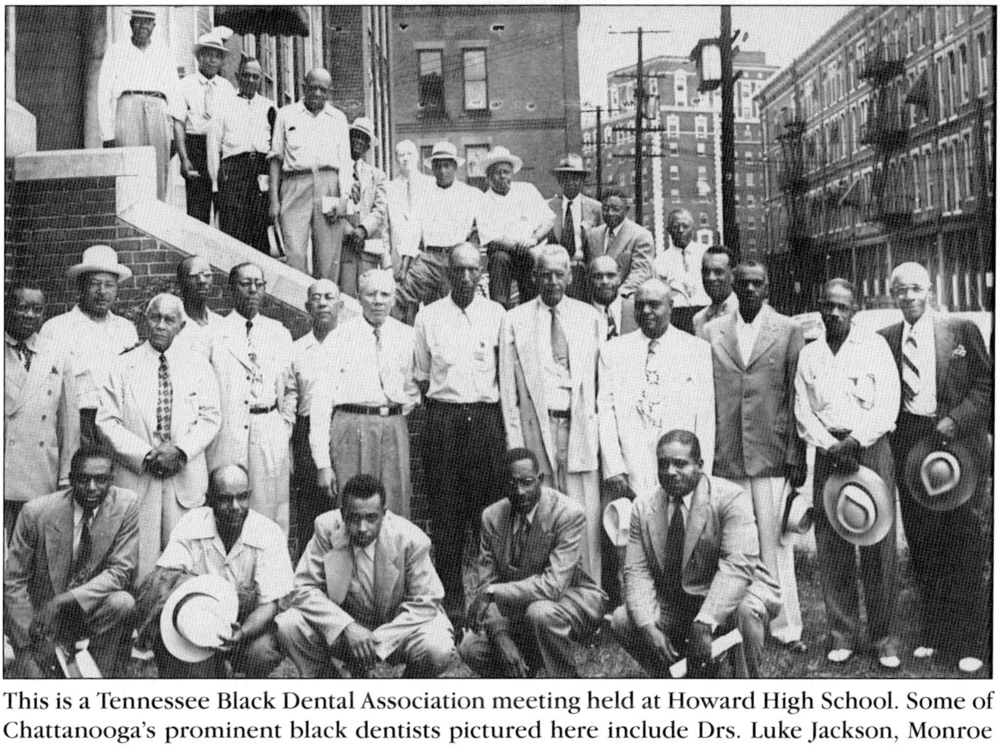

This is a Tennessee Black Dental Association meeting held at Howard High School. Some of Chattanooga's prominent black dentists pictured here include Drs. Luke Jackson, Monroe Bynes, and James Young.

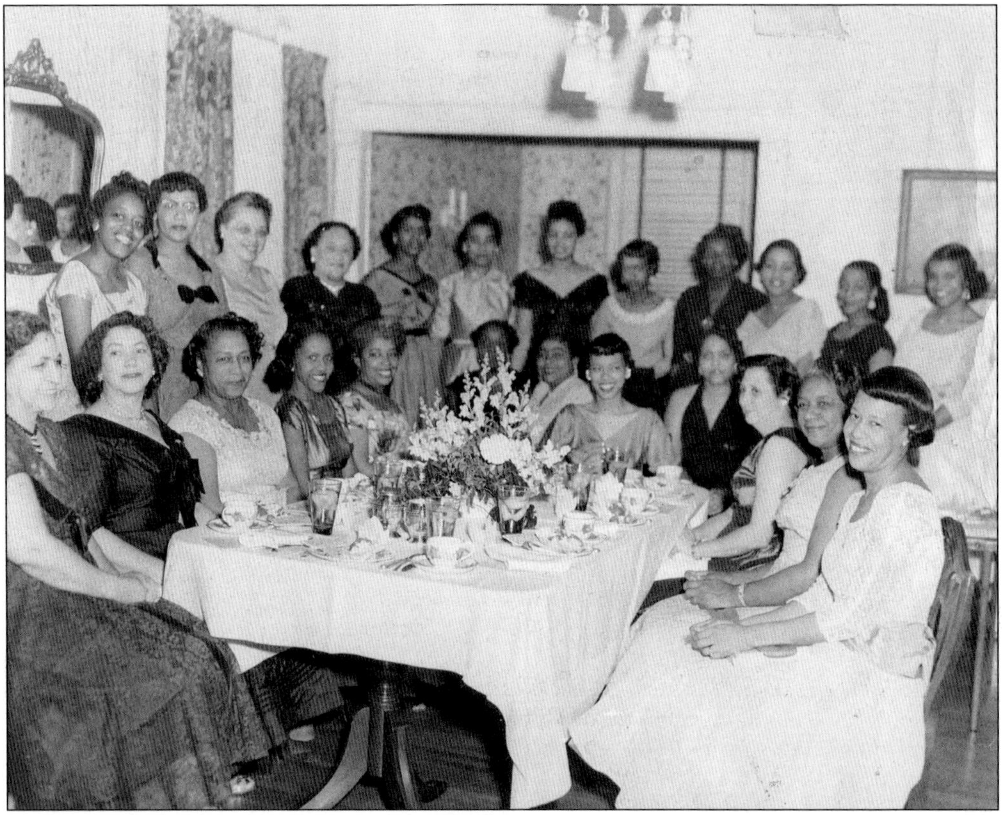

Members of the Pi Omega chapter of Alpha Kappa Alpha Sorority, Inc., are pictured *c.* 1959 at a regional planning committee meeting.

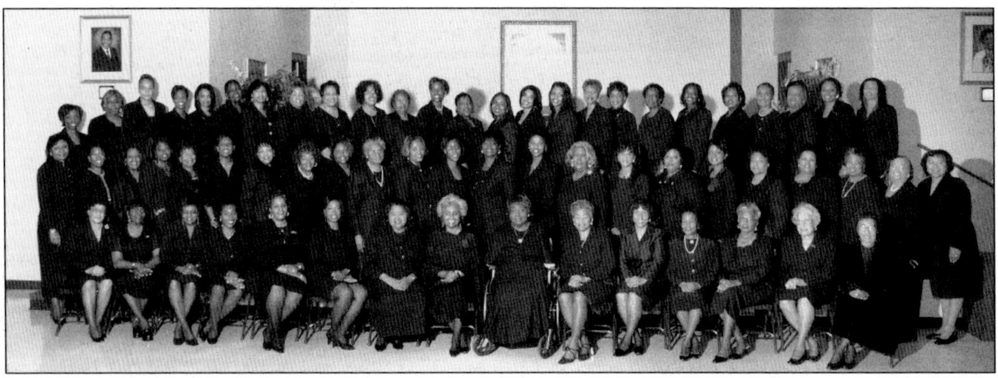

The Pi Omega chapter of Alpha Kappa Alpha Sorority, Inc., was founded on June 25, 1925, at First Congregational Church. Founding members included Dr. Emma Wheeler, Alma Howse, Lucille Diggs, Delolah Harris, and the chapter's first president, Emma J. Henry, daughter of James A. Henry.

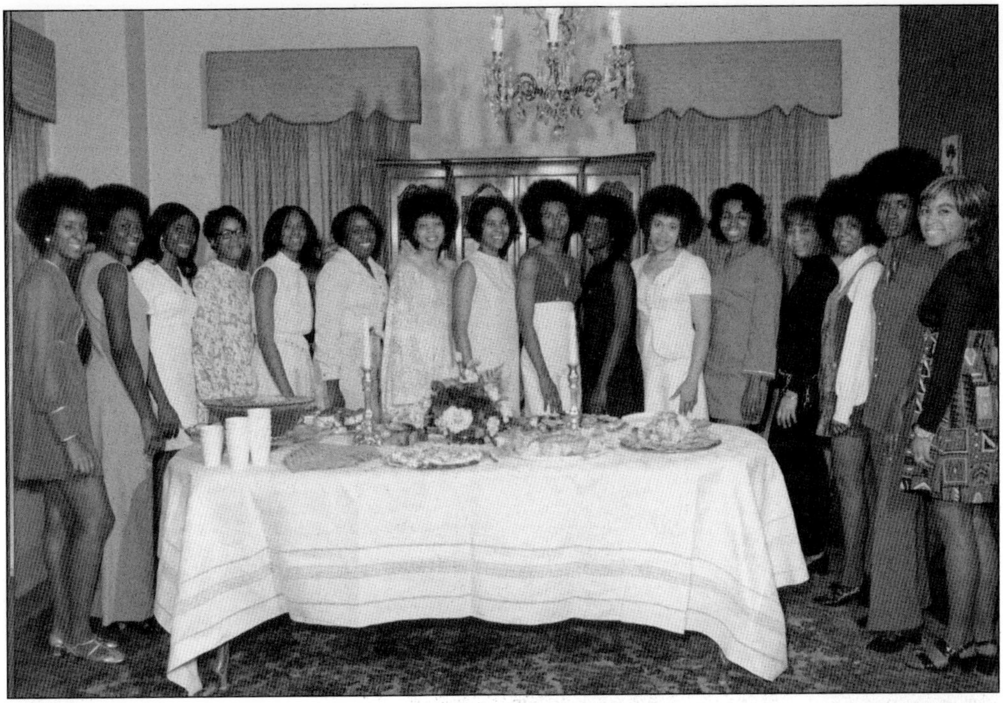

Members of the Zeta Kappa chapter of Alpha Kappa Alpha are seen here around 1971. This chapter was founded in 1970 under the direction of Dorothy Scruggs Jones and Vilma Scruggs Fields.

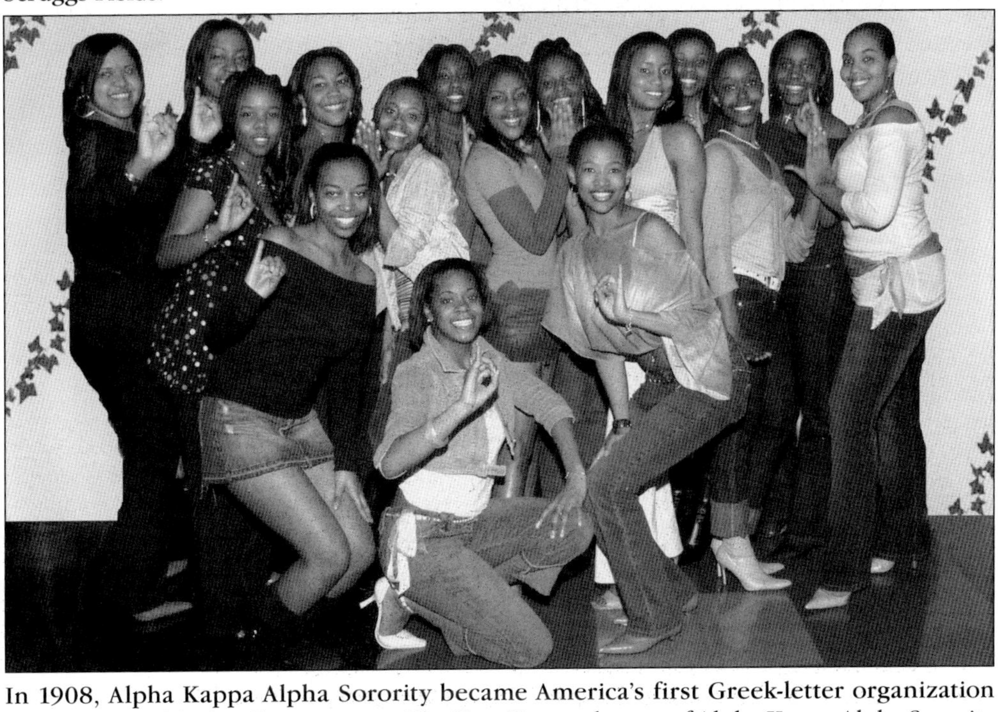

In 1908, Alpha Kappa Alpha Sorority became America's first Greek-letter organization established by black college women. The Zeta Kappa chapter of Alpha Kappa Alpha Sorority was founded at the University of Tennessee at Chattanooga (UTC) in 1971.

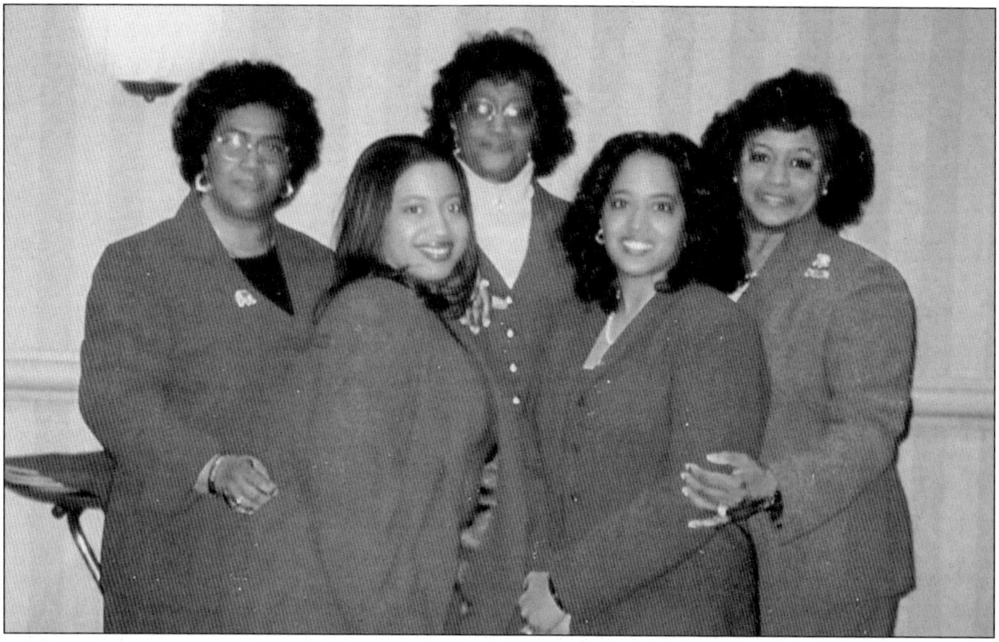

The Kilgore family, members of Chattanooga Alumnae chapter of Delta Sigma Theta Sorority, Inc., are pictured here from left to right: Linda (Kilgore) Logan, Kellie Logan, Joyce (Kilgore) Overton, Stephanie Logan-Tate, and Carol (Kilgore) O'Neal are all active members in this chapter.

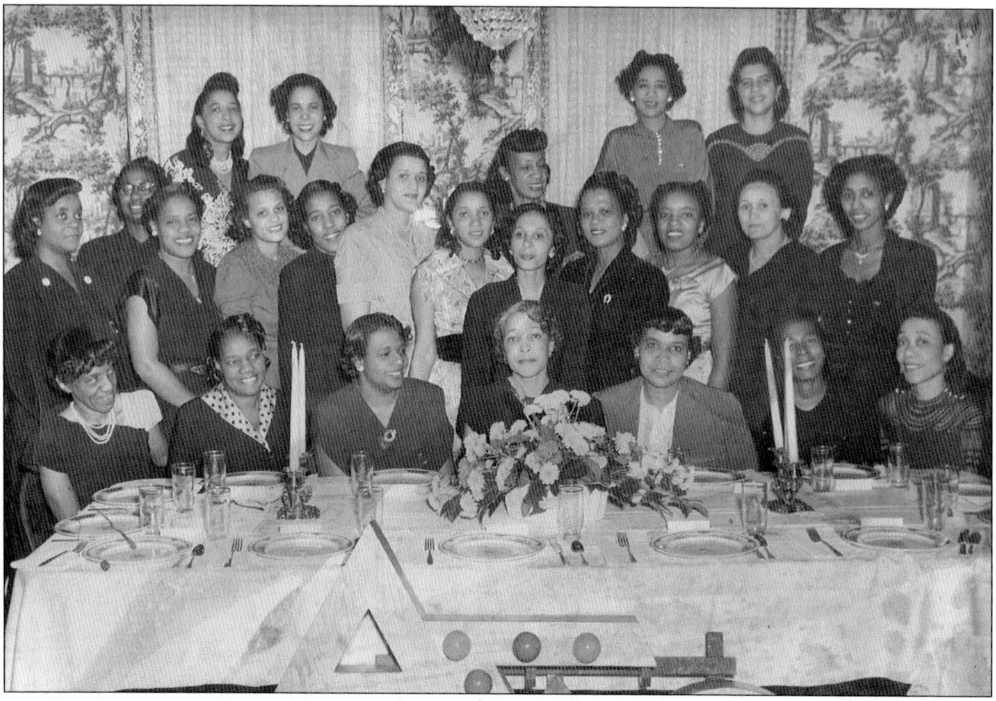

In 1935, eight female college graduates applied for a charter to begin a chapter of Delta Sigma Theta Sorority, Inc. Six years later, the Beta Epsilon (now Chattanooga Alumnae) chapter was formed.

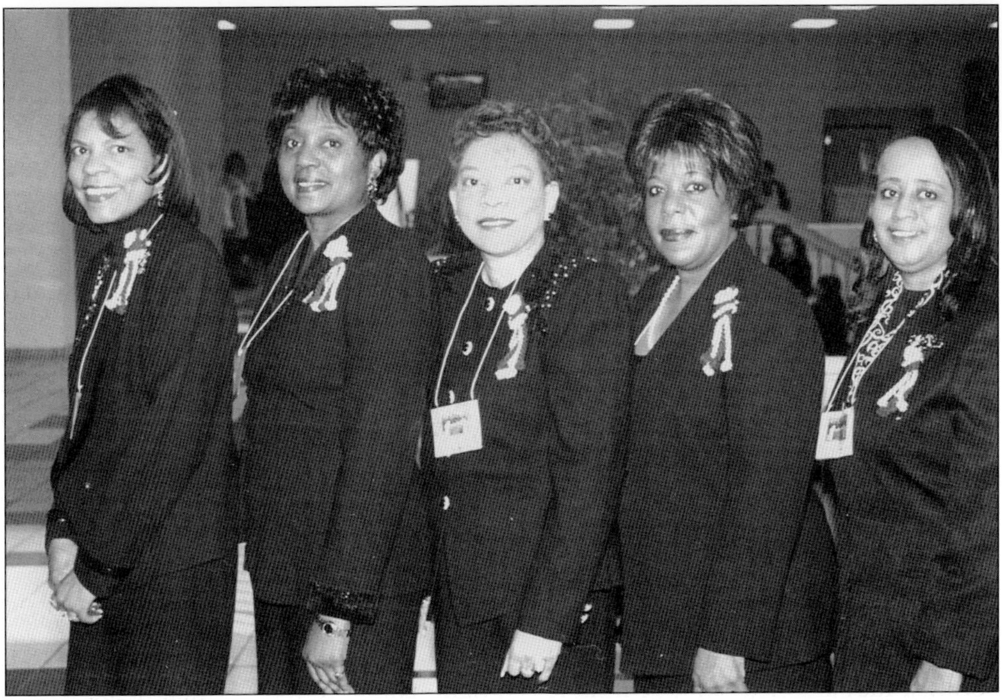

Deltas from across the state of Tennessee were present to give honor to the 22 founders of Delta Sigma Theta. The 2005 Founders Day host chapters were the Chattanooga Alumnae and Theta Rho (UTC) chapters.

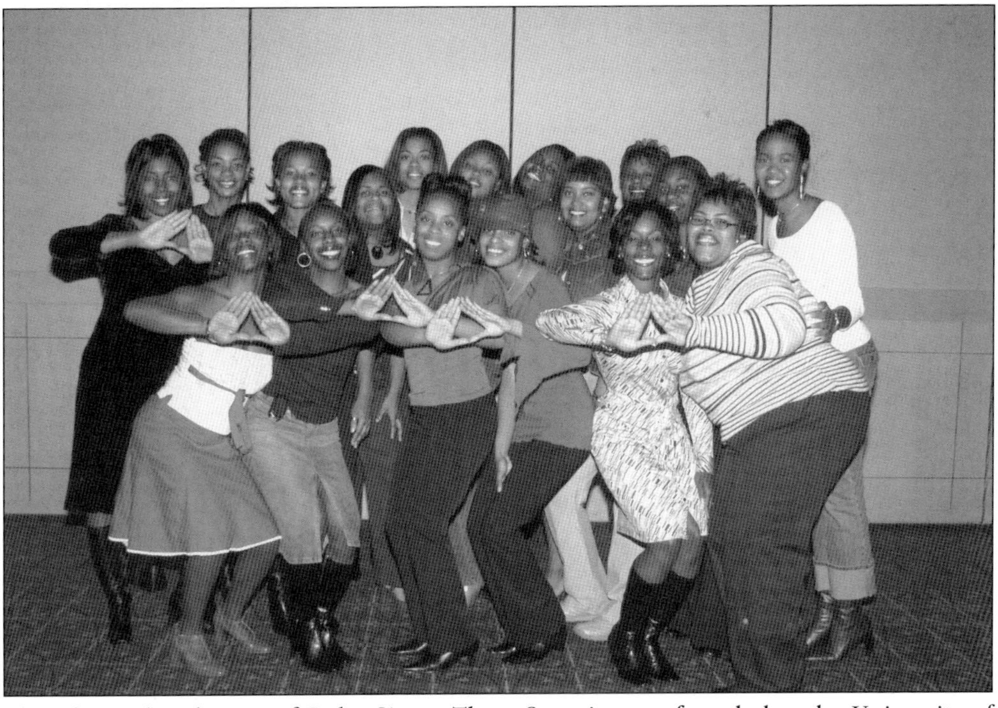

The Theta Rho chapter of Delta Sigma Theta Sorority was founded at the University of Tennessee at Chattanooga in 1971.

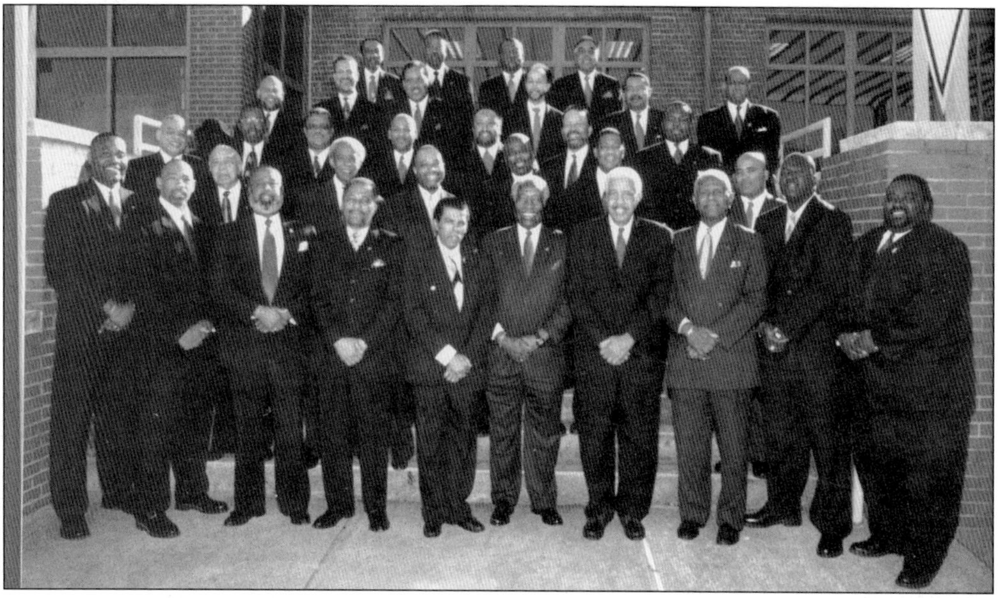

The Chattanooga Alumnae chapter of Kappa Alpha Psi Fraternity, Inc., was founded on June 1, 1946. Values of the alumni chapter include leadership, achievement, and brotherhood. They are committed to youth and community involvement through spiritual, social, and cooperative partnership.

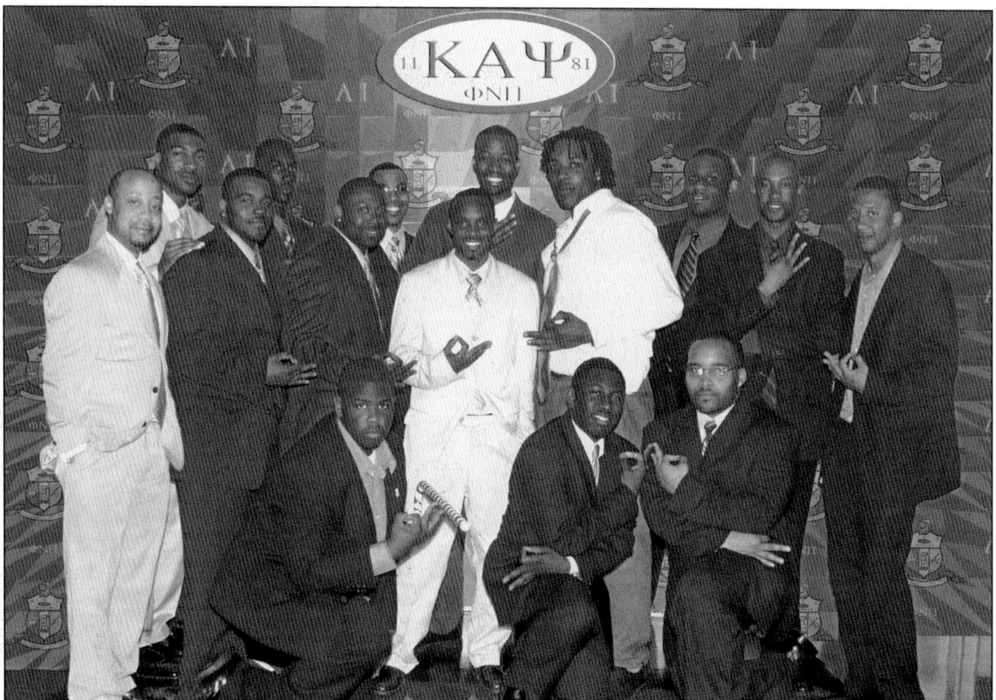

The Lambda Iota chapter of Kappa Alpha Psi Fraternity was founded at the University of Tennessee at Chattanooga in 1981. Fashioning achievement as its purpose, Kappa Alpha Psi began uniting college men of culture, patriotism, and honor in a bond of fraternity.

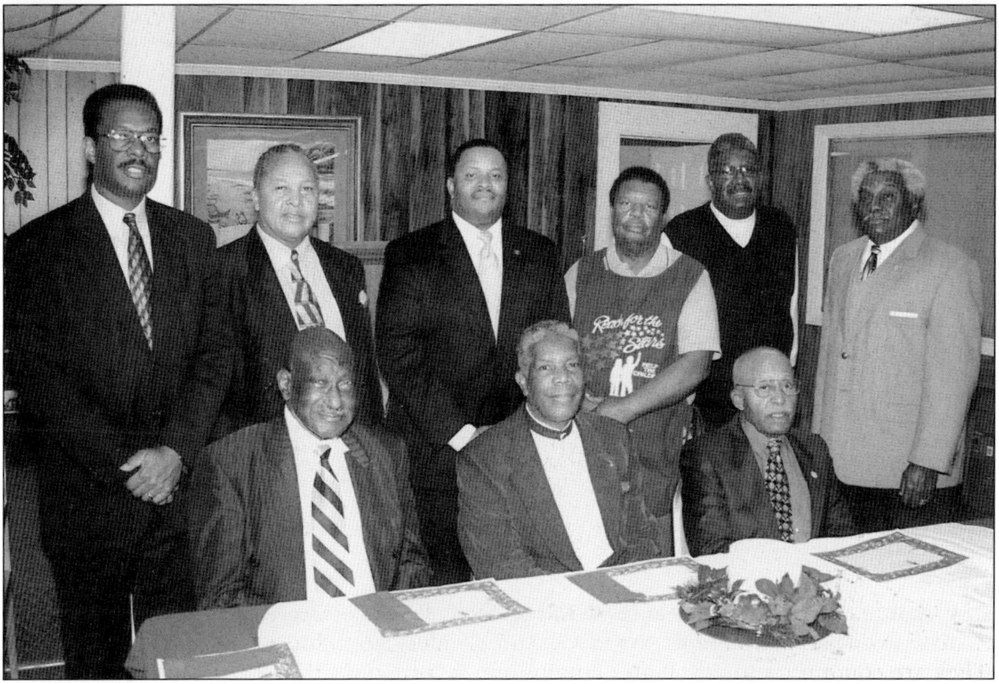

The Psi Lambda chapter of Alpha Phi Alpha Fraternity, Inc., was founded in 1926. Members of the fraternity participate in their annual adopt-a-grandparent Christmas dinner, one of the many community activities that the fraternity participates in annually.

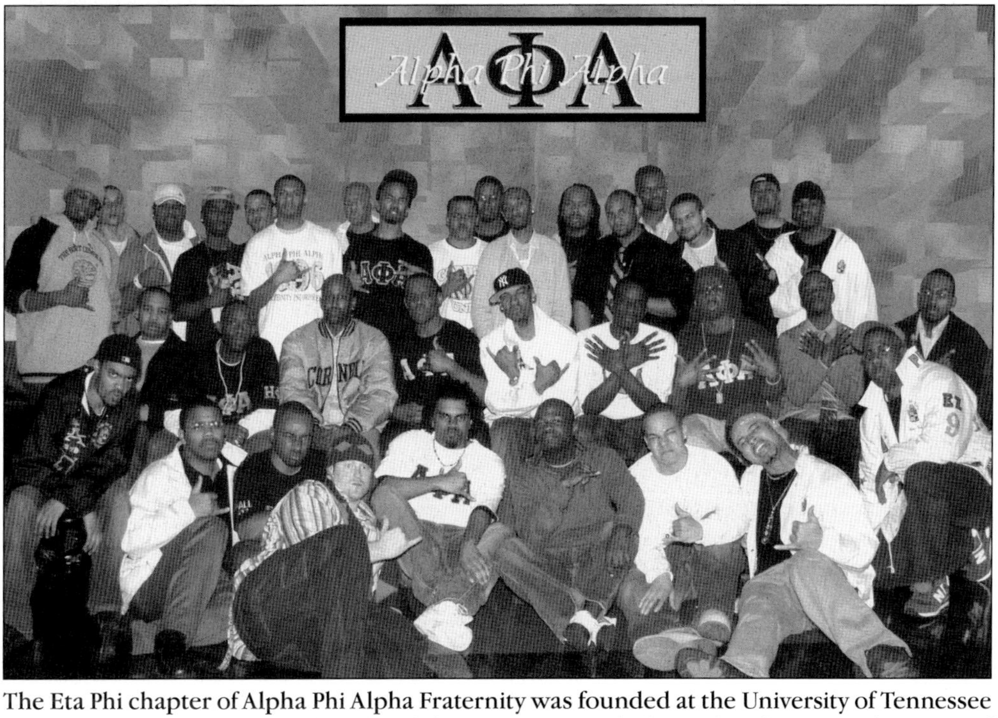

The Eta Phi chapter of Alpha Phi Alpha Fraternity was founded at the University of Tennessee at Chattanooga in 1971. Alpha Phi Alpha Fraternity is dedicated to fostering the spirit of brotherhood and training a new generation of leaders.

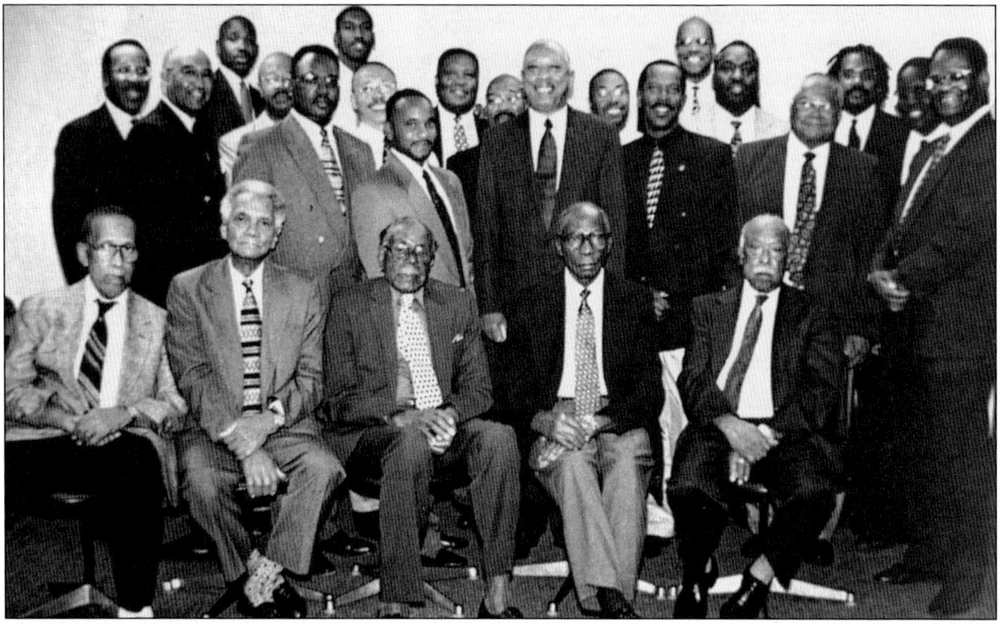

From the initials of the Greek phrase meaning "Friendship is Essential to the Soul," the name Omega Psi Phi was derived. This international fraternity's Chattanooga chapter, Kappa Iota, was formed in the fall of 1945. Kappa Iota provides the following programs: Achievement Week, scholarships, Talent Hunt, memorial services, Reclamation (a program to reclaim members who for one reason or another had to drop out of the chapter), and United Negro College Fund (UNCF).

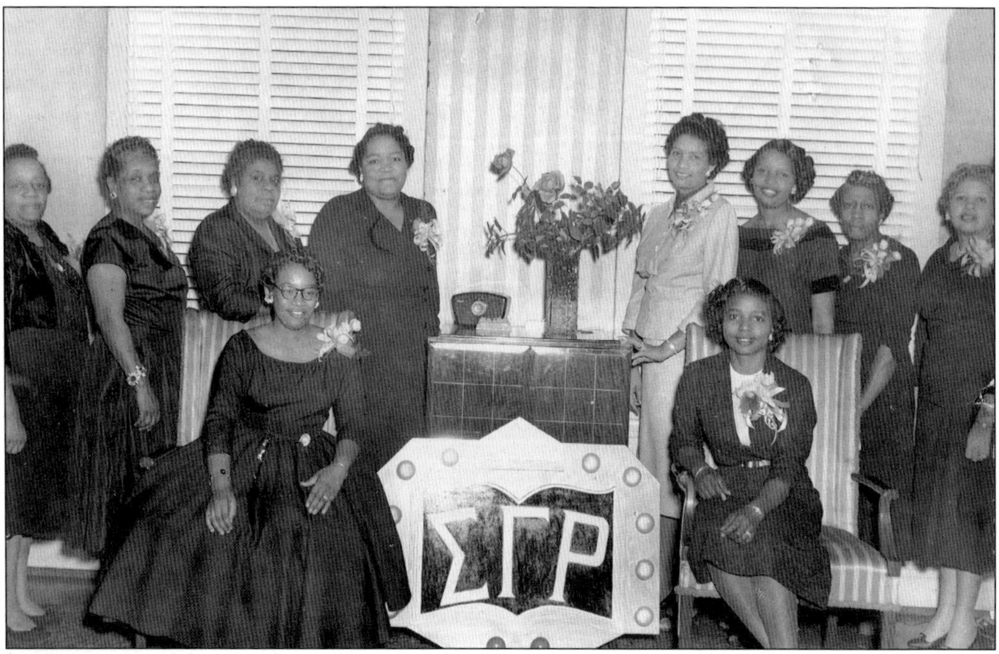

Sigma Gamma Rho Sorority's aim is to enhance the quality of life within the community. Public service, leadership development, and education of youth are hallmarks of the organization's programs and activities. This is a late-1950s photograph of the Chattanooga Alumni chapter of Sigma Gamma Rho Sorority, Inc.

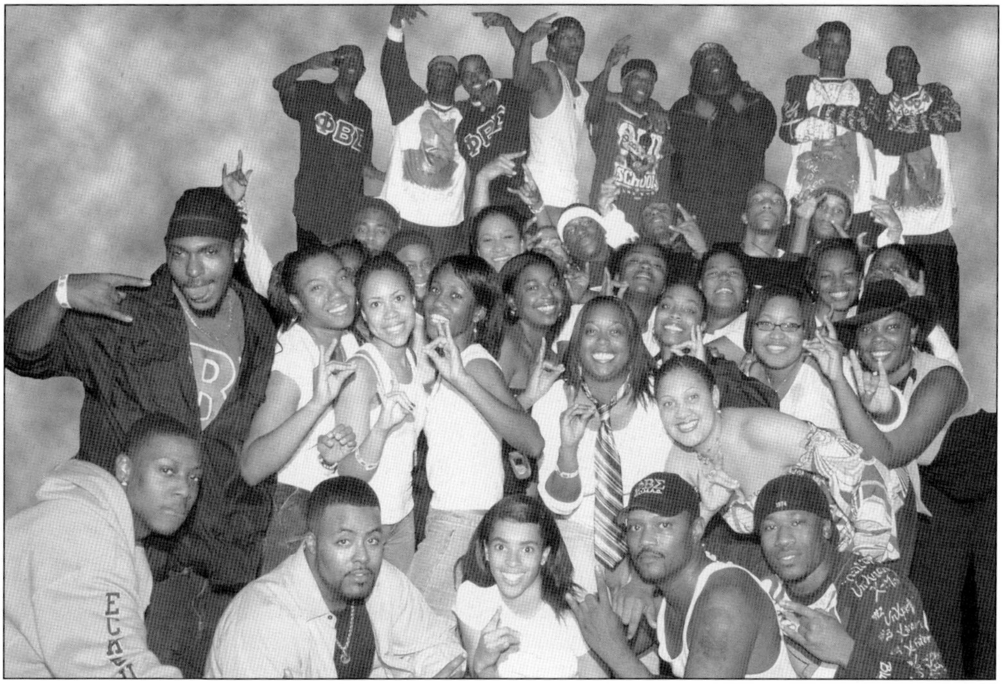

Pictured here are members of the Xi Upsilon chapter of Phi Beta Sigma Fraternity, Inc., along with their sister organization, Zeta Phi Beta Sorority, Inc., both from the University of Tennessee at Chattanooga. Phi Beta Sigma Fraternity holds a constitutional bond with Zeta Phi Beta Sorority, the only black Greek-letter organizations to do so.

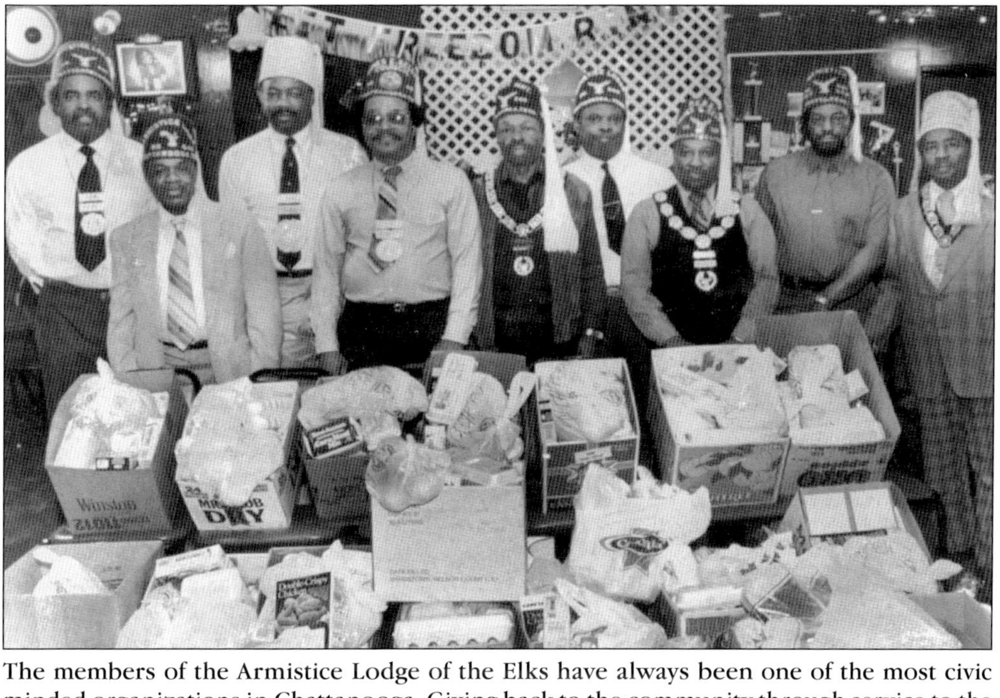

The members of the Armistice Lodge of the Elks have always been one of the most civic minded organizations in Chattanooga. Giving back to the community through service to the needy was always evident in their community projects.

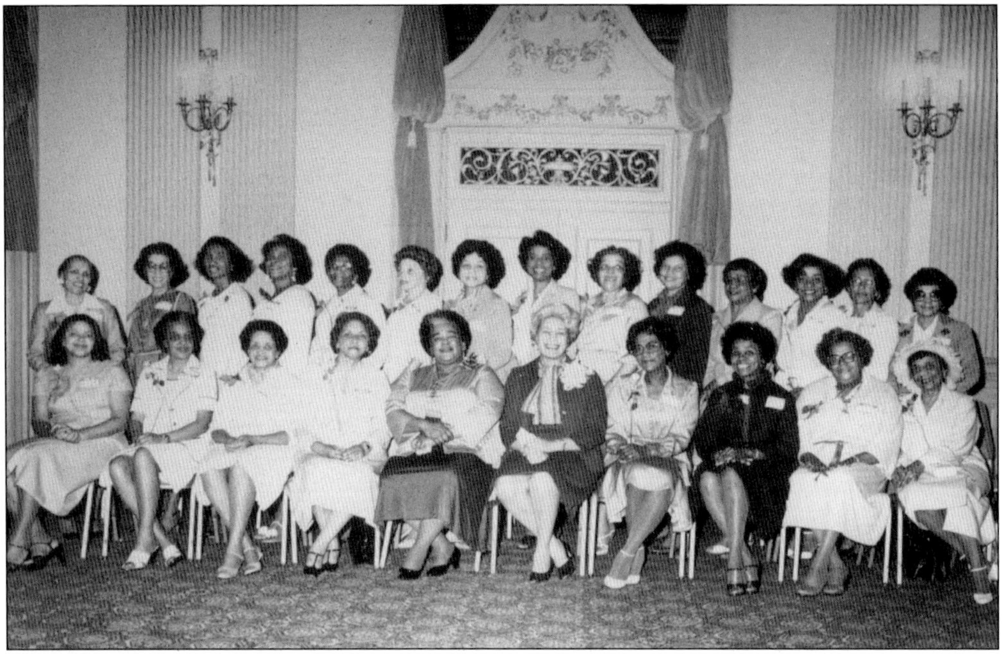

The Chattanooga chapter of Links, Inc., is a volunteer service organization of African American women. The membership seeks to improve the quality of life for the greater community and its members through education and civic and cultural activities. The Chattanooga chapter was the fifth Links chapter established in Tennessee and is one of nearly 250 chapters nationwide.

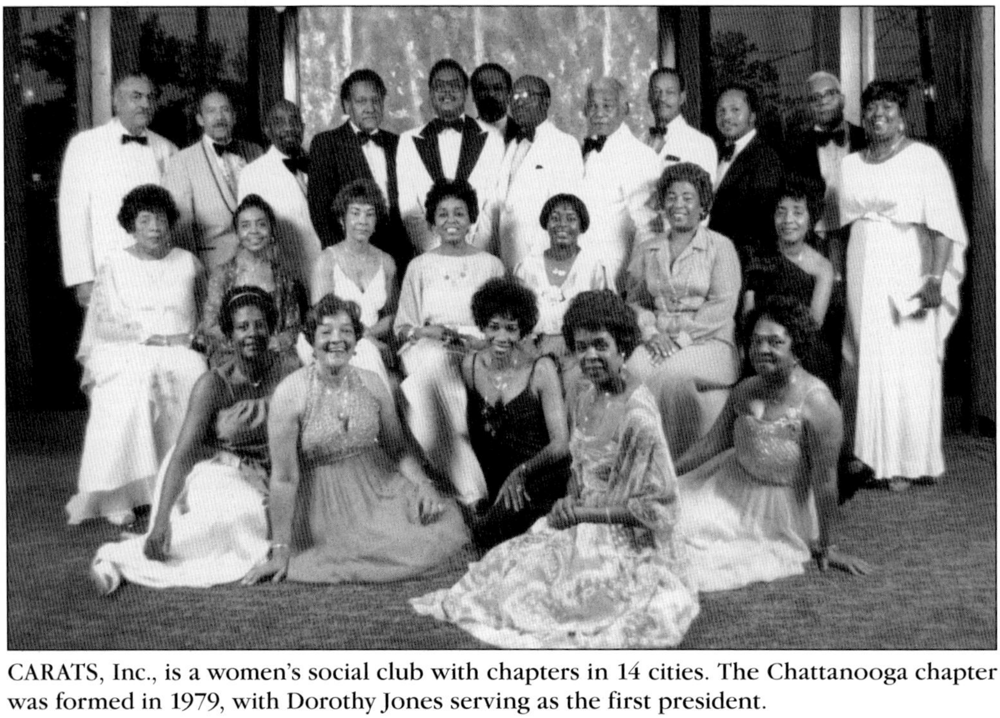

CARATS, Inc., is a women's social club with chapters in 14 cities. The Chattanooga chapter was formed in 1979, with Dorothy Jones serving as the first president.

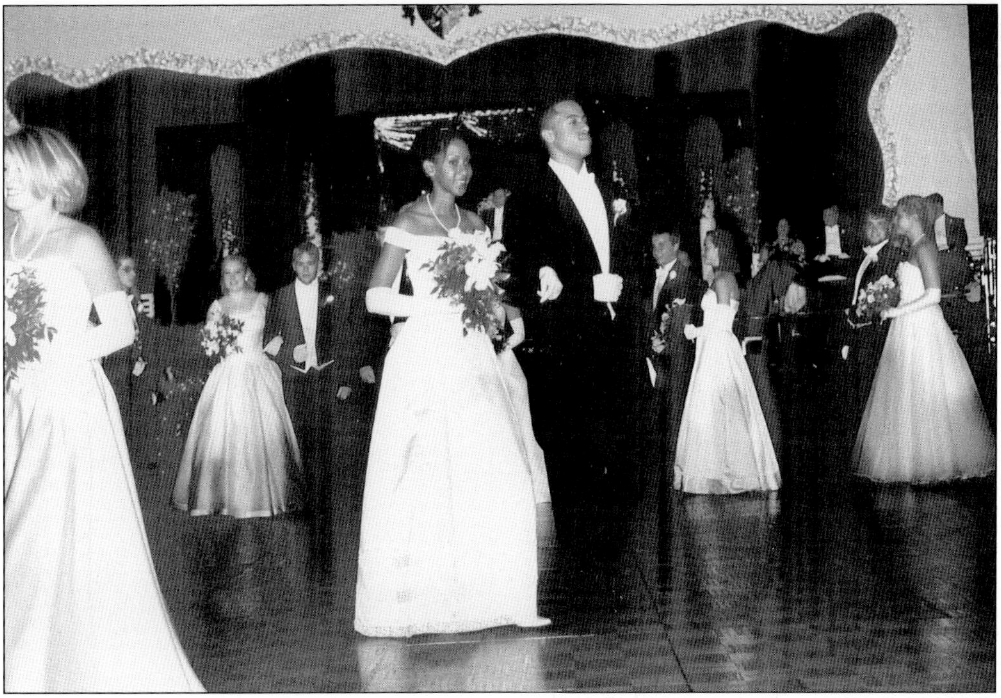

Hilary Williams, escorted by James Andrew Bradley, was the first African American "belle" to be presented at the Cotton Ball in the 40-plus years of all-white presentations. She is the daughter of Judge Walter Williams and Gwen Williams.

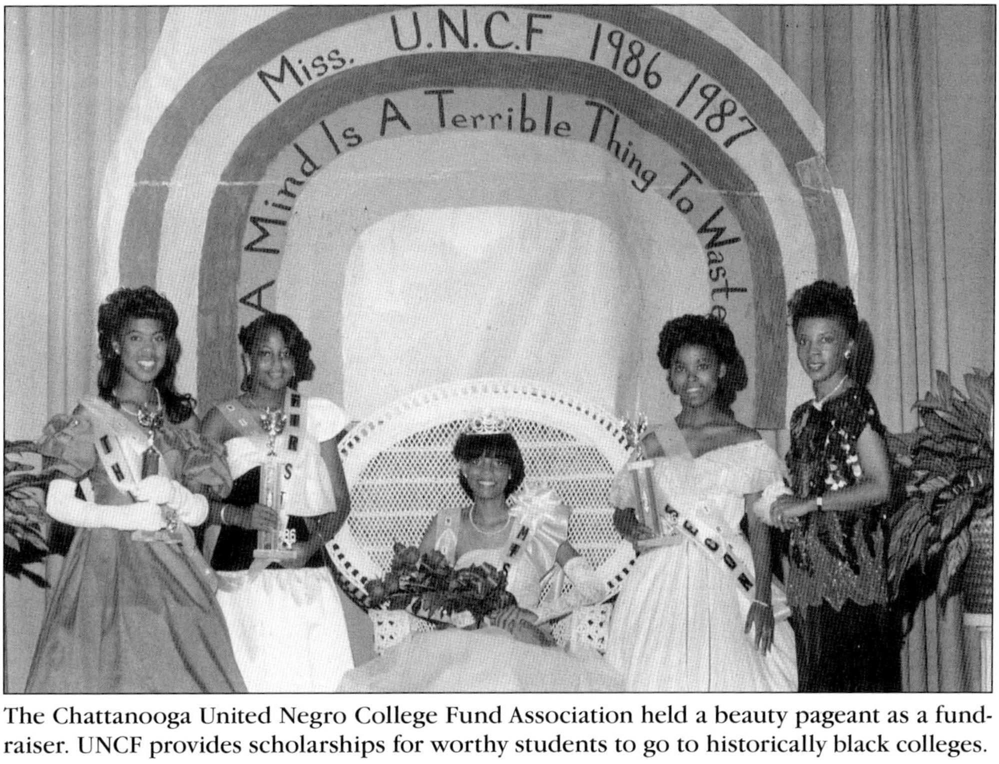

The Chattanooga United Negro College Fund Association held a beauty pageant as a fund-raiser. UNCF provides scholarships for worthy students to go to historically black colleges.

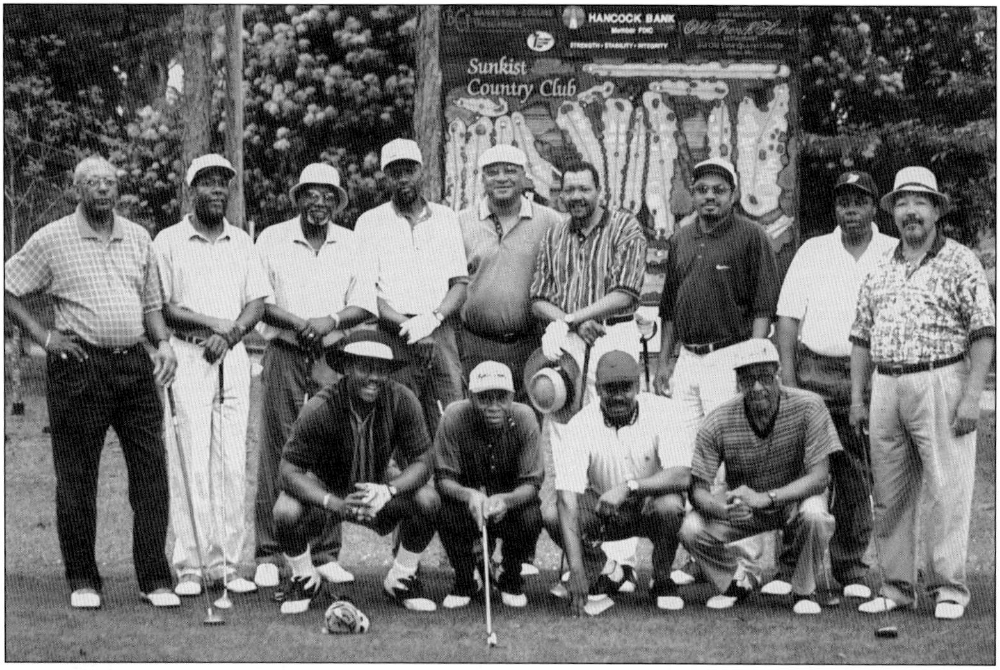

The 19th Hole Golf Association was formed to create an outlet for minority players and to make golf available and accessible to all people through youth clinics, community outreach, and scholarships.

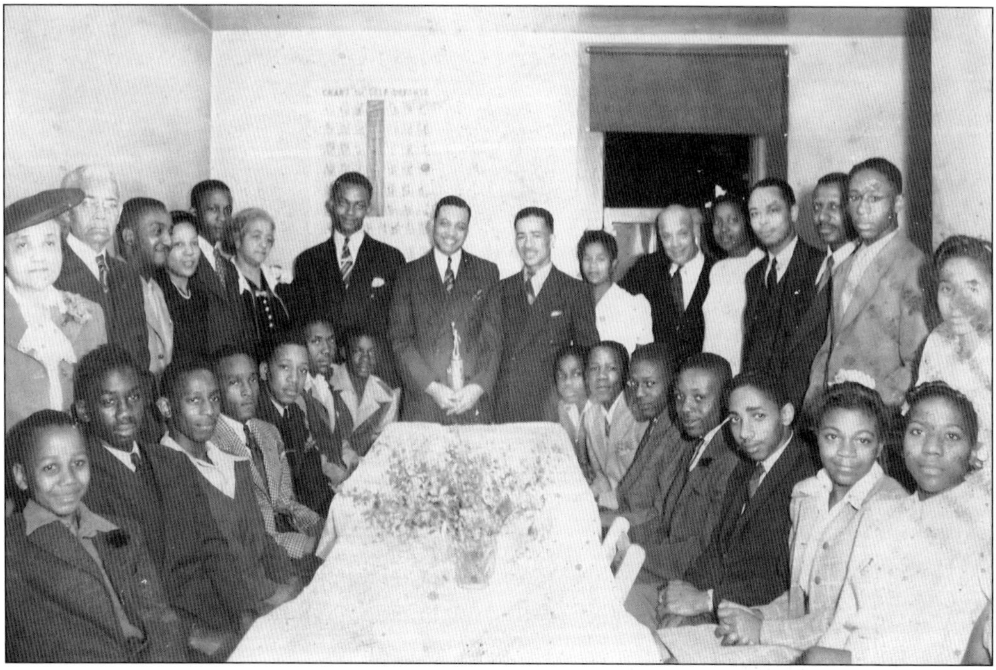

Chattanooga Black Athletic Association was formed in 1951 to benefit both African American coaches and athletes and to foster lifelong values, good citizenship, ethics, and a fair-play approach to life among student-athletes while promoting safe and sporting-like athletic environments.

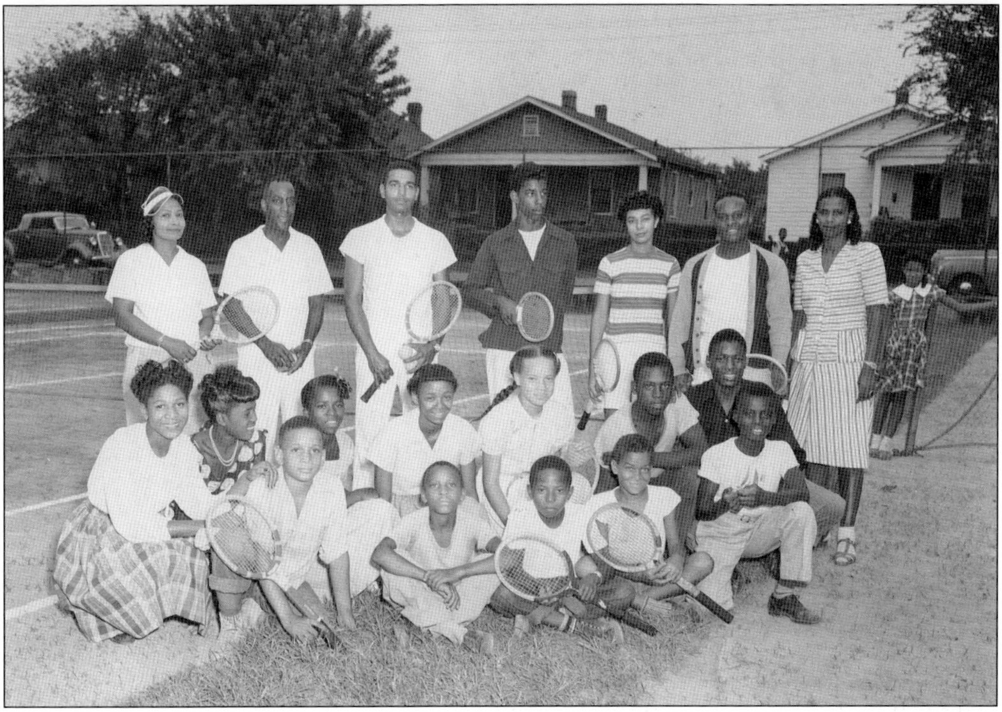

Lincoln Park Tennis Association was formed in 1947, when a group of youths expressed interest in the game of tennis. One of the biggest success stories out of this group was the discovery of the talent that Wylhma McGhee-Reid had. McGhee-Reid won city, state, and national championships at Tuskegee, Alabama. McGhee-Reid went on to play tennis professionally for many years.

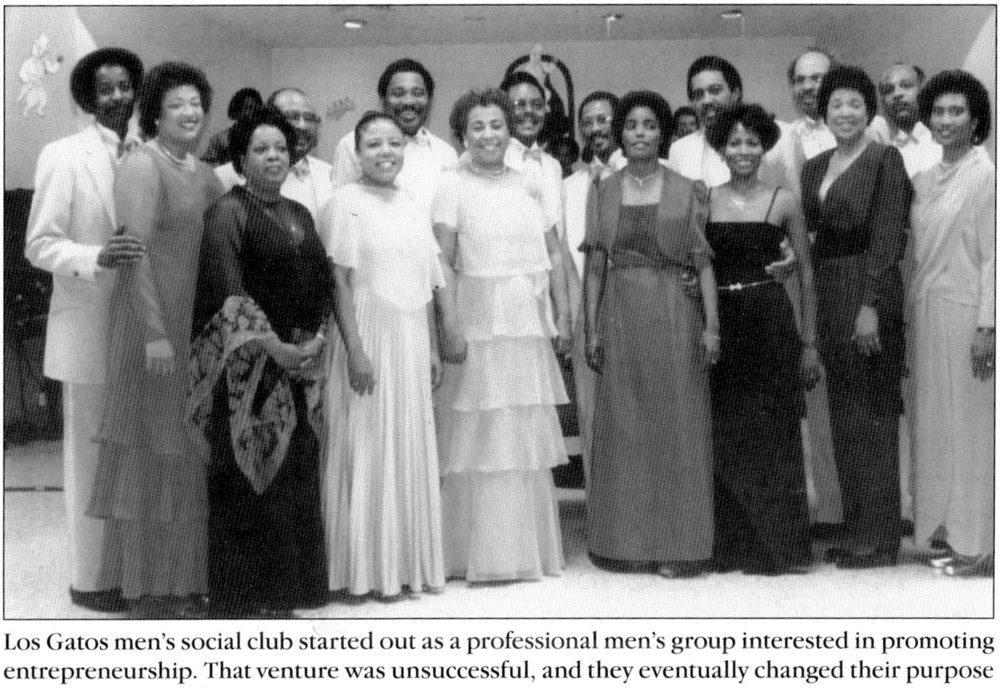

Los Gatos men's social club started out as a professional men's group interested in promoting entrepreneurship. That venture was unsuccessful, and they eventually changed their purpose to become a social club.

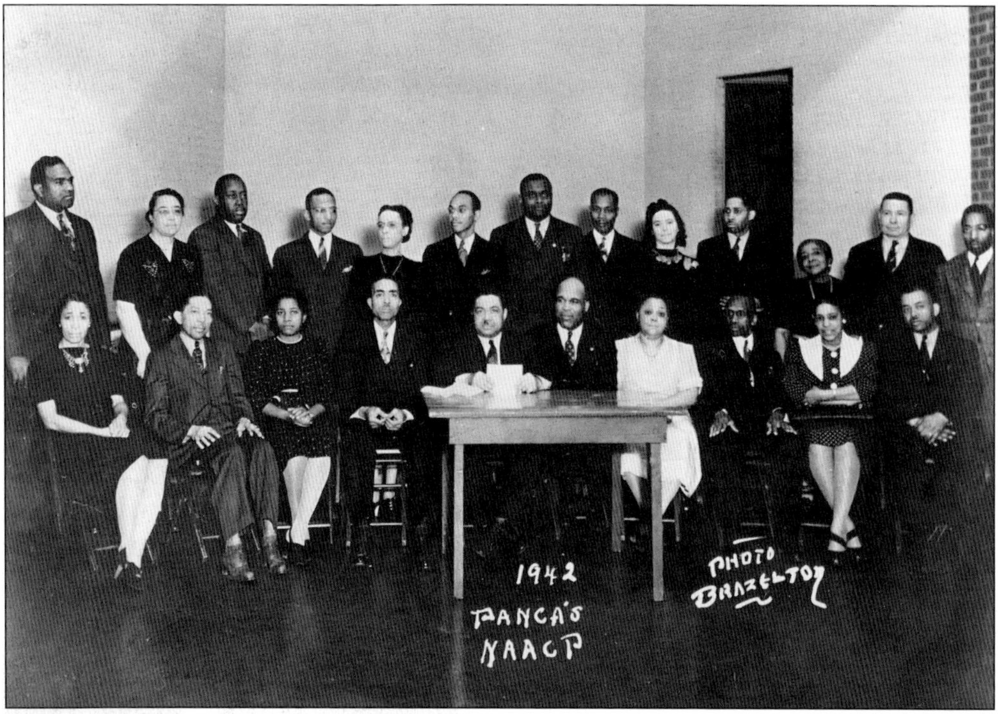

Here is a 1942 picture of the Chattanooga chapter of the National Association for the Advancement of Colored People. The National Association for the Advancement of Colored People, or NAACP, is one of the oldest and most influential civil rights organizations in the United States.

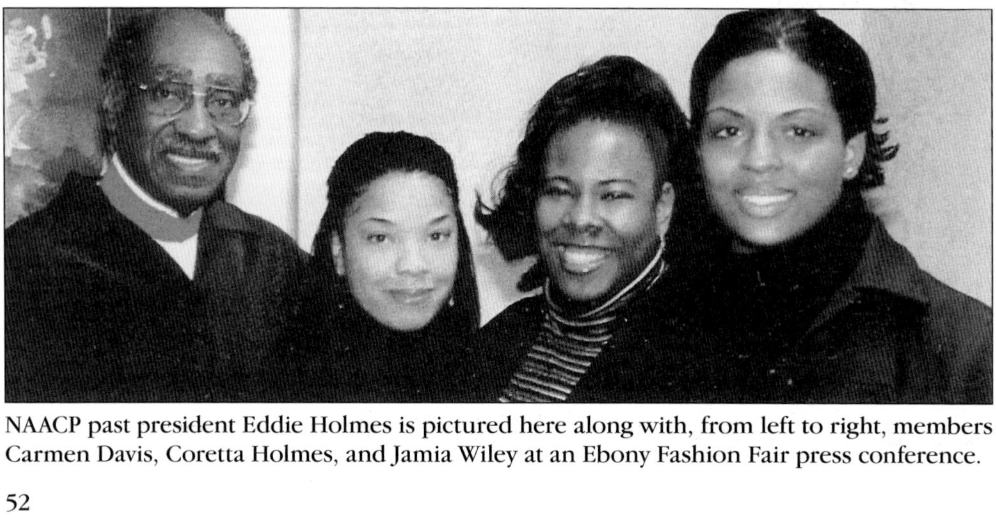

NAACP past president Eddie Holmes is pictured here along with, from left to right, members Carmen Davis, Coretta Holmes, and Jamia Wiley at an Ebony Fashion Fair press conference.

Jesse Jackson formed two nonprofit organizations, Operation PUSH (People United to Serve Humanity) and the National Rainbow Coalition. Both groups merged in 1996. The combined organization keeps its national headquarters in Chicago and has branches throughout the United States. Johnny Holloway, pictured at right, served as the former head of the Chattanooga chapter of the Rainbow/PUSH Coalition.

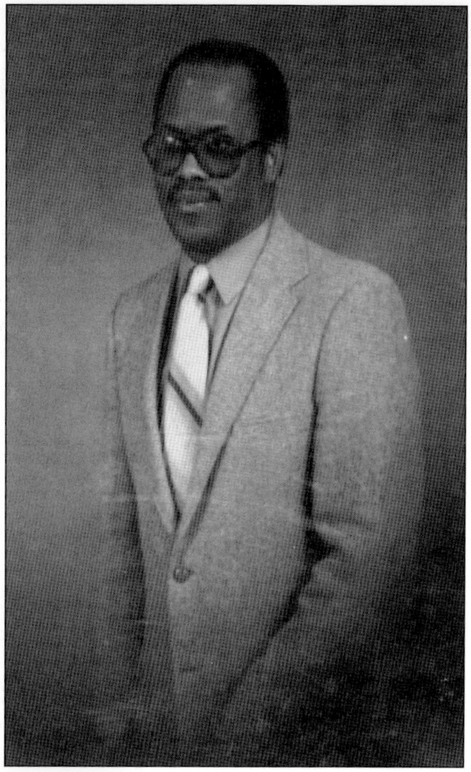

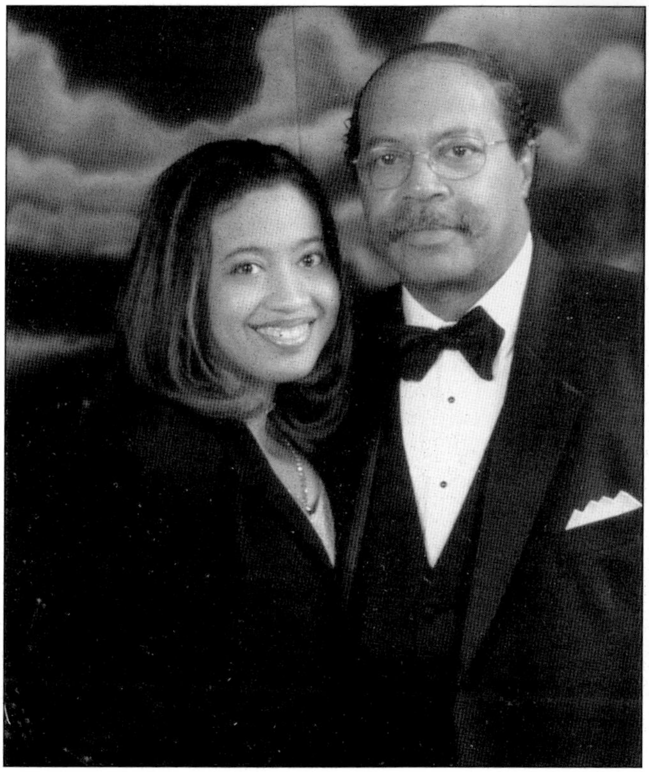

Kellie Logan is shown here with her father, Warren Logan, president of the Urban League of Greater Chattanooga (ULGC), at the 2003 Equal Opportunity Dinner. ULGC's mission is to enable African Americans and other disadvantaged persons to secure economic self-reliance, parity, power, and civil rights.

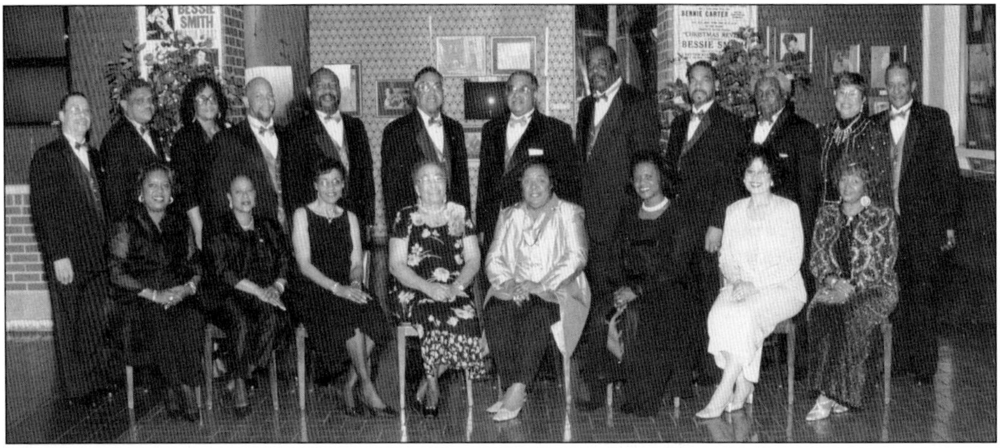

Couples Club of Chattanooga is seen here at a March 2002 social. This social club, which holds dances and other activities for its members, started in 1972 and still exists today.

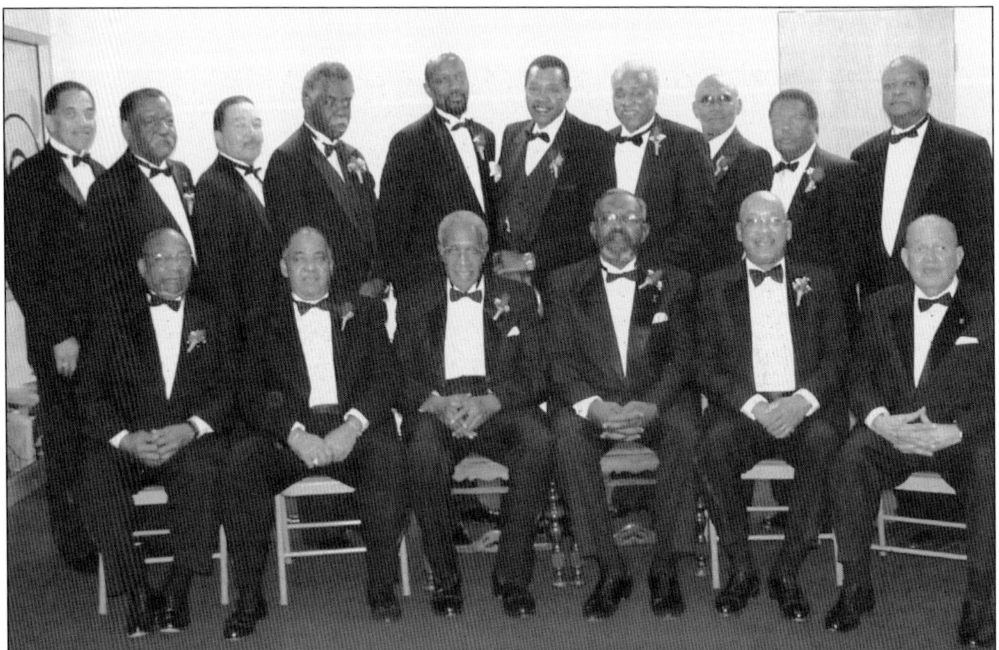

Esquire Club is a social club for men only. The club holds socials twice a year for members and their spouses.

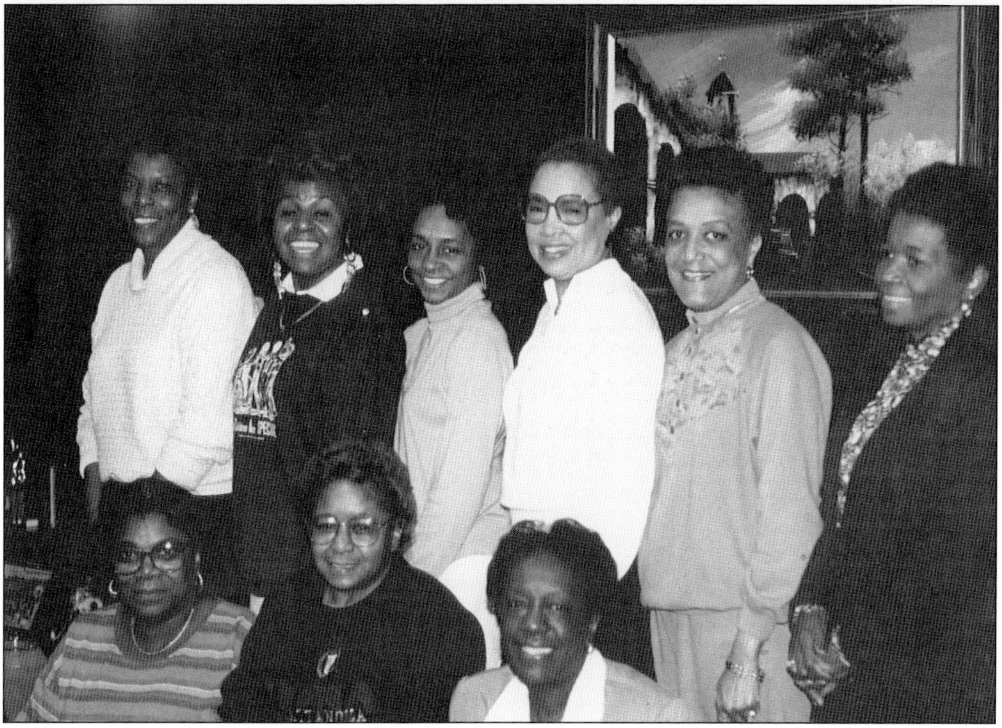

Les Sophisticates Bridge Club dates back to 1961. Bridge clubs served as another social outlet for African American women. Many of these clubs still exist today.

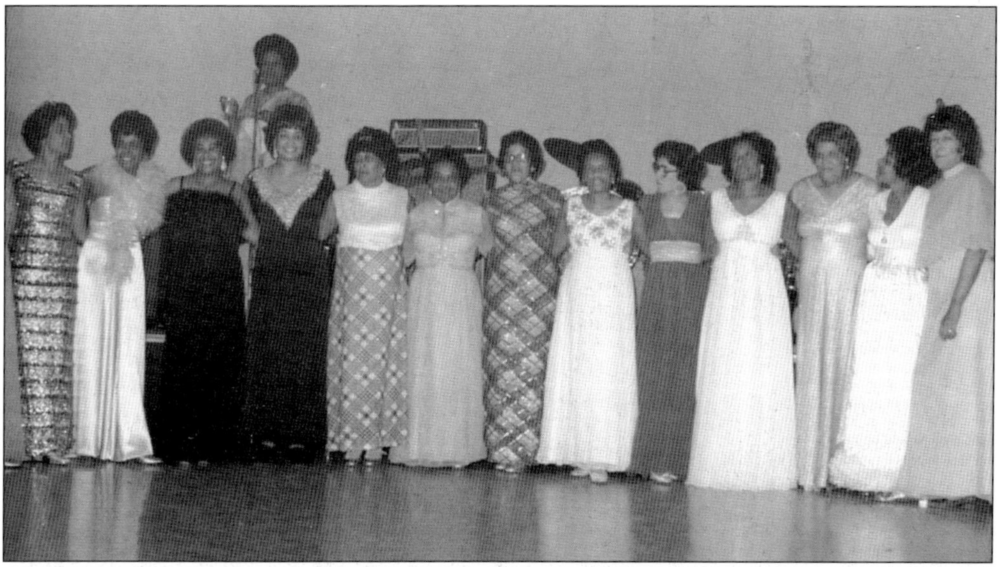

Members of the Witoka Bridge Club, which dates back to the 1950s, are pictured at a social function in the late 1970s. Bridge clubs became popular in the 1950s in middle-class African American communities throughout the nation. These clubs serve as another social outlet for the female members of the black elite.

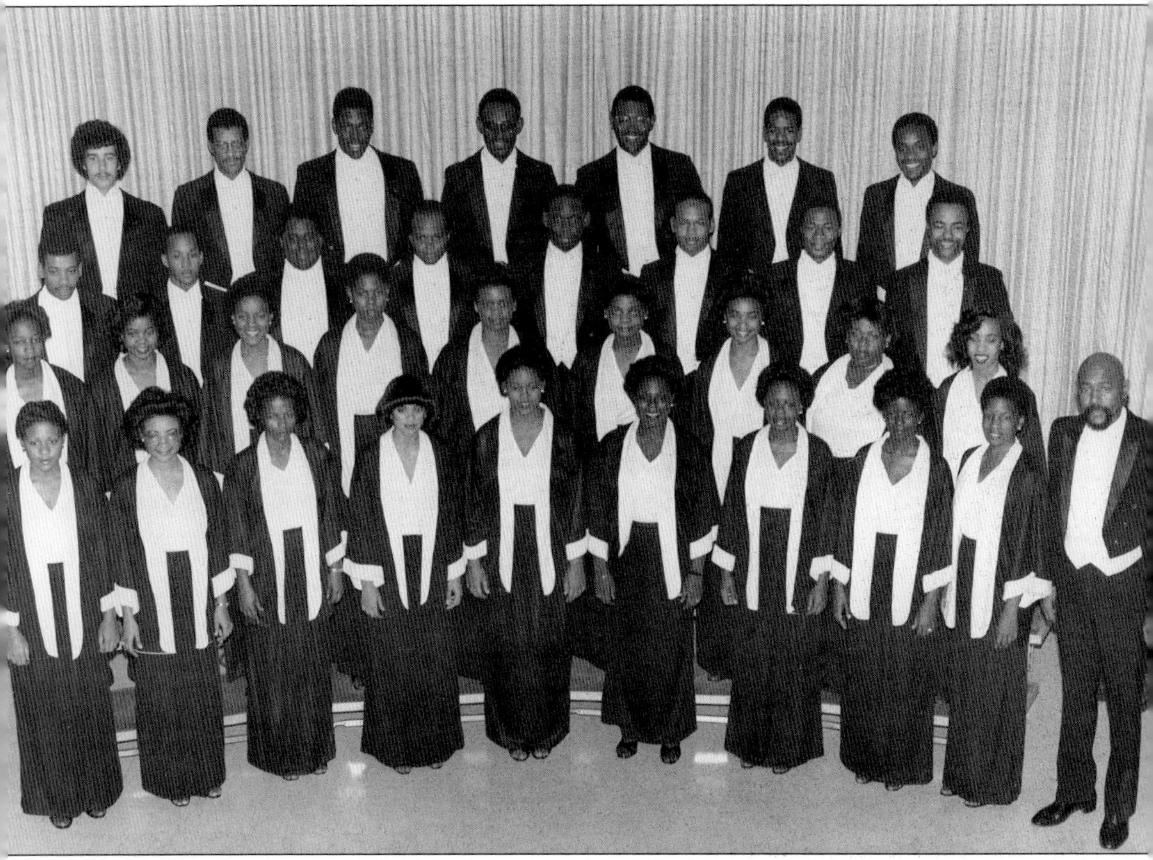

The Chattanooga Choral Society for the Preservation of African American Song is a group formed to preserve the rich heritage of African American songs with special emphasis on Negro spirituals. Under the direction of Roland Carter, this diverse group is comprised of different professional backgrounds, including students, professors, professional musicians, and others, who all share a love of music and a desire to perform with an emphasis on quality.

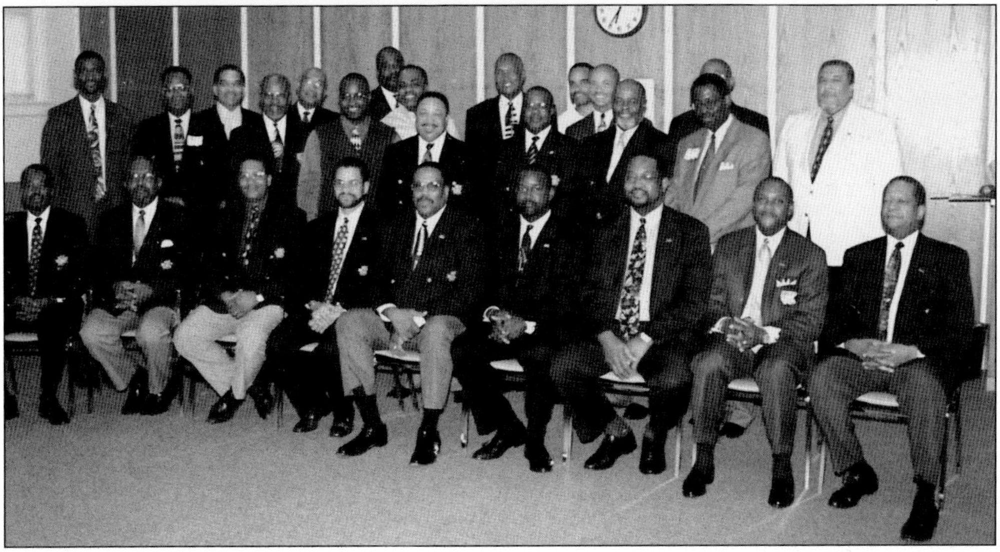

Due to the encouragement of Ruby Key, the 25th chapter of 100 Black Men was established in 1992. The mission of 100 Black Men of Chattanooga, Inc., is to improve the quality of life of our citizens and enhance educational and economic opportunities for all African Americans.

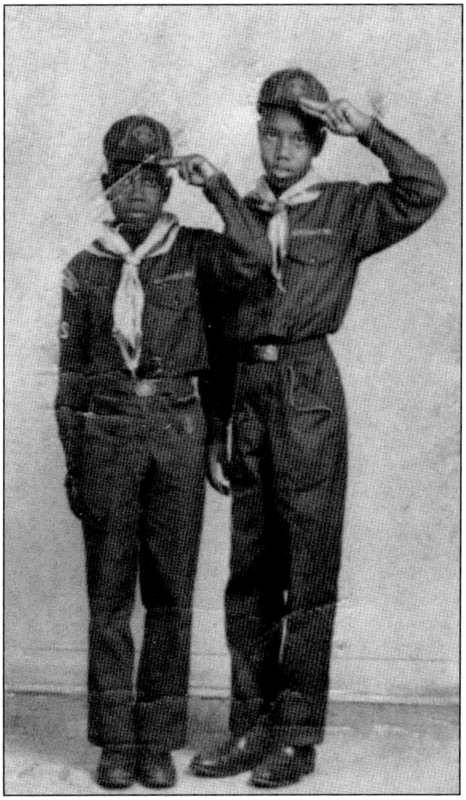

Success in life for many young black males began with the Scouts. The mission of the Boy Scouts of America is to prepare young people to make ethical and moral choices over their lifetimes by instilling in them the values of the Scout Oath and Law.

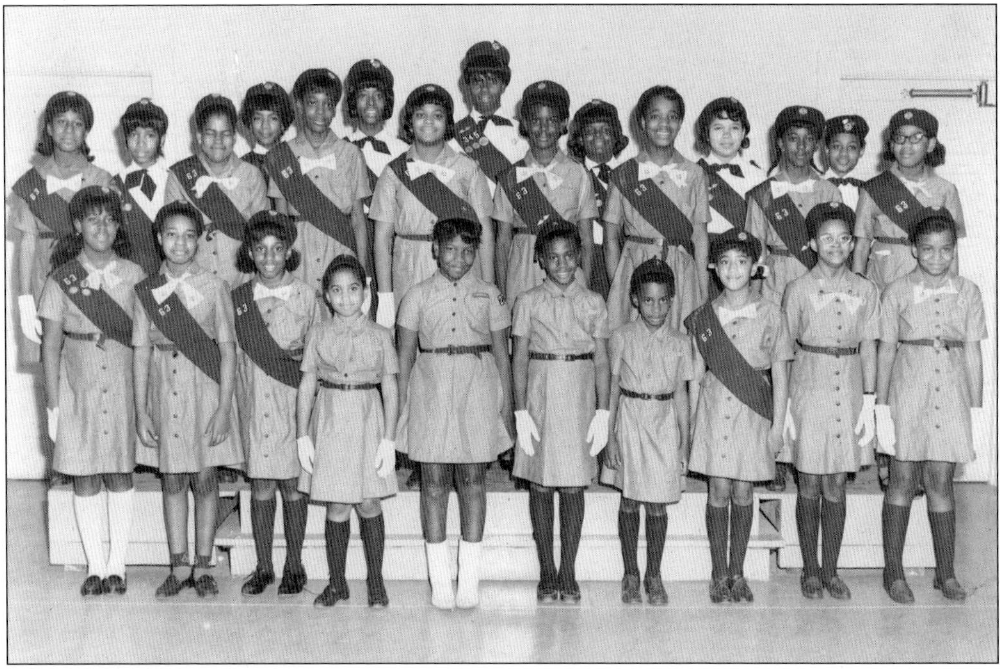

The Girl Scouts offered many activities that taught discipline and built character for young black females. The purpose of Girl Scouting is to inspire girls with the highest ideals of character, conduct, patriotism, and service that they may become happy and resourceful citizens.

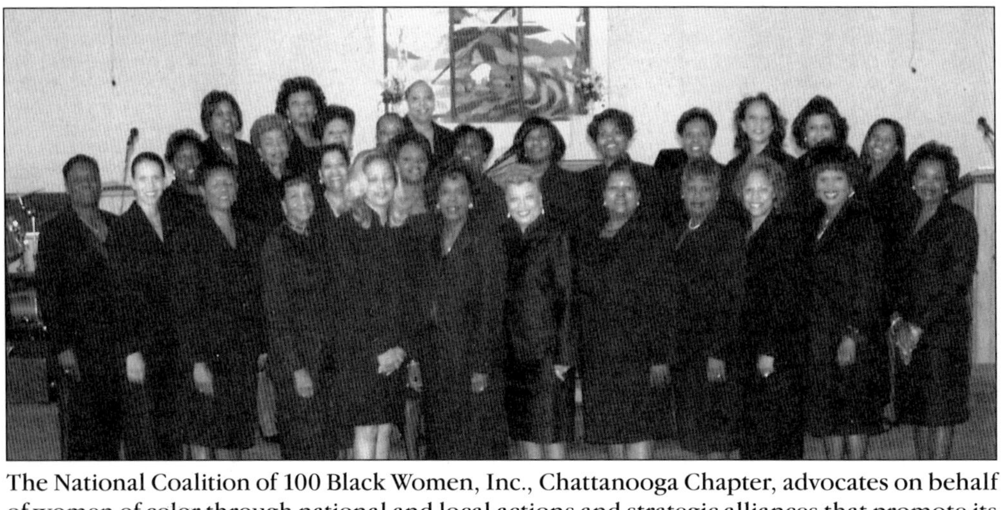

The National Coalition of 100 Black Women, Inc., Chattanooga Chapter, advocates on behalf of women of color through national and local actions and strategic alliances that promote its national and international agendas on leadership and on gender equality in health, education, and economic development.

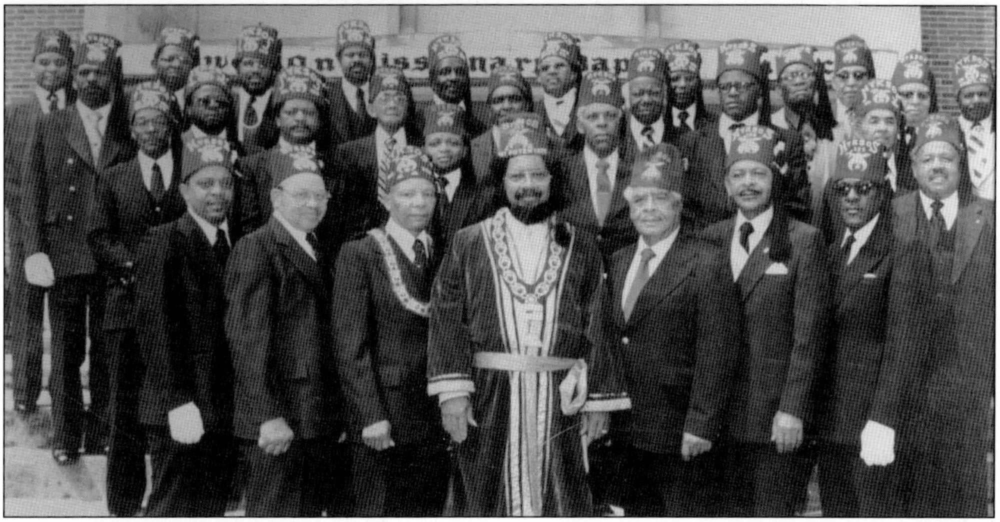

This is the Chattanooga chapter of the Shriners, a national organization of men that focuses on pride and leadership.

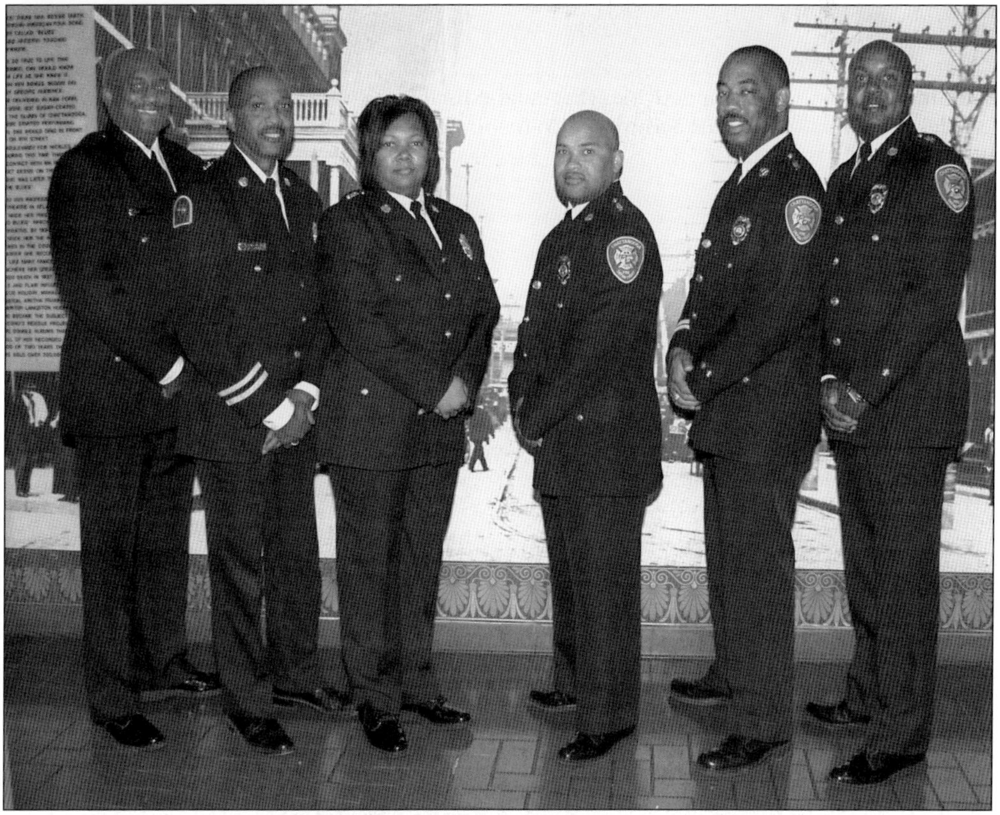

Pictured here are the 2005 officers of the Chattanooga Chapter of the International Association of Professional Black Fire Fighters (IAPBFF). IAPBFF maintains a continuous effort to provide leadership through service, commitment, and example. Pictured here, from left to right, are Freddie Brooks, Cecil Barker, Joyce Haynie, Randy Stargin Jr., David Brooks, and Danny Usher.

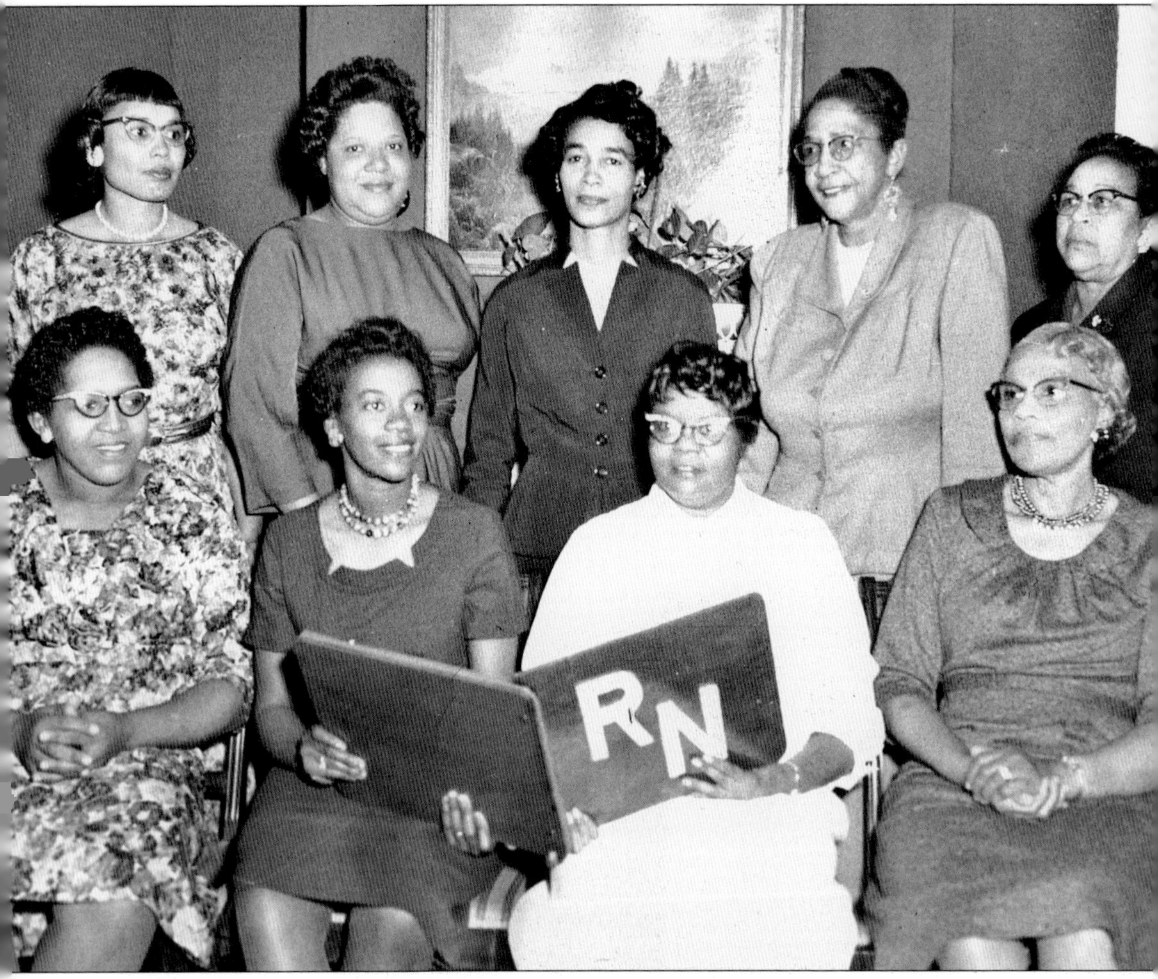

In 1959, the registered black nurses of Chattanooga banded together to form the Registered Nurses Club. The organization was formed to encourage black nurses to join other nursing organizations, offer loans to students with an interest in becoming nurses, and inform the public about the profession of nursing.

Four

Religion

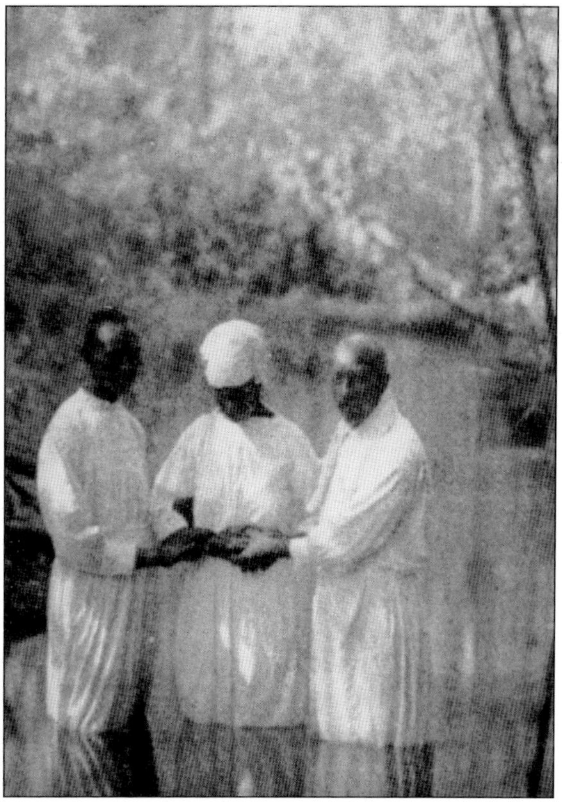

Religion and the black church are significant dimensions to the African American experience in the United States, both past and present. The church historically was significant to the survival and liberation of the African American community.

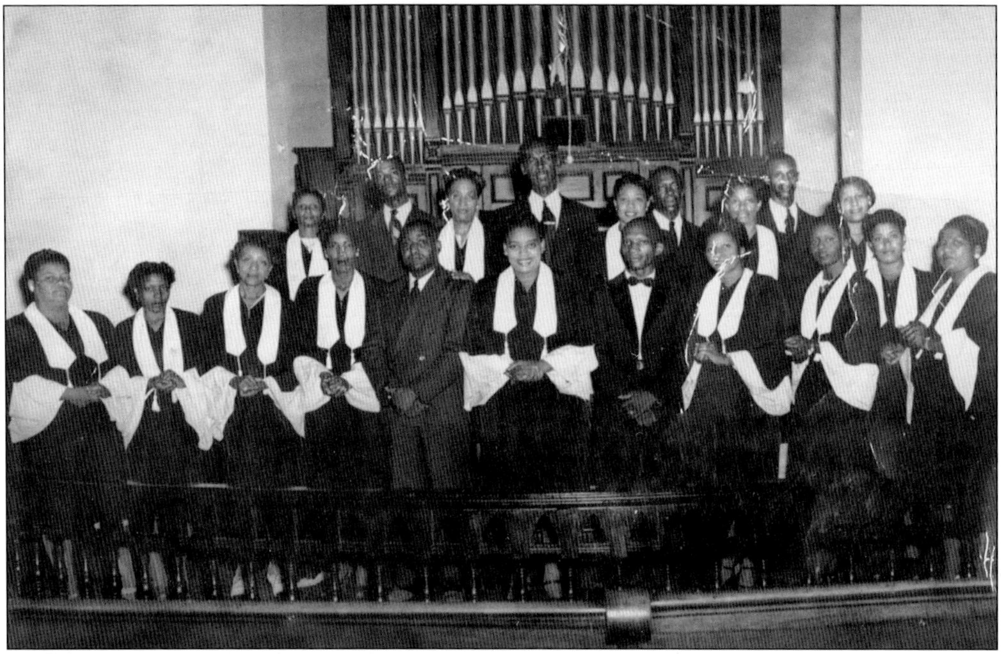

In 1847, at the corner of Lookout Mountain and 4th Streets, the Methodists held a fund-raiser to finance the construction of a new building in which to worship. It was called the Pepper Box Church. Both blacks and whites worshiped together in the same church with 100 white members and 12 black. The church later became Wiley Memorial Methodist Church, the oldest church in Chattanooga.

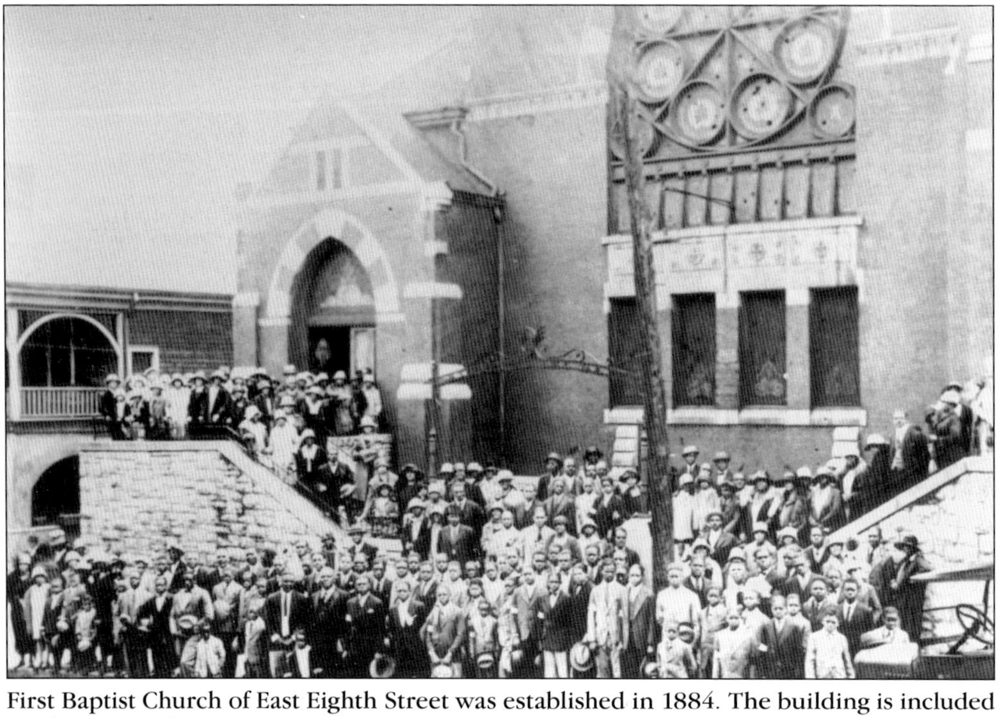

First Baptist Church of East Eighth Street was established in 1884. The building is included on the National Historic Register.

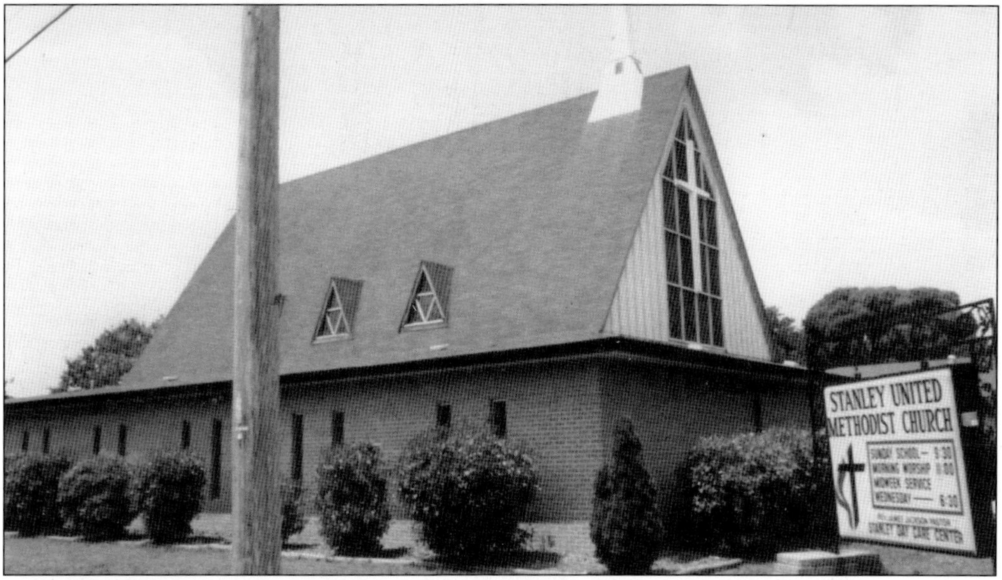

The AME Church, which operates internationally, was founded in 1796 by black members of the Methodist Episcopal Church in New York City and was organized as a national body in 1821. Thompkin Chapel Metropolitan African Methodist Episcopal Zion Church, pictured here and located in Chattanooga, was founded in 1865.

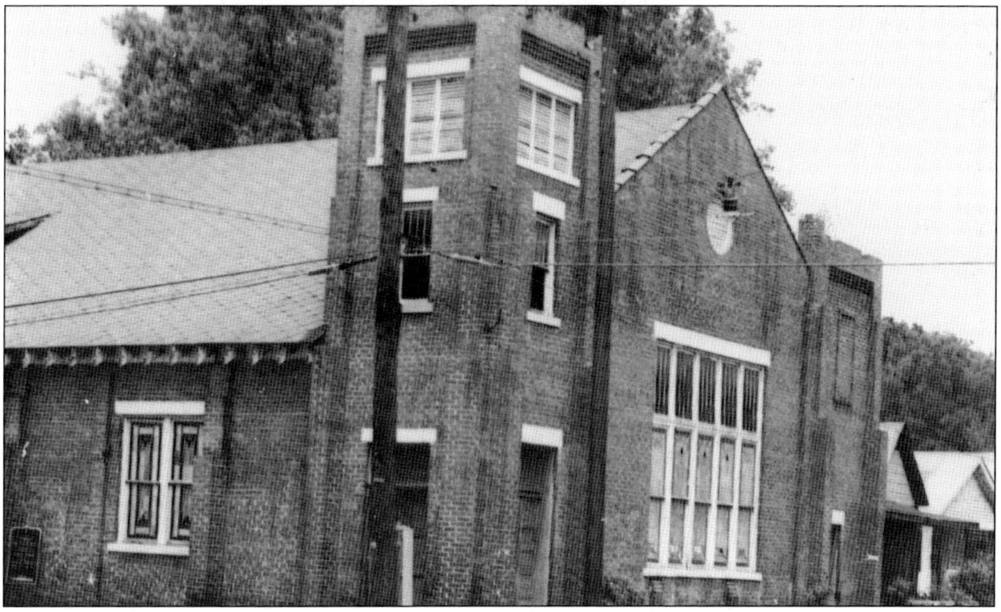

In the late 1860s, a group of Christians began to meet as a prayer band in local homes in an area of Chattanooga. Charles Stanley, recognizing the persistence and dedication of the worshipers, donated land to the Methodist Episcopal Church in July 1886 for a place of worship located at Sixth and Pike Streets. Mr. Stanley gave land for churches of various denominations in the area; thus, this area became known as Churchville. At first all the various denominations met at the Methodist site, which was in a "brush arbor" structure. Around 1960, that structure later became Stanley Chapel Methodist Episcopal Church, which is now Stanley United Methodist Church (SUMC).

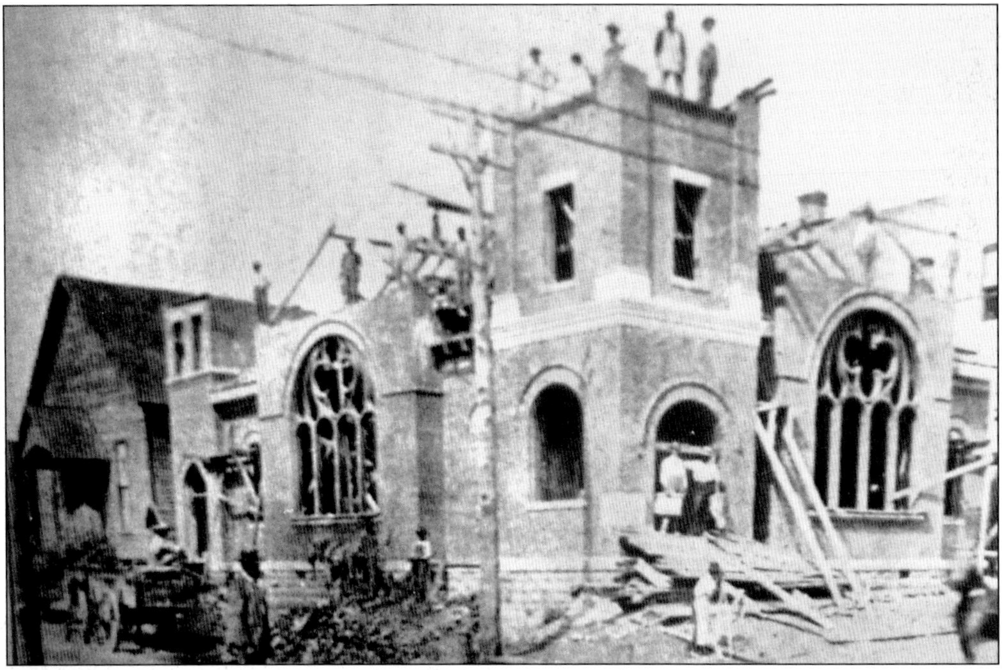

This is First Congregational Church under construction during the early 20th century. It was located at what was then Ninth and A Streets (now East Martin Luther King and Lindsay). Black contractors L. C. Alston (wood work) and A. J. Johnson (brick work) handled the construction of the building.

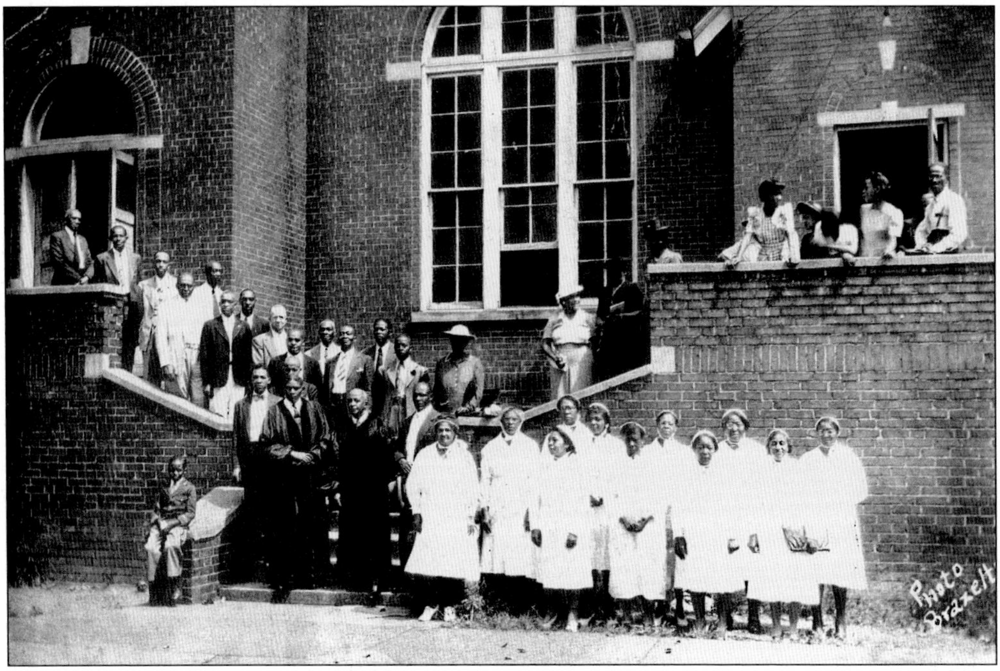

St. Paul African Methodist Episcopal Church was established in 1889. The church is a connectional church created from the First AME Mother Church (Bethel) in Philadelphia as one body, under one name.

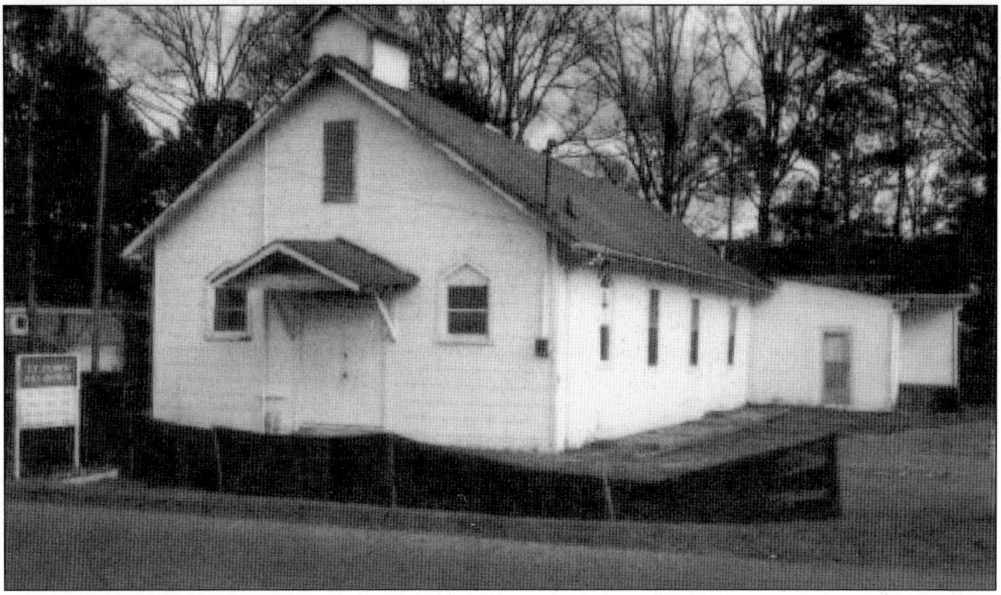

Reverend Hanson of the North Georgia Annual Conference of the AME Church organized St. James African Methodist Episcopal Church (SJAMEC) in 1898. On May 20, 1901, the property was deeded over to the trustees of the SJAMEC from Mr. and Mrs. B. Bedell.

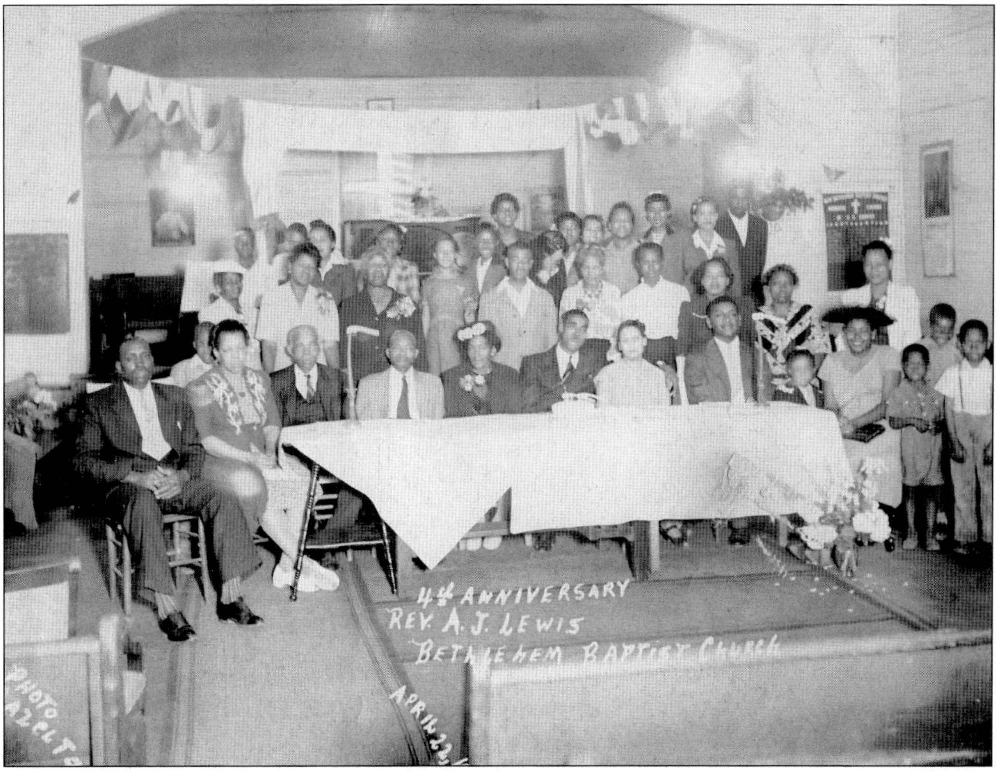

In 1882 in Hill City, Tennessee, the foundation was laid and the creation of Bethlehem Baptist Church began in a two-room house that was owned by the late Mr. and Mrs. Will Bryson. Rev. J. P. Love and Will Martin served as the first pastors of the church.

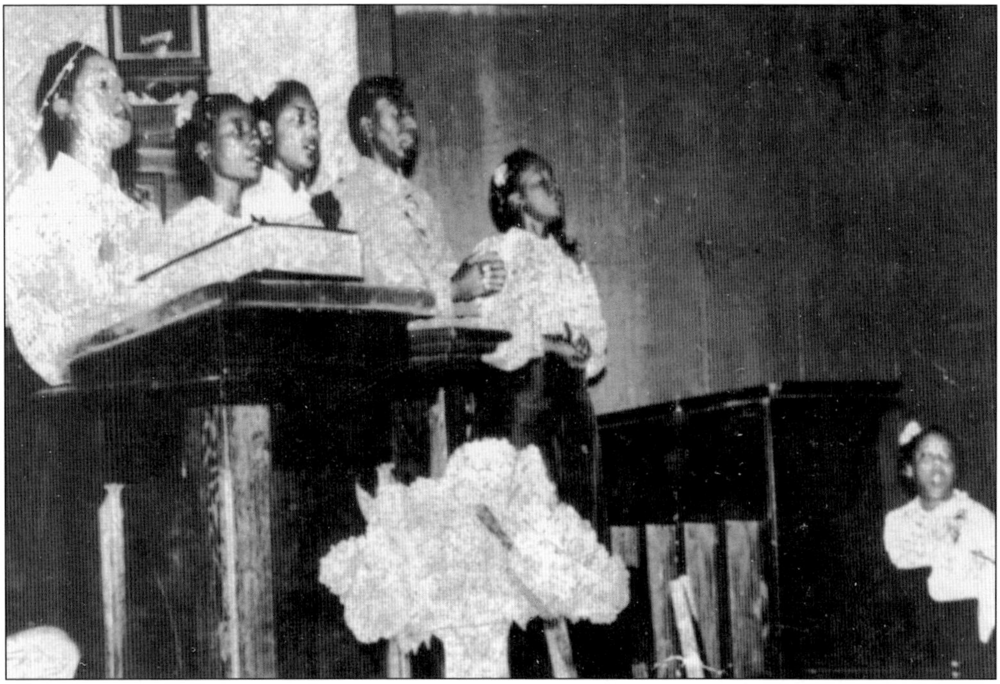

Derrick Singers perform in a church under the direction of Cleavant Derrick around 1941. Derrick was helping his mother sweep out a theater in Chattanooga when he found $5 and the inspiration to write the gospel classic "Just a Little Talk with Jesus." Derrick is also the author of a widely read book on race relations, *Crumbs from the Master's Table*.

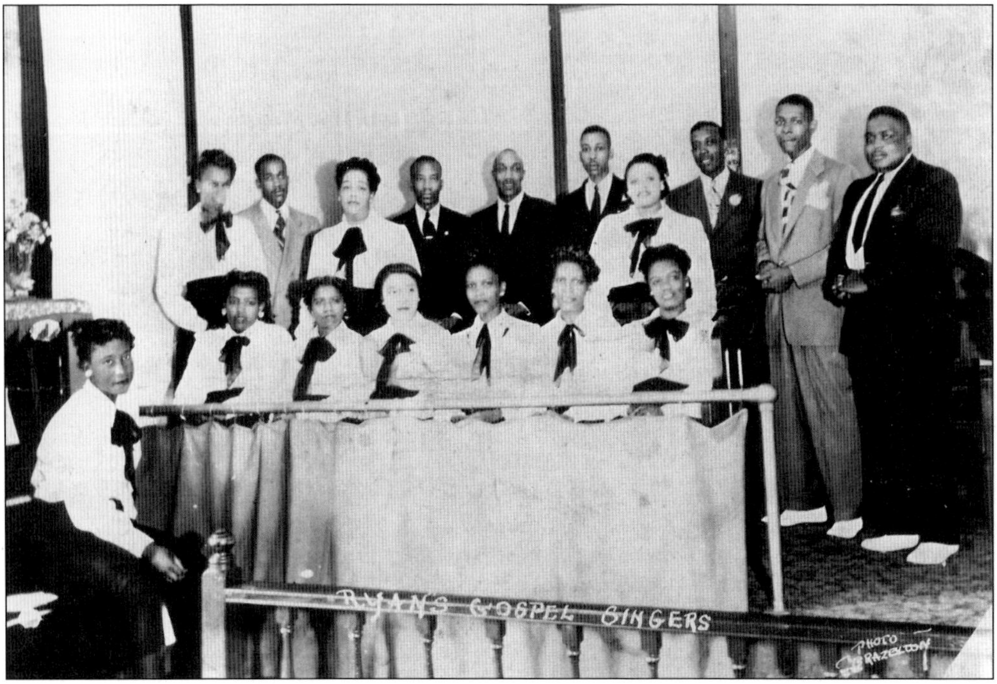

Rev. William "The Singing Preacher" Ryan was a graduate of Zion College, located in Chattanooga, and leader of the Ryan Gospel Singers.

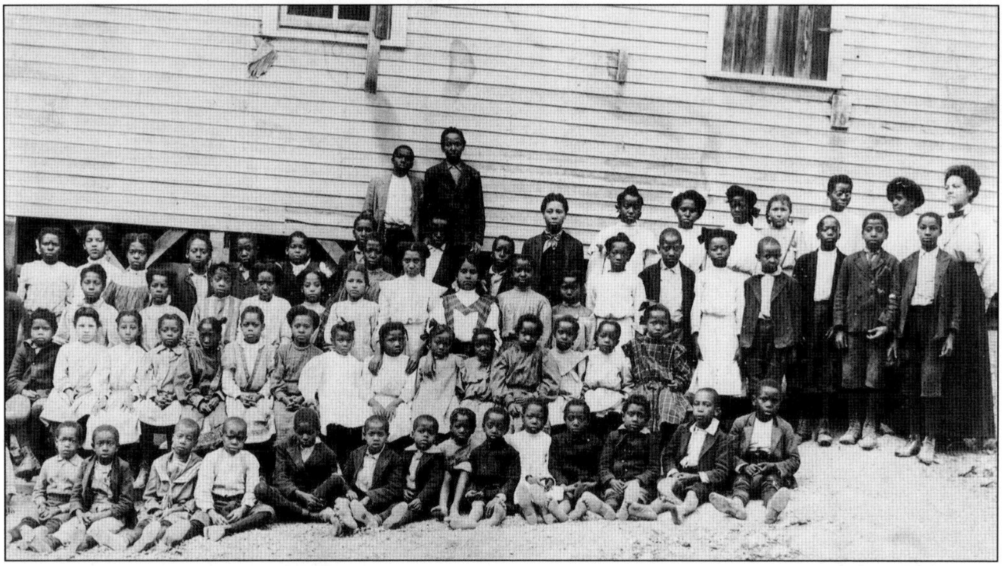

Hurst United Methodist Church (HUMC) was originally named Jackson Chapel and located on a site near Bell Avenue. In 1883, it was dedicated as New Hope United Methodist Church. Now located at Dallas Road, the church laid the cornerstone in 1906 and was dedicated as Hurst Memorial Methodist Episcopal Church.

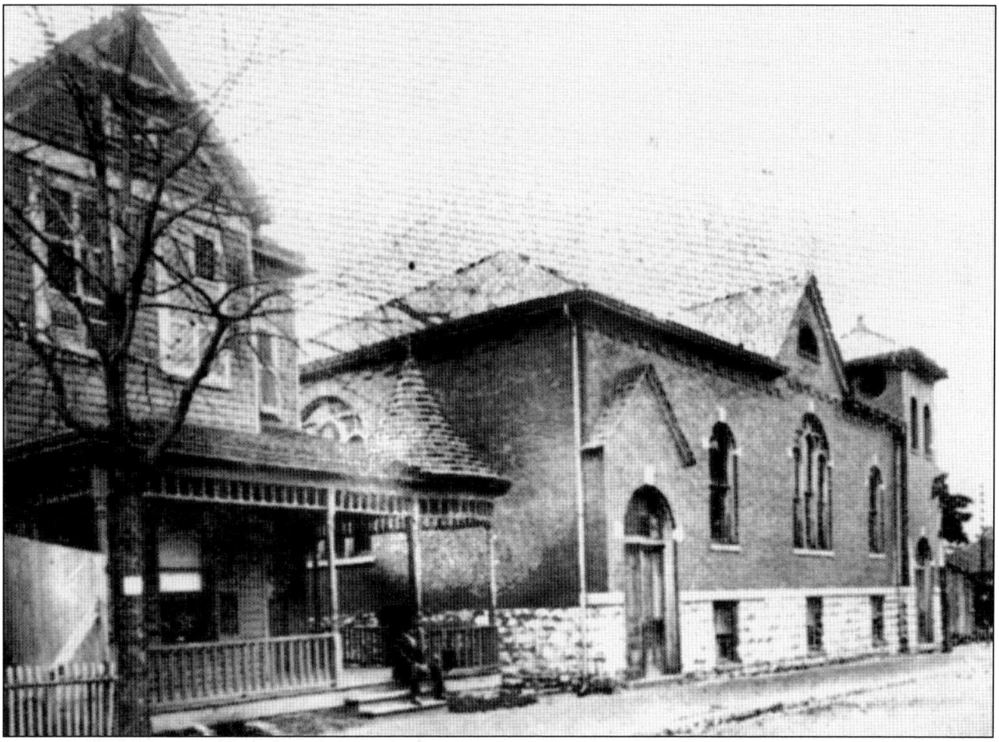

The Leonard Street Presbyterian Church was organized on August 12, 1888, under the name of Pleasant Union Presbyterian Church. In 1896, after a name change, a lot was purchased at Leonard and Vaughn Streets, and the dedication of the brick structure pictured above happened on May 13, 1900.

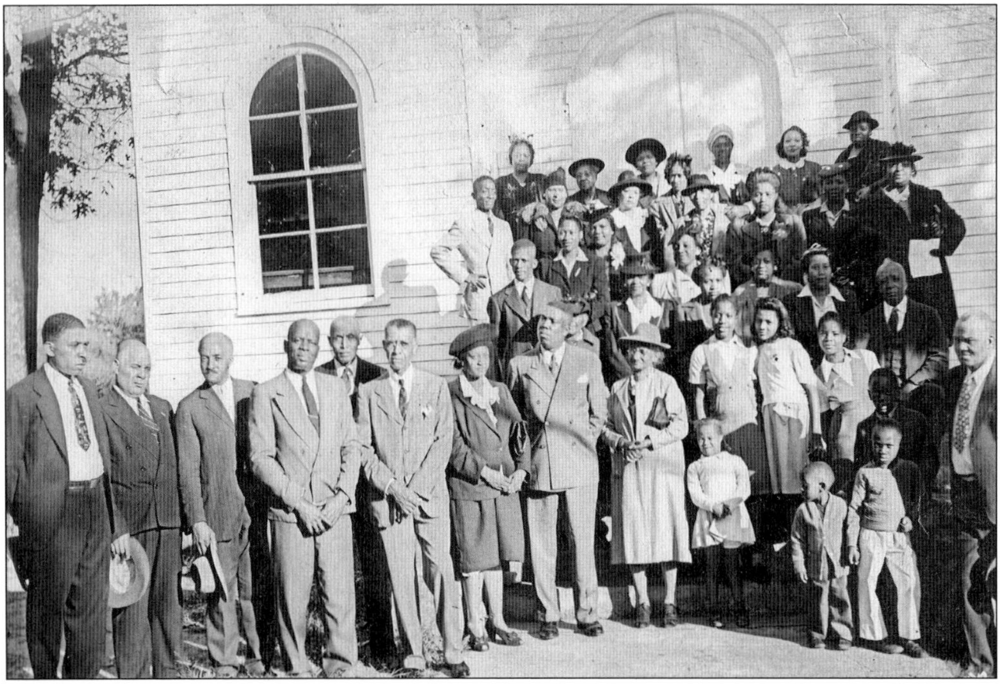

In 1904, a small group of Baptists among the black community on Lookout Mountain, wanting a place of their own to worship, formed First Baptist Church of Lookout Mountain. A small one-room house at the corner of Scenic Highway and Forrest Avenue served as the church's first building, with Rev. E. H. Dial as the first pastor.

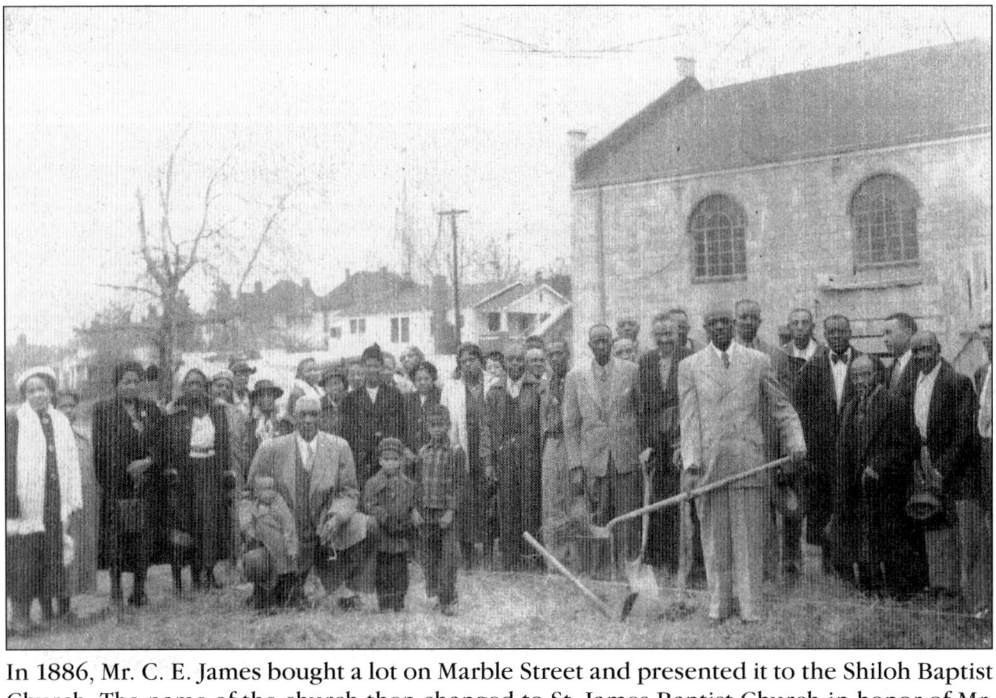

In 1886, Mr. C. E. James bought a lot on Marble Street and presented it to the Shiloh Baptist Church. The name of the church then changed to St. James Baptist Church in honor of Mr. James. This is the property on which the church now stands.

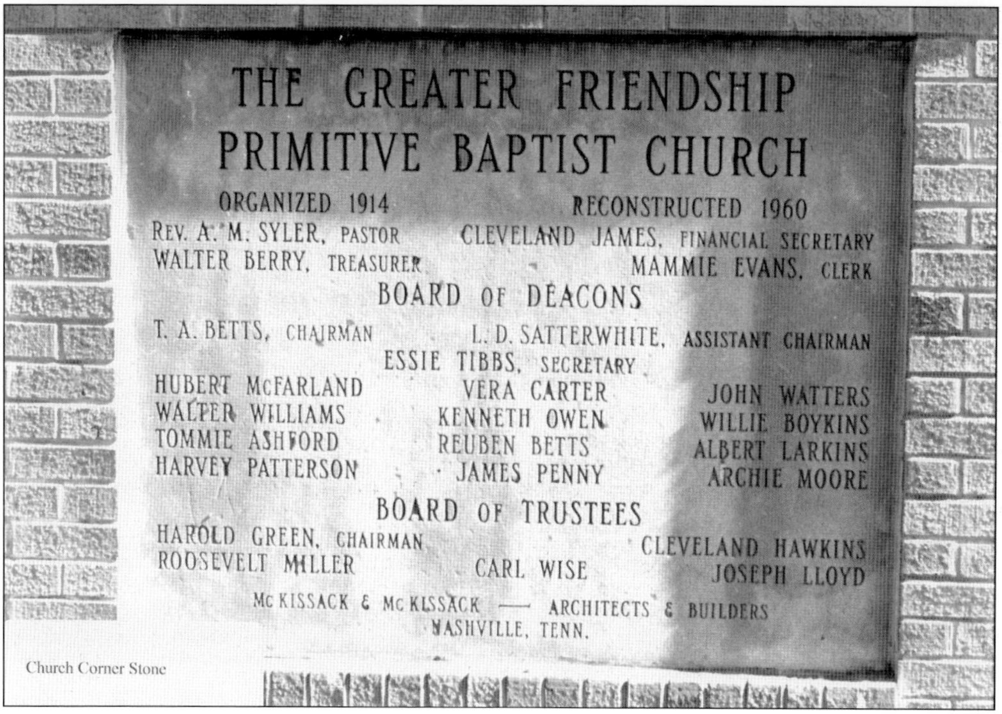

Church Corner Stone

Greater Friendship Primitive Baptist Church was founded in 1904 under the leadership of Rev. Robert Tillman, who also served as its first pastor.

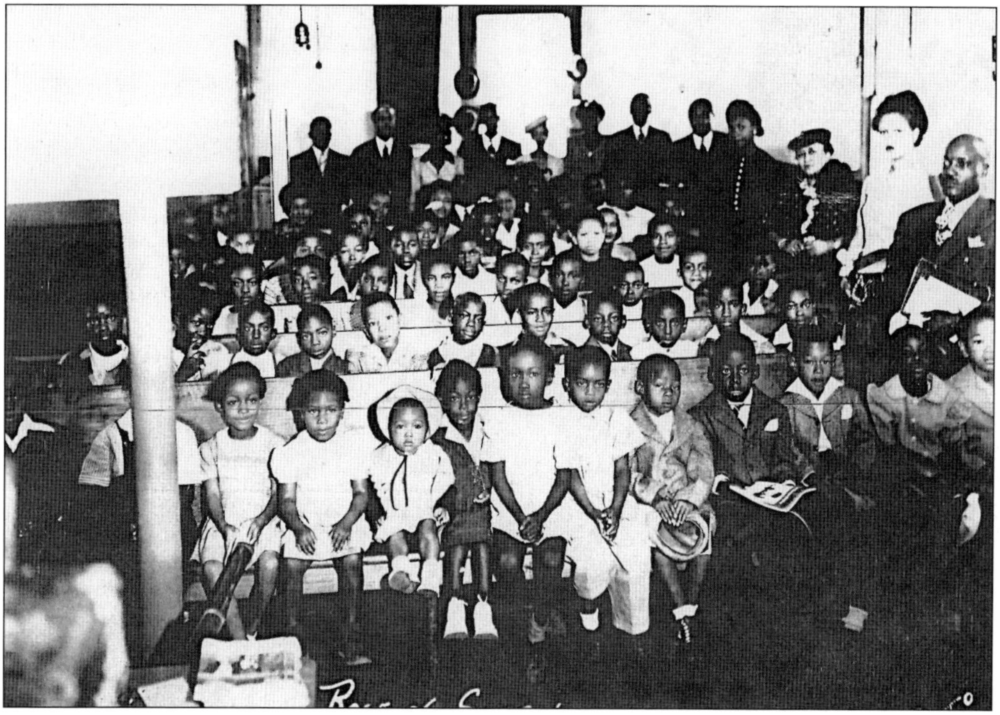
Rose of Sharon Baptist Church was founded in 1930 under the leadership of Reverends Johnson, Keith, Murray, and Brown.

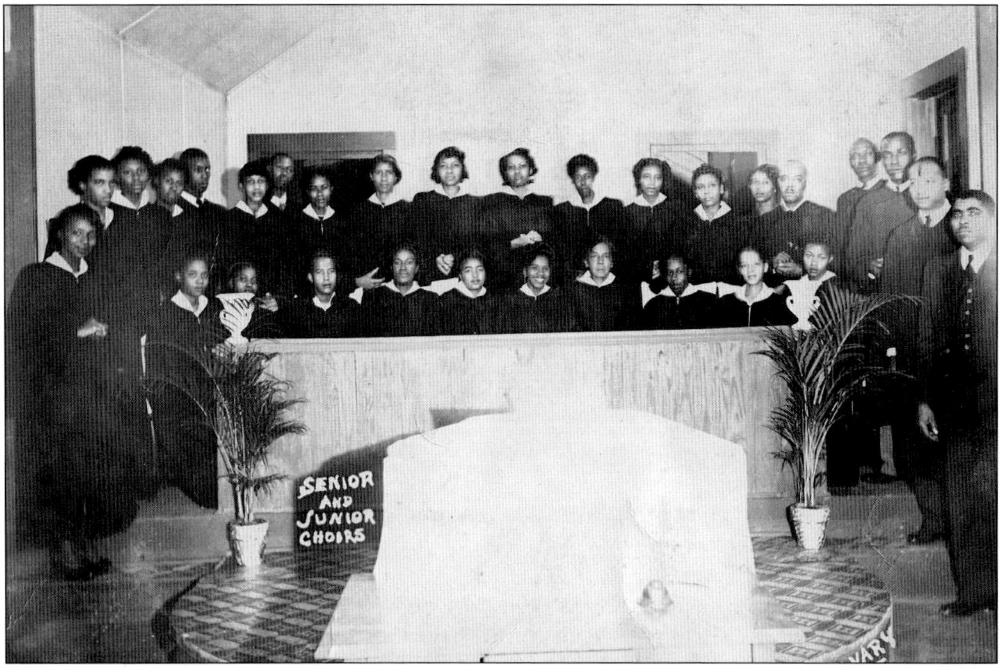

The history of African American church choirs can be traced back to the fields during slavery, when slaves would use "call and response" methods to sing through the workday. More structured choirs, like the Senior and Junior Choir members pictured here from Mount Calvary Baptist Church, were formed after the Civil War.

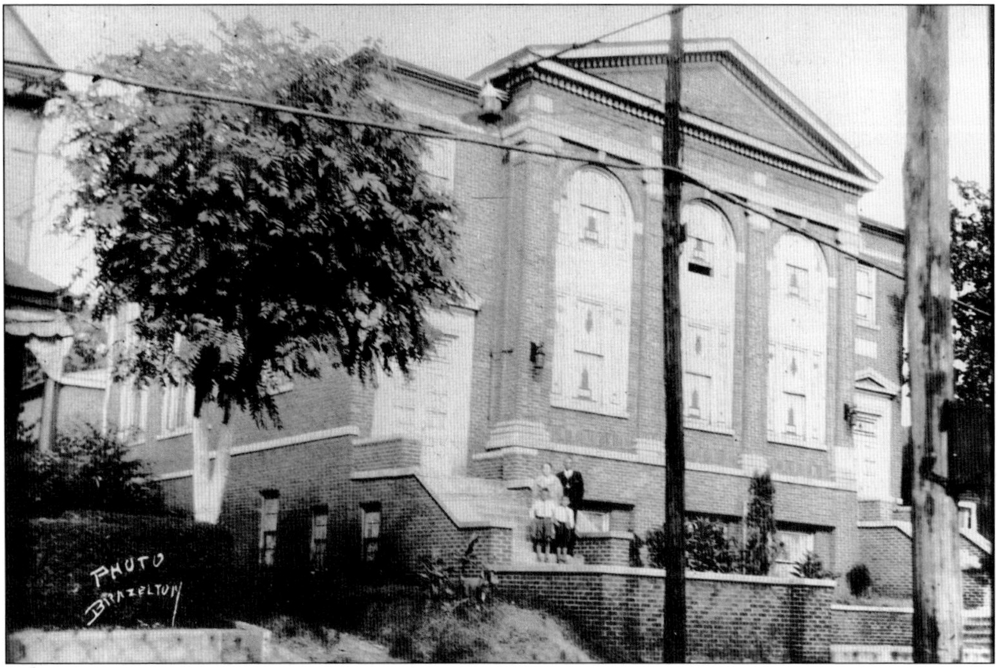

New Monumental Baptist Church is located on East Eighth Street. This is also the site of the Roland Hayes historic marker. Rev. Virgil Caldwell and his family are standing on the front steps of the old facility.

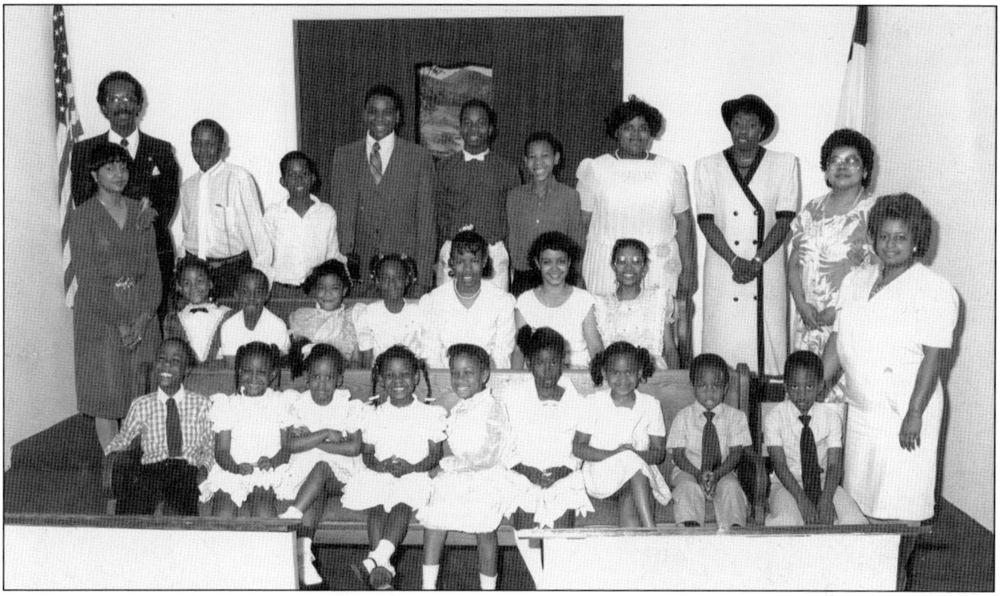

The New United Church Youth Choir is seen here with Pastor and Mrs. William McKinley Holloway around 1986. The church is built upon the theme of "Word In, Glory Out." Celebrating 20 years, New United is now in the beginning stages of building affordable houses on over 173 acres of land for deserving families.

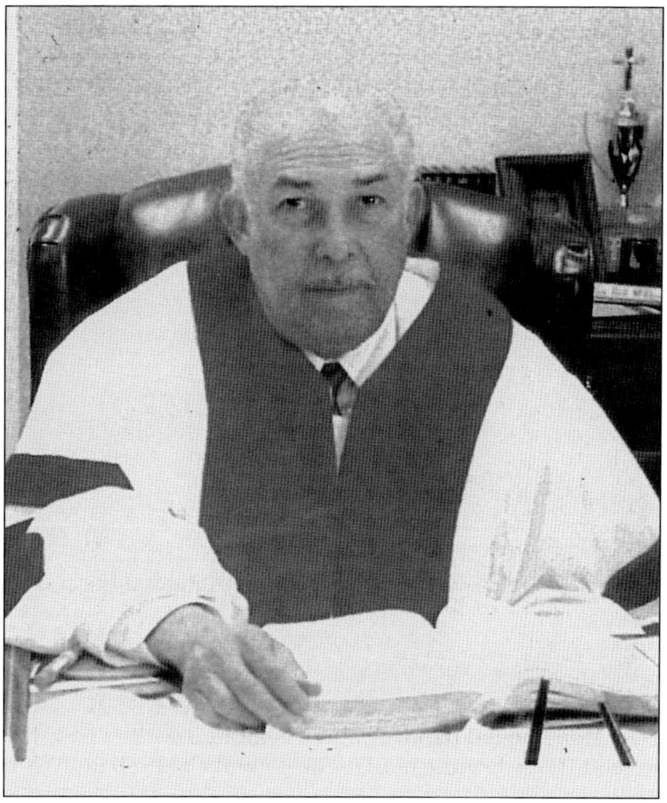

Rev. Paul A. McDaniel Sr., pastor of Second Missionary Baptist Church, is the first African American to serve as chairman of the Hamilton County Commission, and he won the Supreme Court decision that provided for a minister to be seated at the State Constitutional Convention.

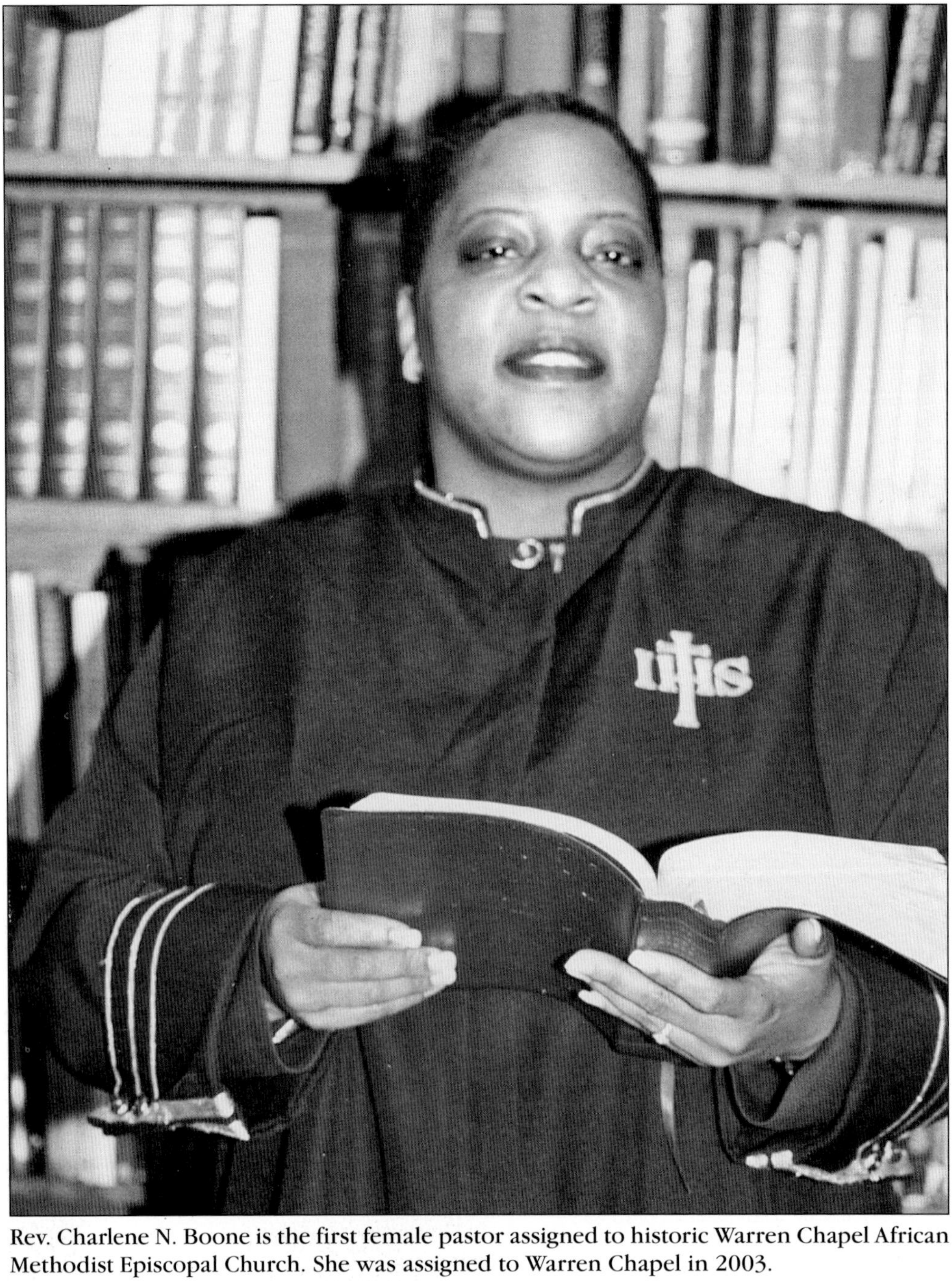

Rev. Charlene N. Boone is the first female pastor assigned to historic Warren Chapel African Methodist Episcopal Church. She was assigned to Warren Chapel in 2003.

Five

Entertainment and Sports

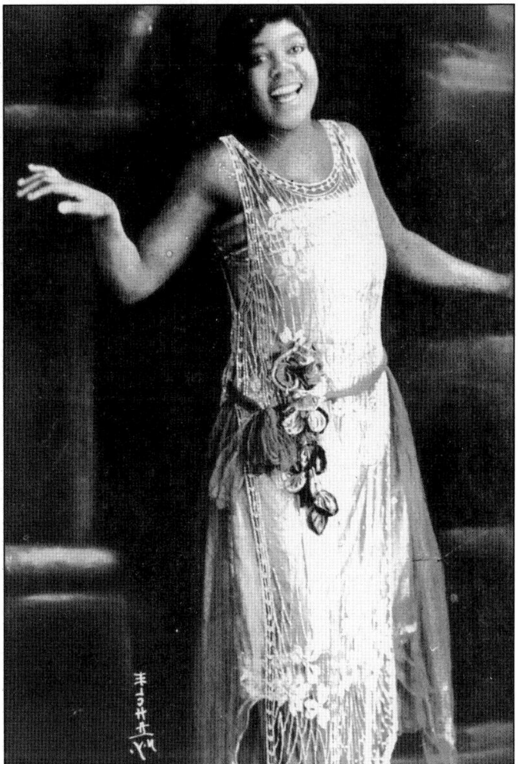

Bessie Smith was born in Chattanooga and grew up on the West Side ("Blue Goose Hollow"). Bessie sang around Chattanooga in the early 20th century and was discovered by Ma Rainey and her Rabbit Foot Minstrel Traveling Show. Bessie was known as the "Empress of the Blues" and has been recognized in the Rock and Roll Hall of Fame for her contribution to music. Bessie died from injuries sustained in a car accident in 1937.

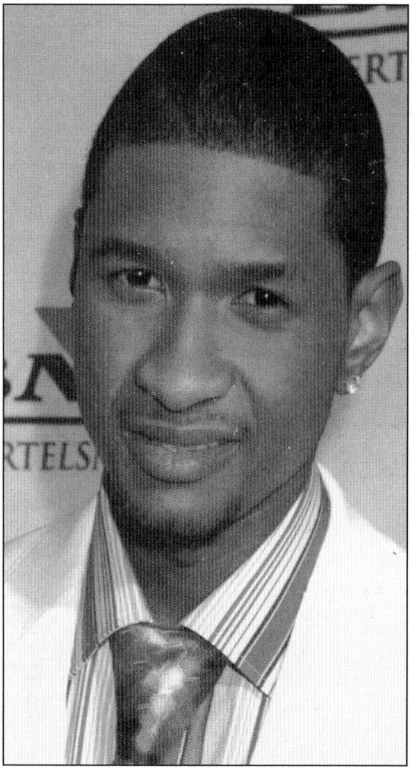

Chattanooga native Usher Raymond IV first started singing in the church choir at the age of six under the direction of his mother, Jonnetta Patton. Today Raymond is a multi-platinum recording artist, actor, dancer, entrepreneur, and Grammy Award winner.

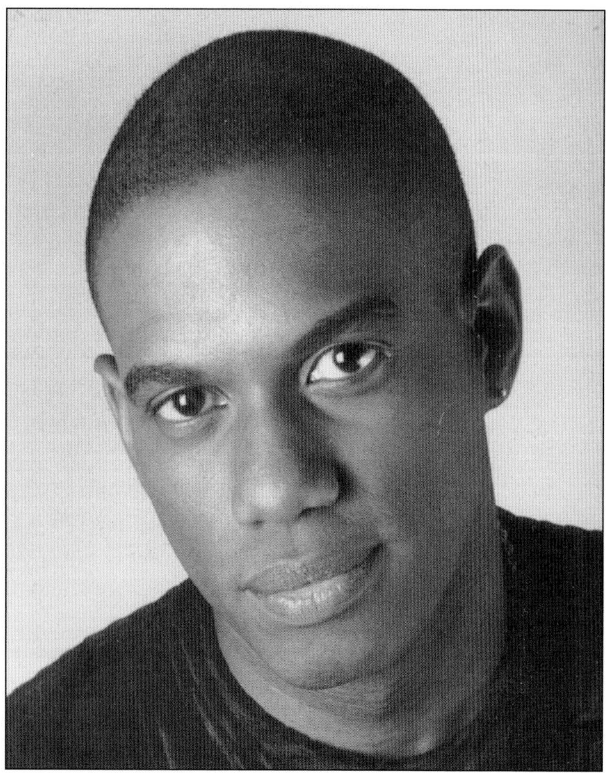

Musician, singer, and songwriter Sam Sims was born and raised in Chattanooga. He has toured with Janet Jackson, Backstreet Boys, Michael Jackson, and Paula Abdul, to name a few. He received a gold record for writing the song "Second Time for Love" for artist Freddie Jackson.

Oscar-nominated actor Samuel L. Jackson was raised in Chattanooga and is a graduate of Riverside High School. His performance in the movie *Jungle Fever* was so acclaimed, the 1991 Cannes Film Festival created a supporting actor award just for him.

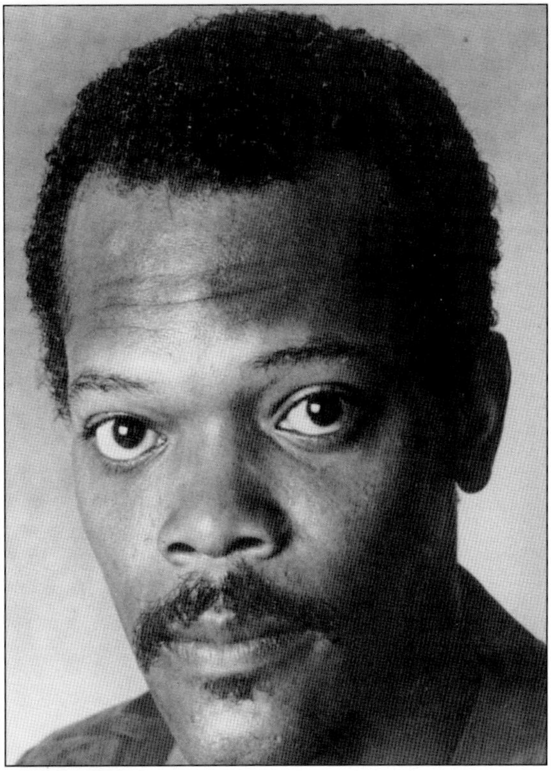

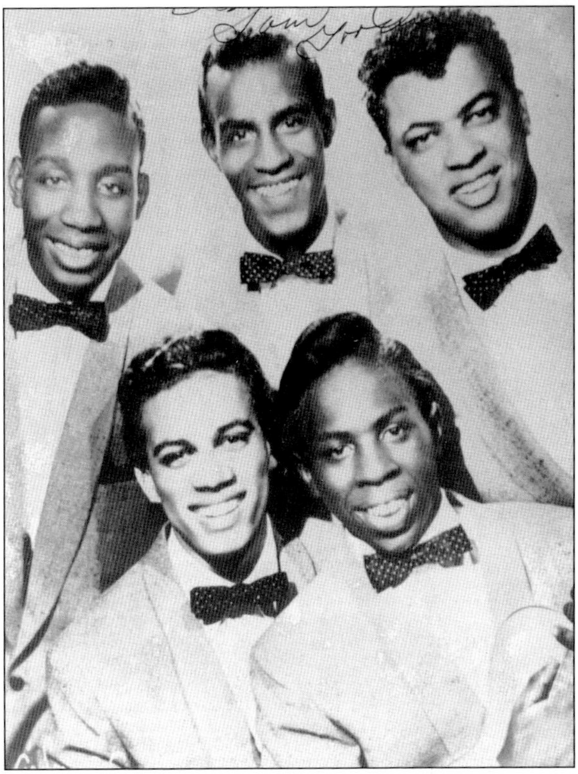

Three of the five original members of the Impressions are from Chattanooga. The Impressions are also in the Rock and Roll Hall of Fame.

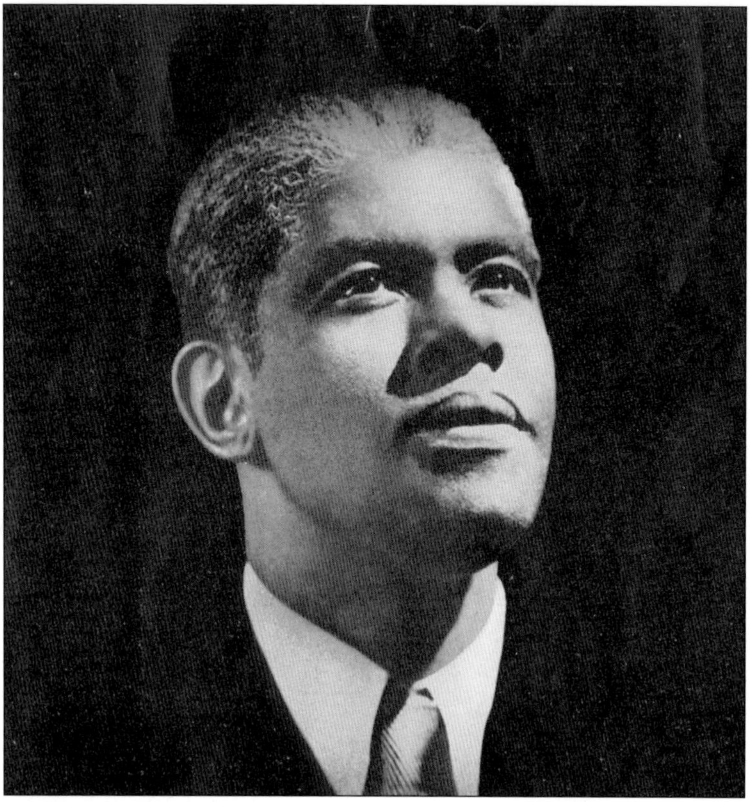

Roland Hayes moved to Chattanooga at the age of 10. Hayes began his career singing at Monumental Baptist Church. He enrolled in Fisk University and performed with the Fisk Jubilee Singers. Hall was the first African American to sing classical music in Carnegie Hall.

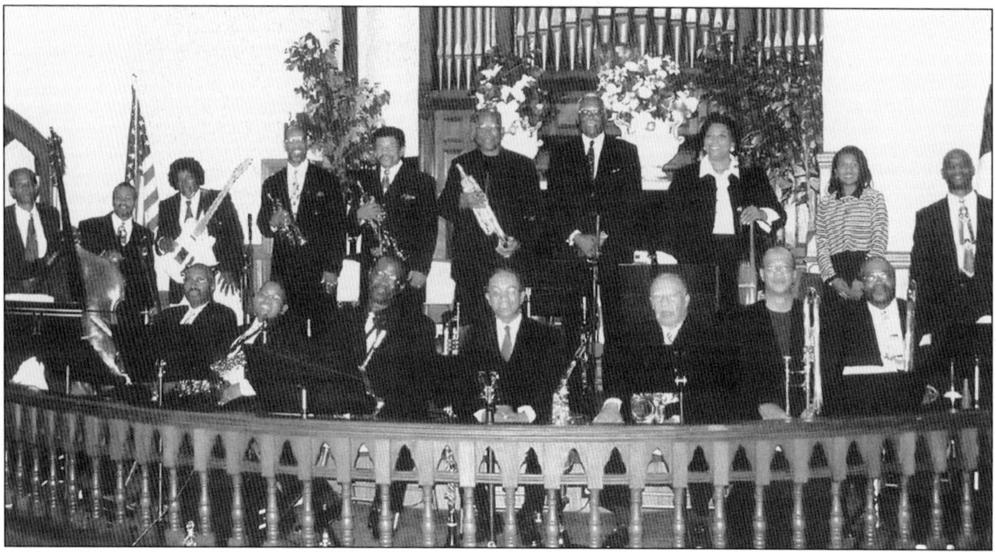

The Gospel Orchestra of Chattanooga was formed to allow musicians to get together and play jazz versions of gospel standards.

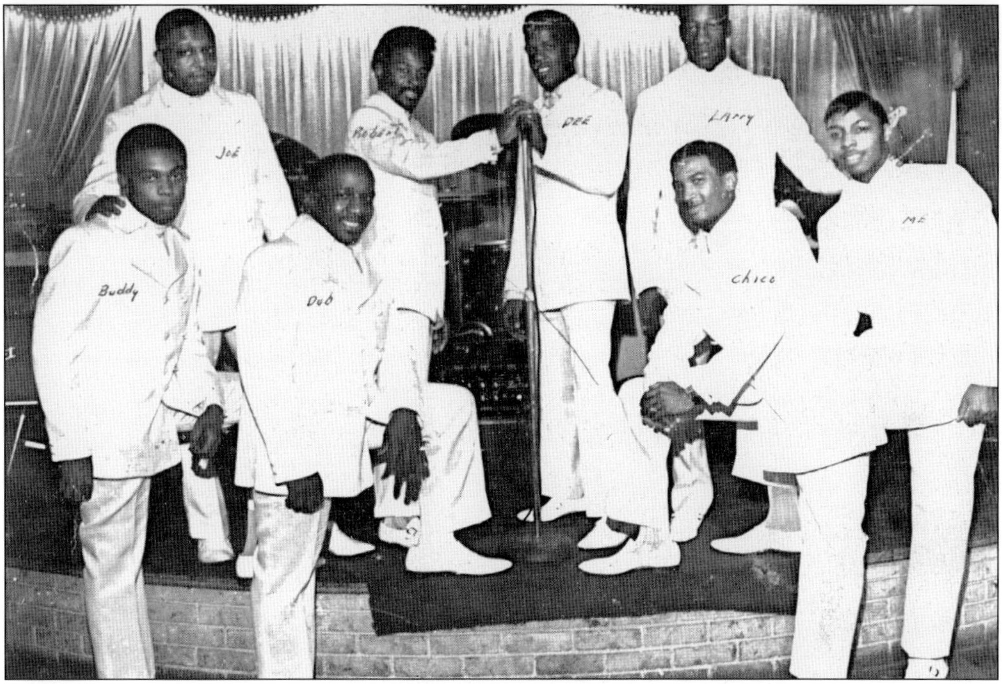

When the Big Nine was a buzzing entertainment district for African Americans in the city, there were many local bands in Chattanooga. Big Joe Dosset and the Mighty Coachmen was one of them.

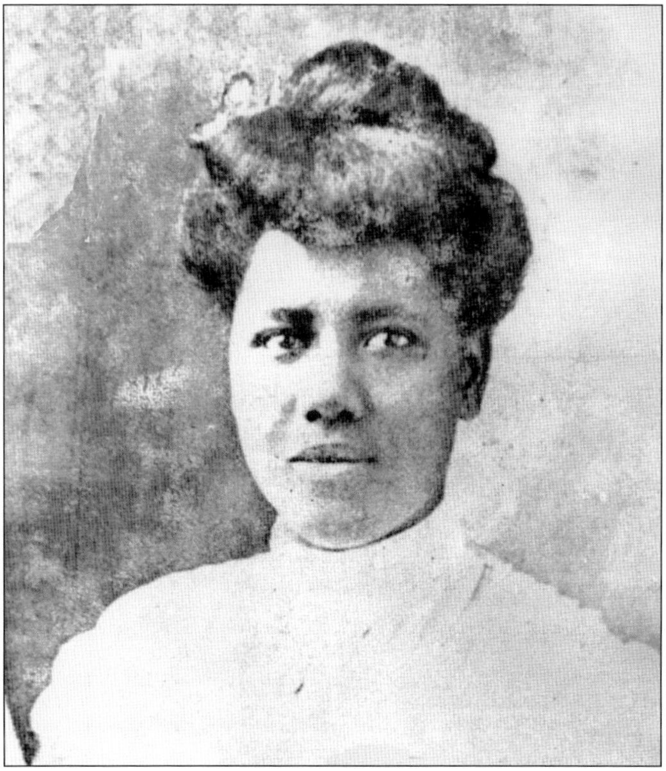

Maude Brown, a graduate of Howard High School, had many successive and successful seasons with the Mason and Downs' Orpheus Jubilee Singers as a mezzo-soprano. It was said by musical critics that her voice was rich, rare, and full of sweetness of quality.

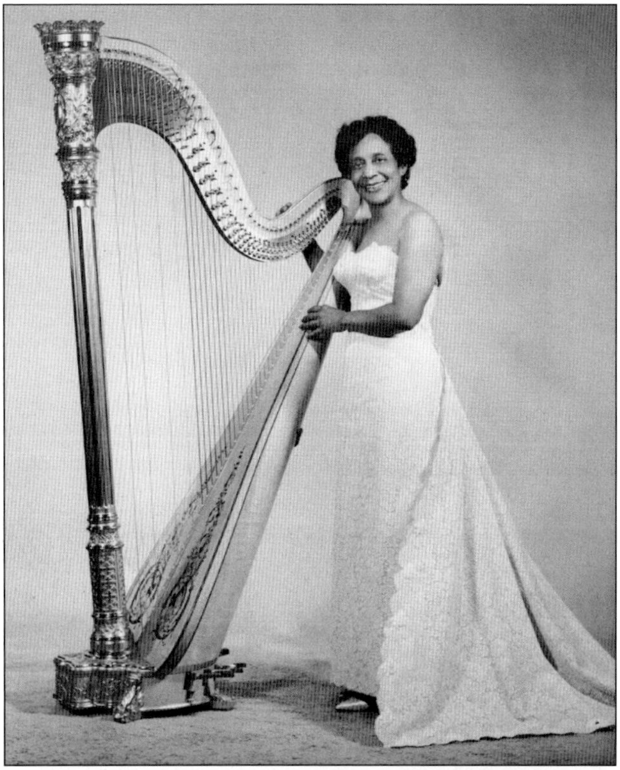

Ann Patton was an internationally known harpist from Chattanooga, Tennessee. Mrs. Patton owned three 24-karat-gold harps and was known for her remarkable stage presence and elaborate costumes.

Valaida Snow was born into a family of musicians in 1909. Although known internationally as the "Queen of the Trumpet," Snow was a versatile artist who claimed talents as a singer, dancer, conductor, arranger, and composer.

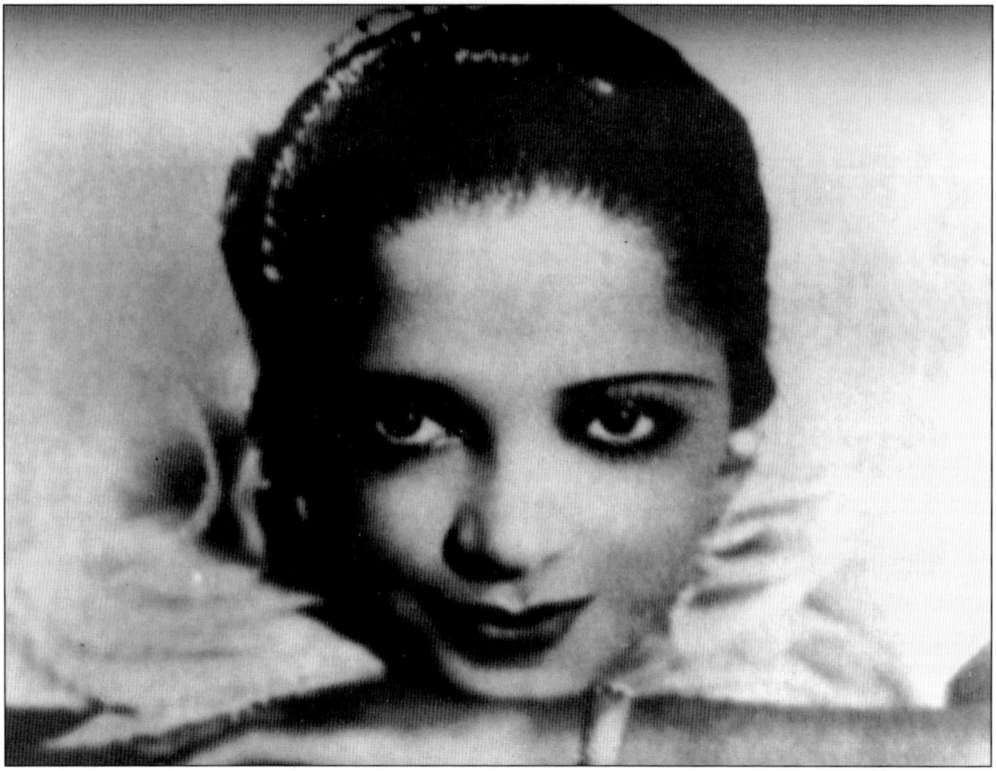

Internationally known opera singer and Howard High School graduate Joyce Mathis was once a member of the New York Metropolitan Opera House performance company.

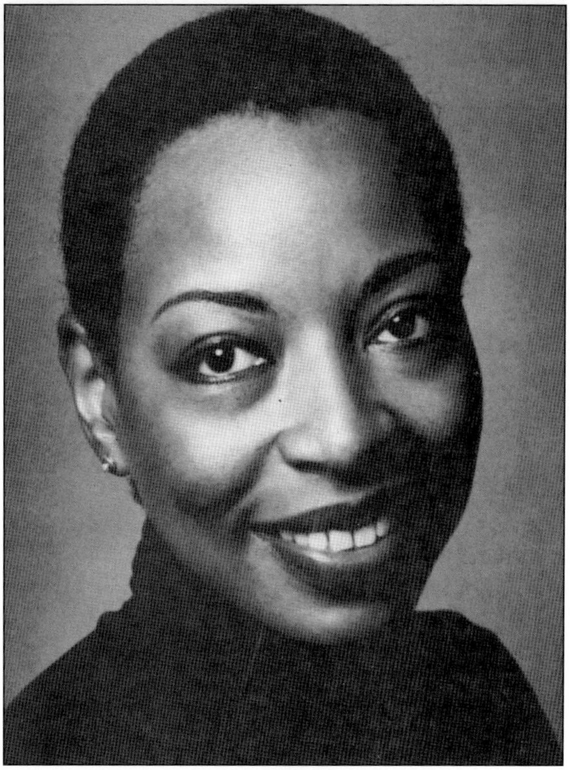

The MaxTiam Jazz Trio is made up of pianist Maxine Bartlett, clarinet player Booker T. Scruggs, and William Price on bass. The trio performs at various functions throughout the city, and proceeds from the sales of their records benefit Upward Bound of Chattanooga.

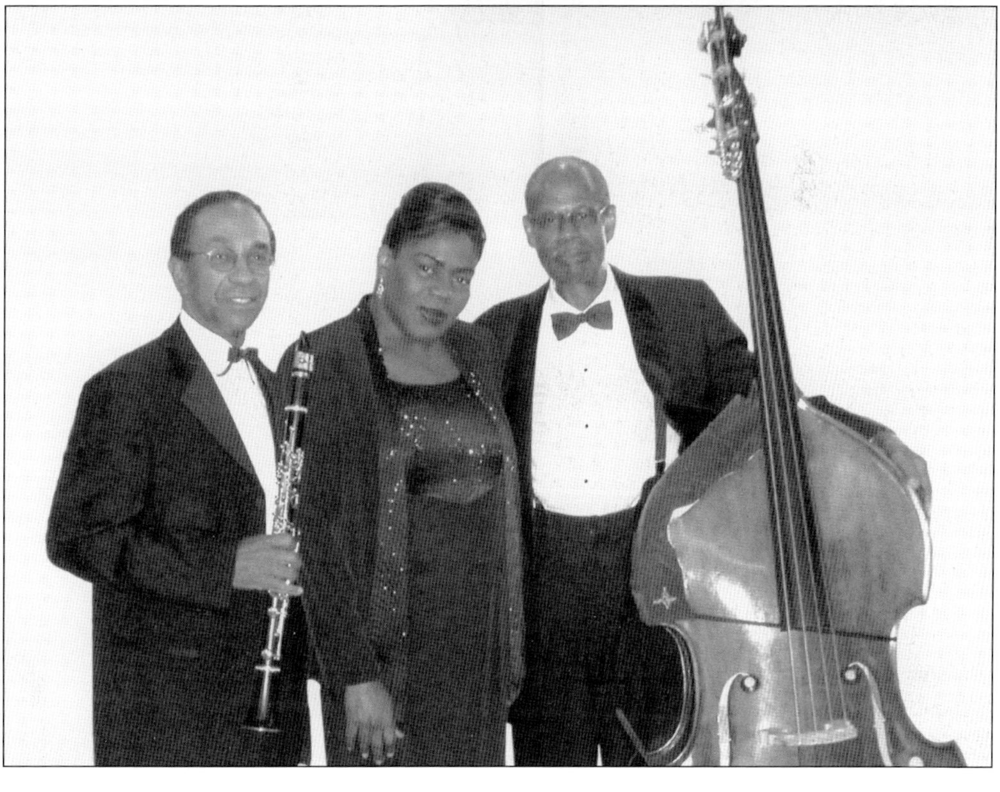

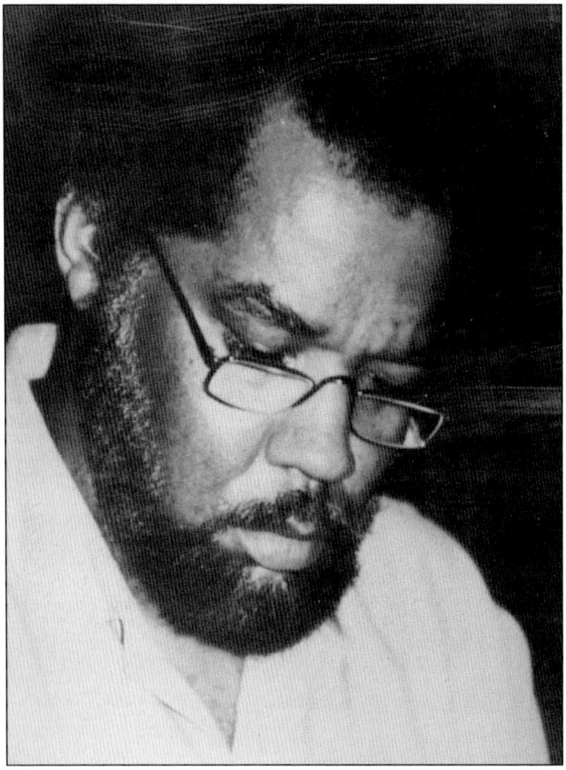

Chattanooga native and jazz musician Butch Cornell has played all over the world with many jazz legends including Freddie Hubbard, George Benson, Grover Washington Jr., Plas Johnson, and Wilfred Middlebrooks.

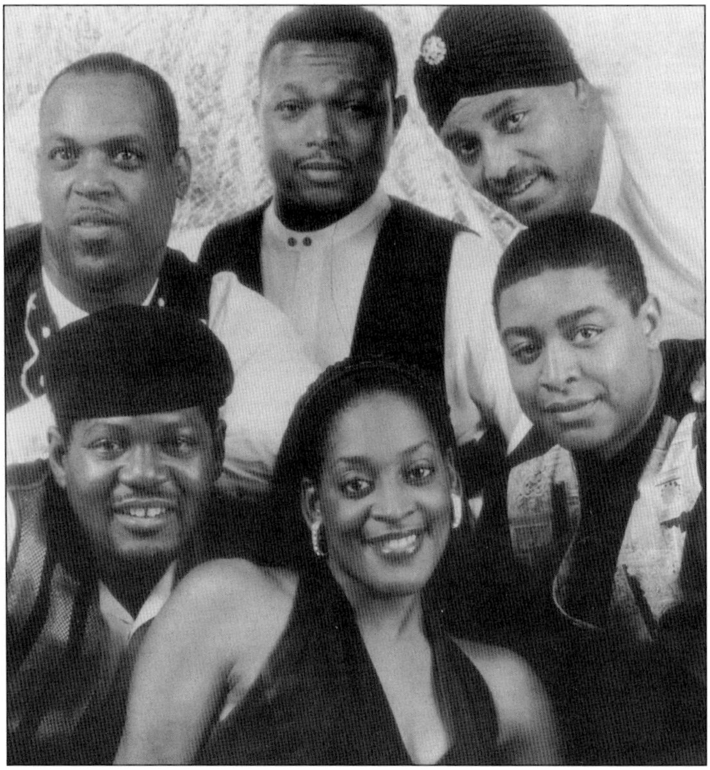

The MaleMen featuring Constance is a versatile musical ensemble based out of Chattanooga.

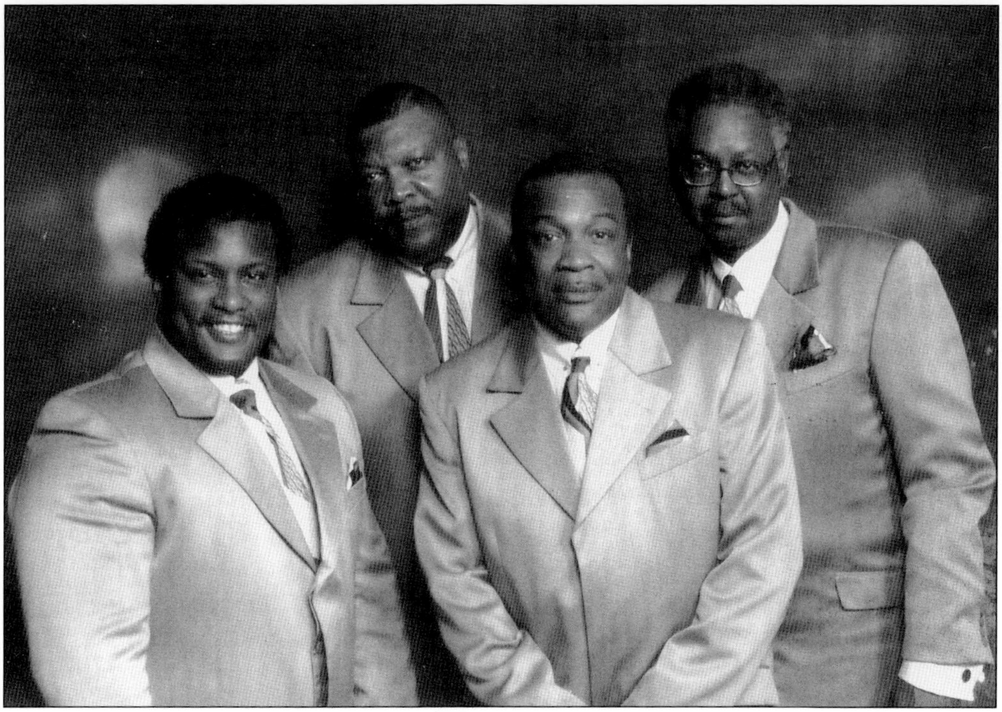

Fire is a singing group composed of local firefighters. They have been together for about seven years and perform all around the city to many fans' delight.

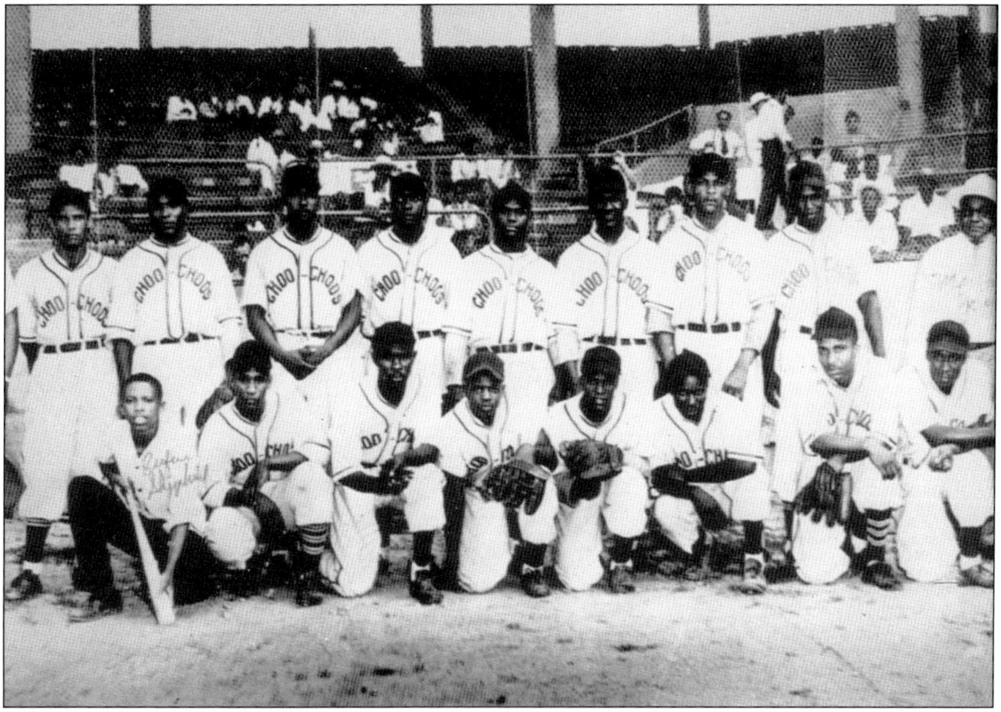

This is a Chattanooga Black Choo Choos team photograph from before 1947. Famous baseball player Willie Mays briefly played with this team and is fourth from the left on the first row.

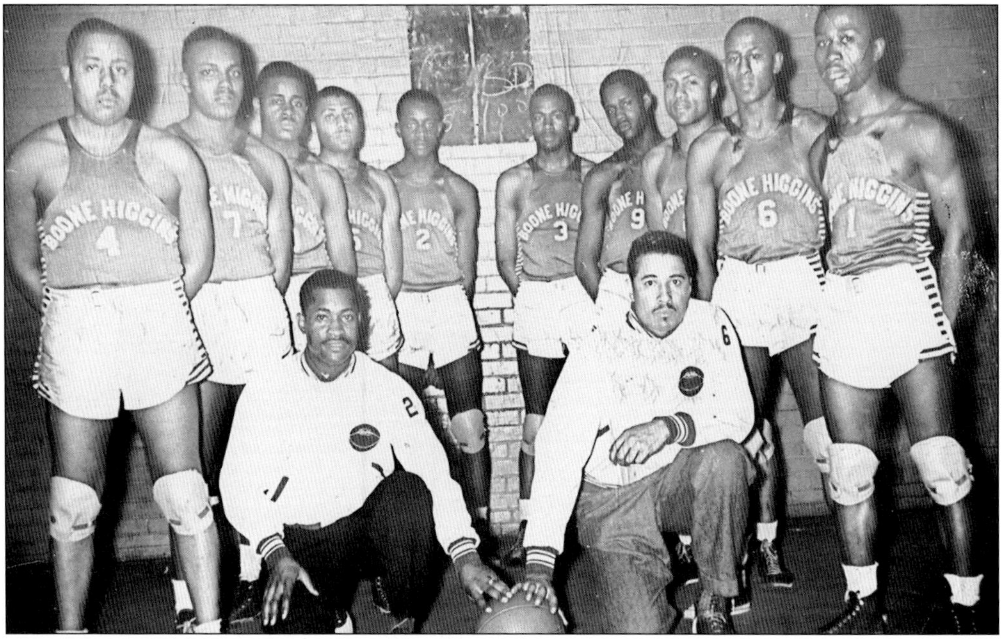

Boone Higgins was an industrial trade school that also offered sports to their students. Pictured here is the basketball team.

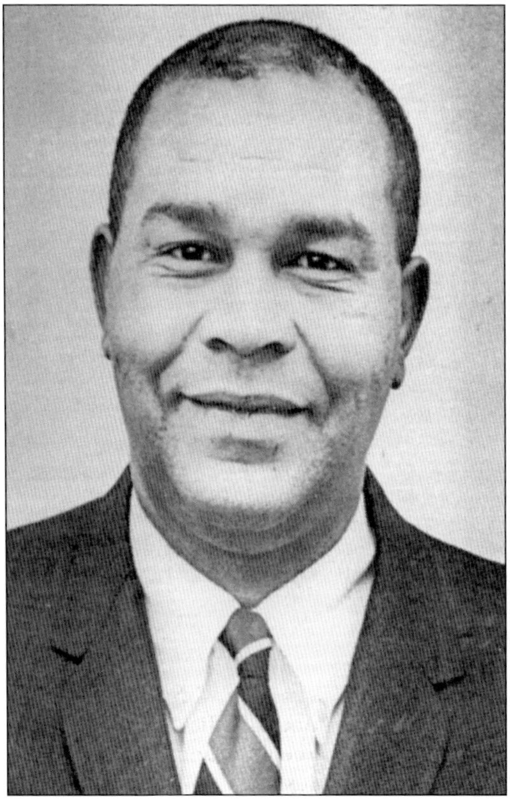

Chubby James, coach at Howard High School during the 1950s, was one of Chattanooga's most respected and acclaimed sports figures and was known as the "Coach of Coaches."

Pictured here is nationally recognized retired coach of Howard High School Henry Bowles. The athletic center at Howard has been named in his honor.

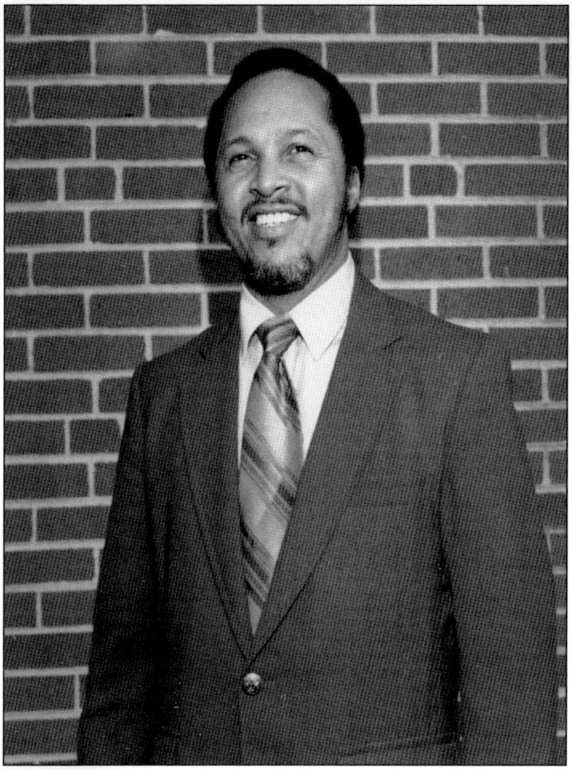

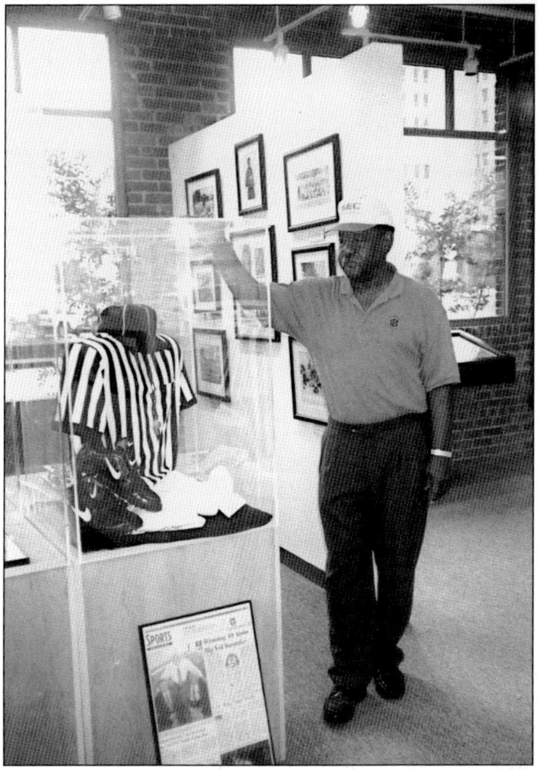

Nathaniel Anderson, Chattanooga's first black SEC football official, donated his uniform to the Chattanooga African American Museum.

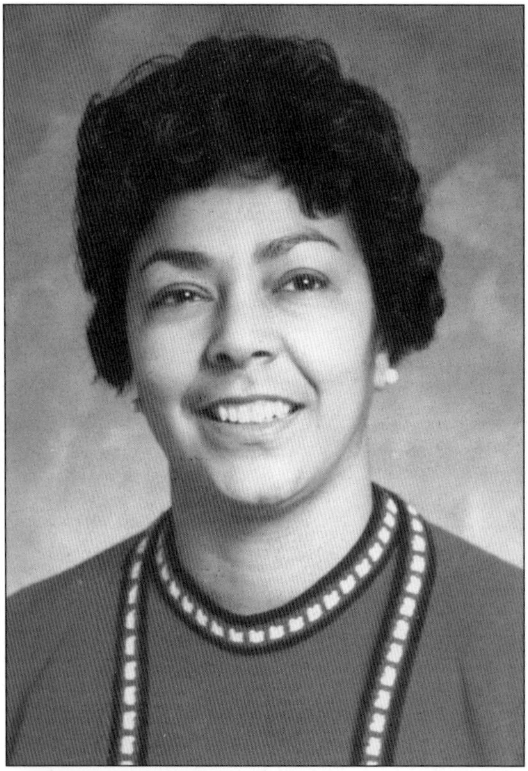

Tennis player Wylhma McGhee Reid won five state tennis championships and one national tournament in Alabama.

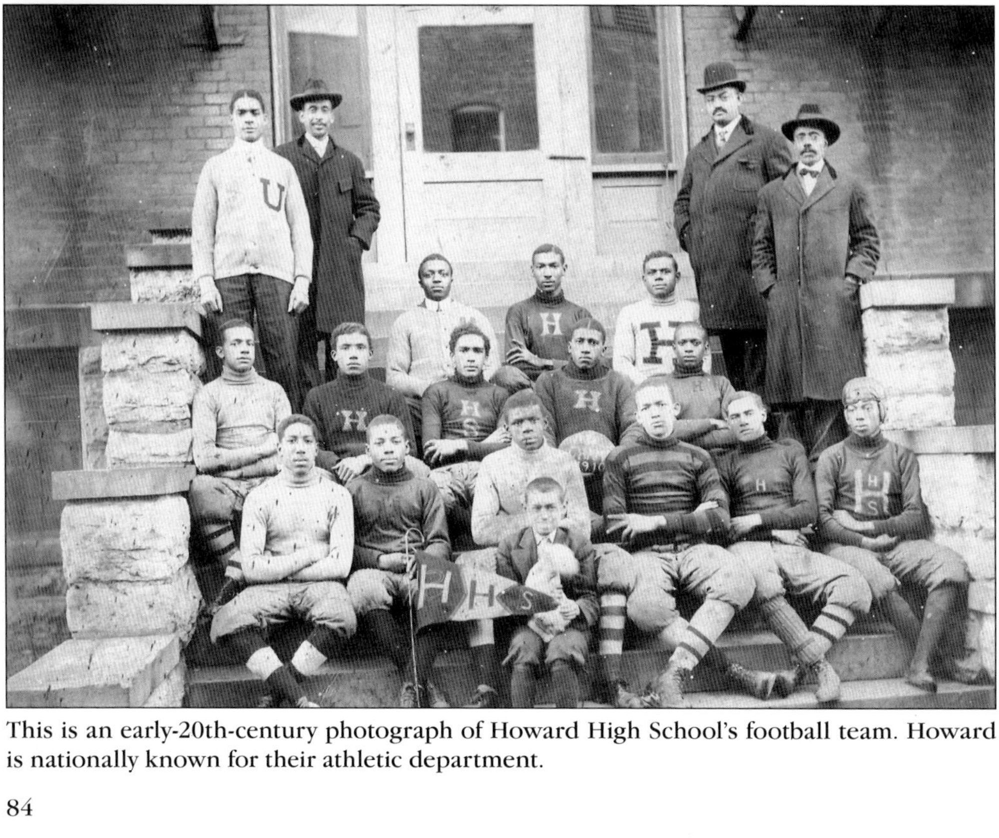

This is an early-20th-century photograph of Howard High School's football team. Howard is nationally known for their athletic department.

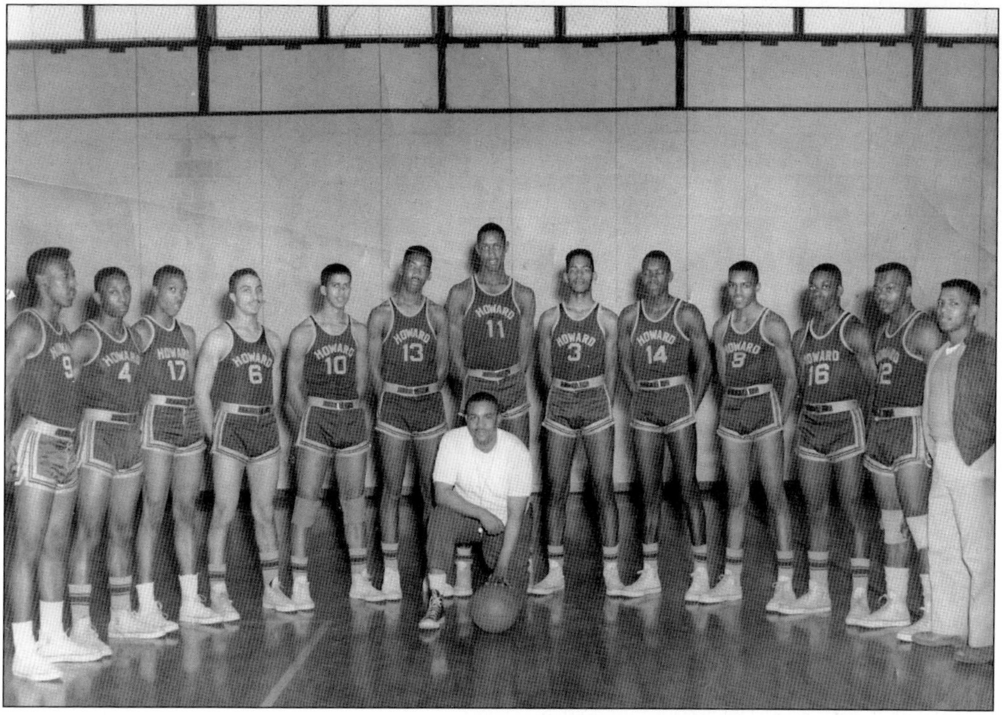

Howard High School offers various sports programs to its students. Pictured here is the basketball team. Howard High School was the first public school in Chattanooga, founded in the early 19th century.

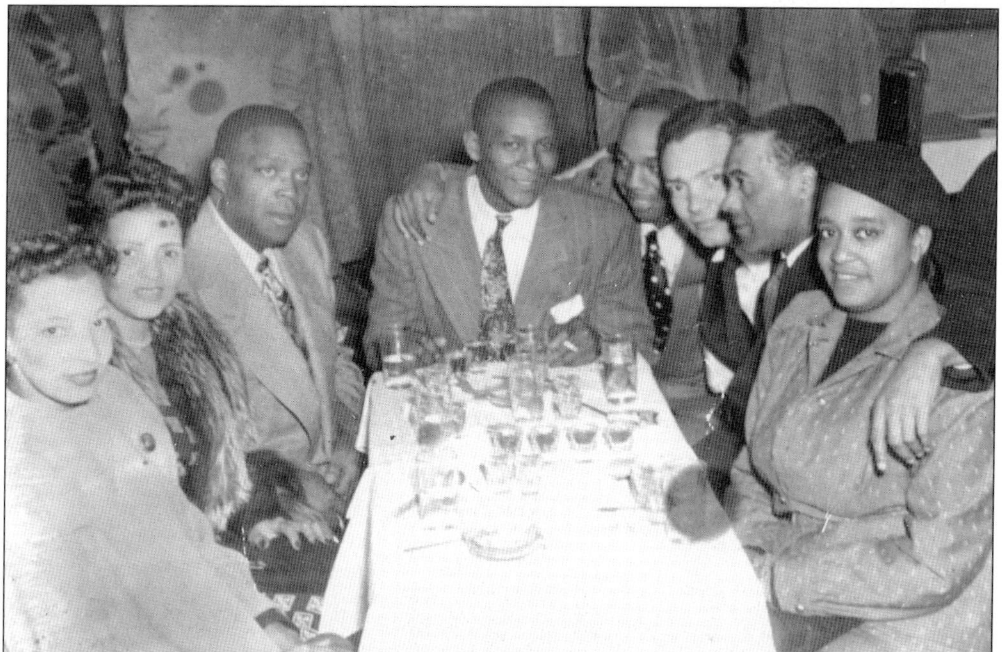

Beck Shepherd (top left) made a New York City recruiting trip for the Chattanooga Black Choo Choos. He brought back Satchel Paige (at the head of the table) as a new player for the team.

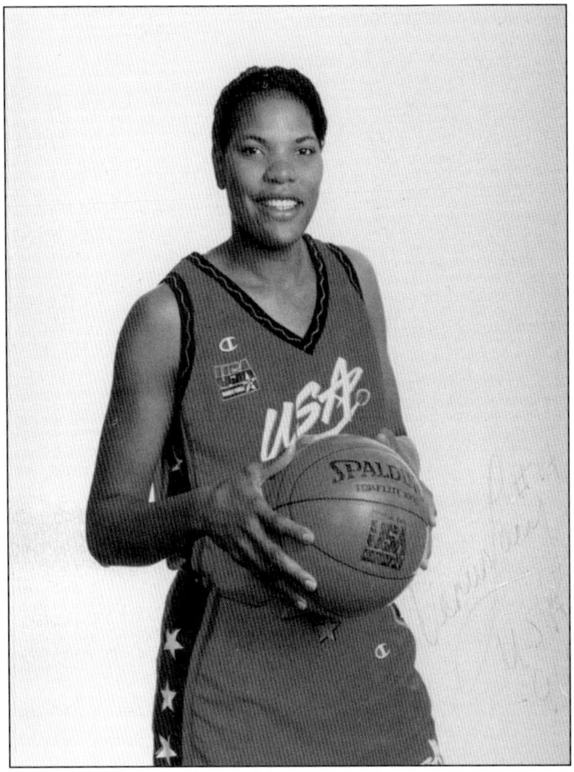

Venus Lacey, a graduate of Brainerd High School in 1986 and Louisiana Tech in 1990, is the first African American from Chattanooga to play on the USA Olympic Basketball Team. Lacey won a gold medal as a member of the 1996 USA Women's Olympic Basketball Team.

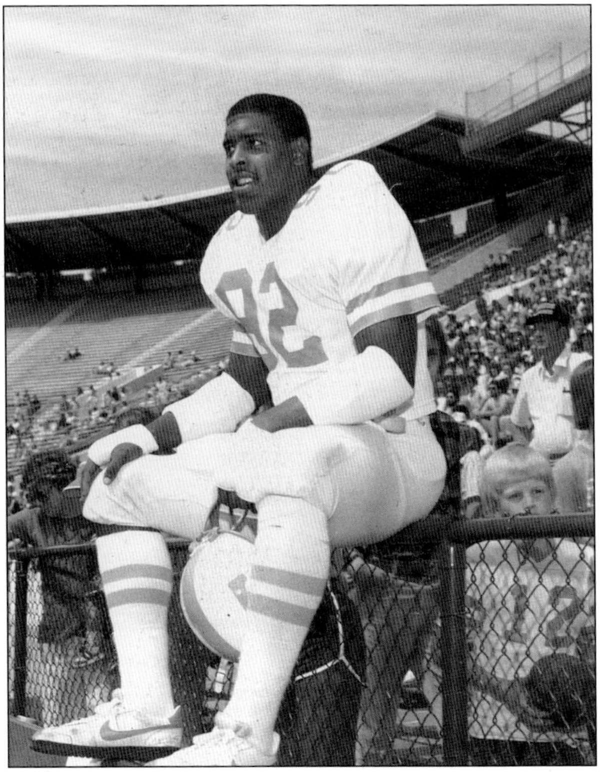

Reginald Howard "Reggie" White, nicknamed the "Minister of Defense" (a dual reference to his football prowess and to his Evangelical Christian ordination), was one of football's most prolific sackers in college, the USFL, and the NFL.

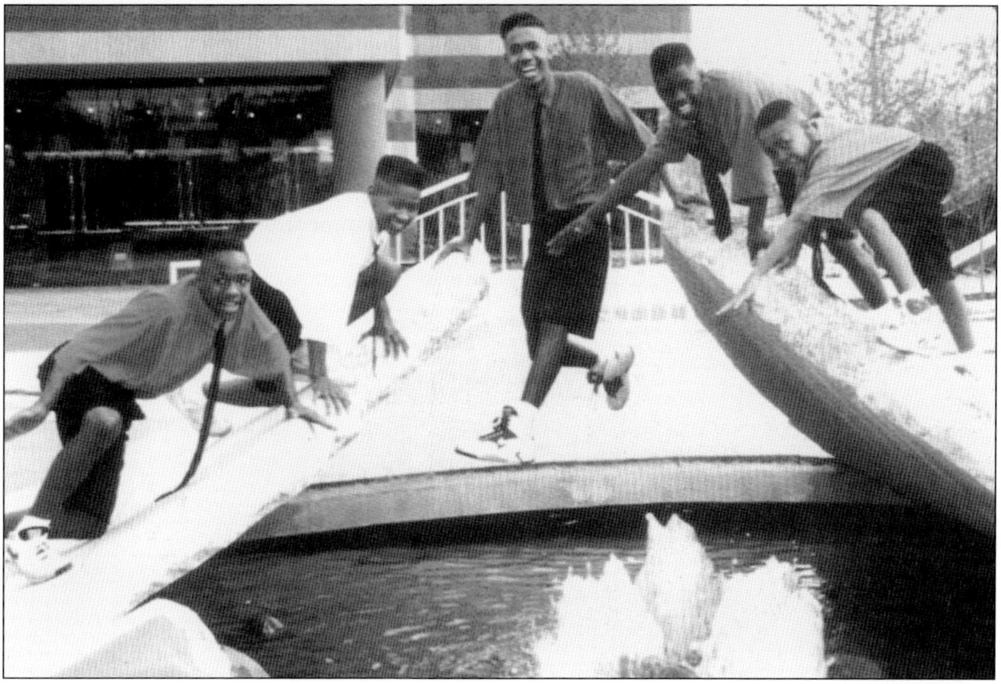

Nu Beginning singing group is where Usher Raymond got his first break in the music business. In 1993, Raymond would go on to sign a solo deal with LaFace Records, leaving this talented group of young men that was put together by Daryl Wheeler Sr.

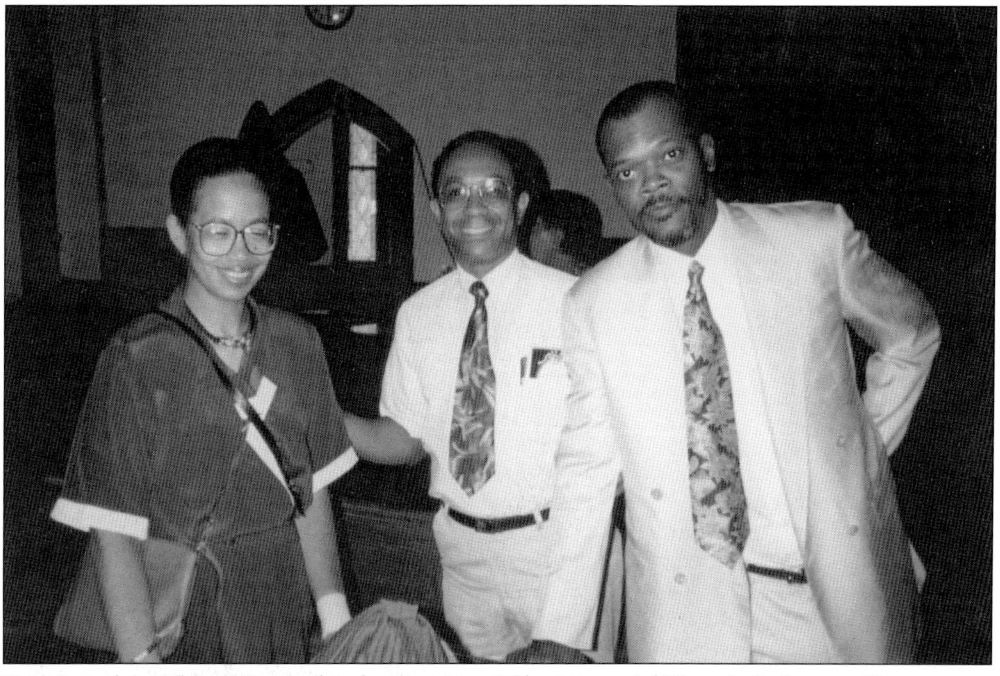

Here is acclaimed actor Samuel Jackson visiting Wiley Memorial Church. Jackson, a Chattanooga native, would often come to Chattanooga to speak at various functions.

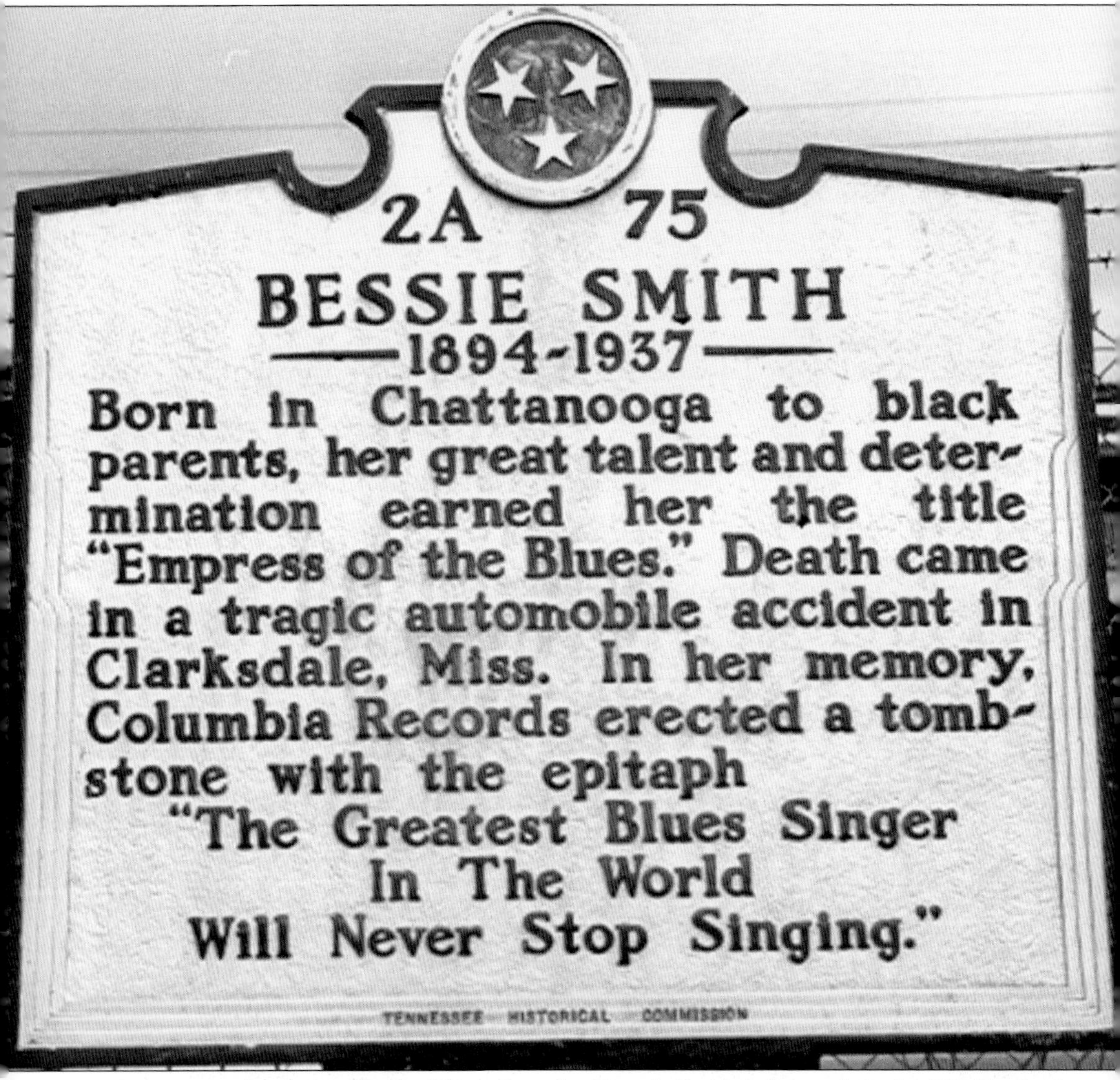

A historic marker honoring the life and work of Bessie Smith is located on the 700 block of Martin Luther King Boulevard.

Six

BUSINESS AND INDUSTRY

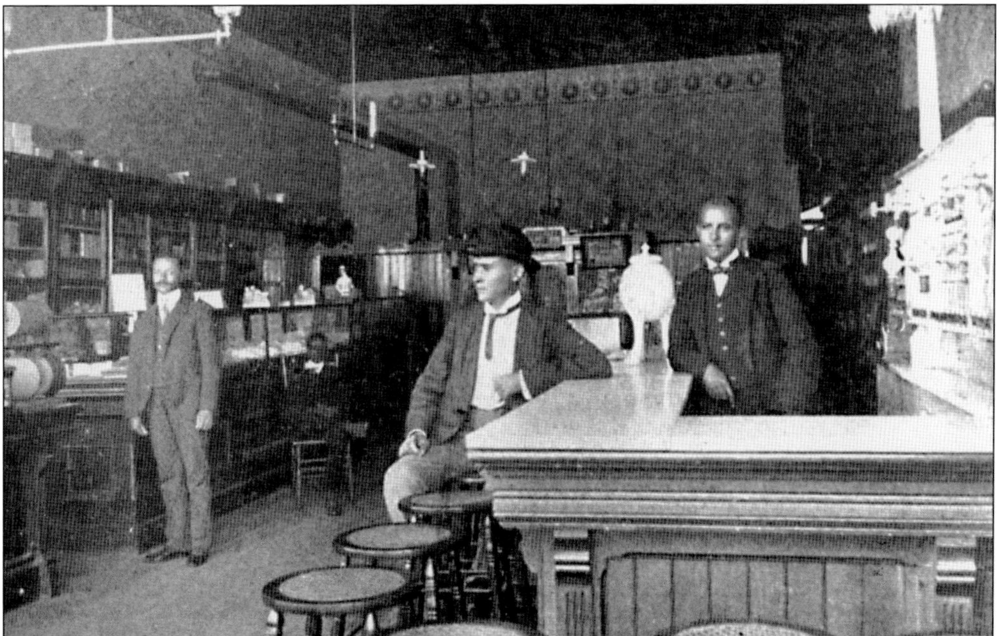

James and Allen Drug Company was a very successful black-owned drug store in downtown Chattanooga.

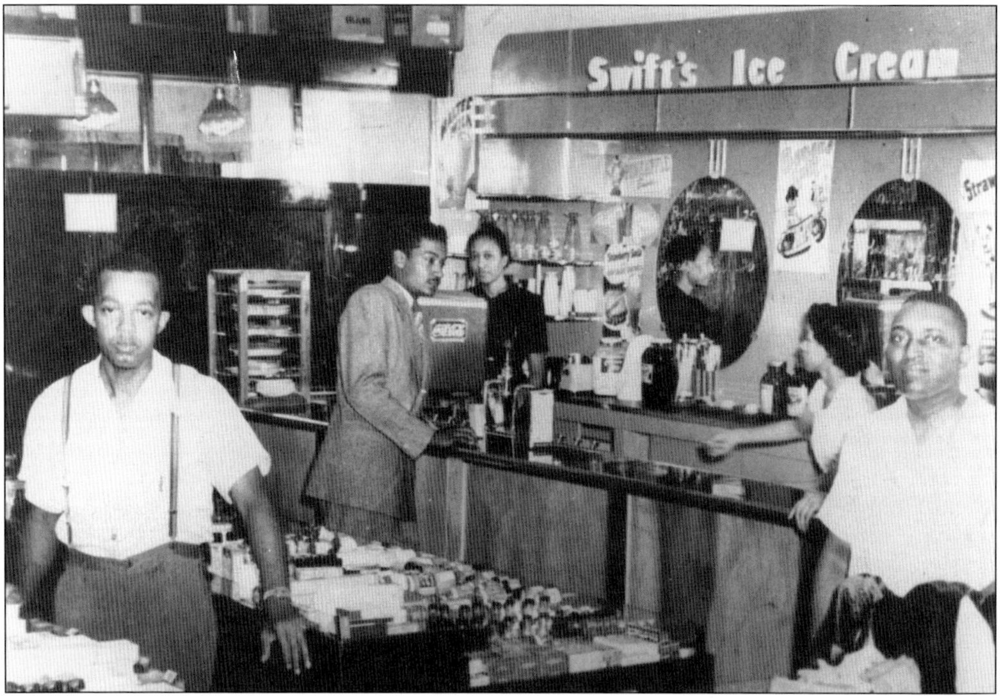

L&G Five and Dime Store, owned by Mr. Gordon, was located on Ninth Street, now Martin Luther King Boulevard.

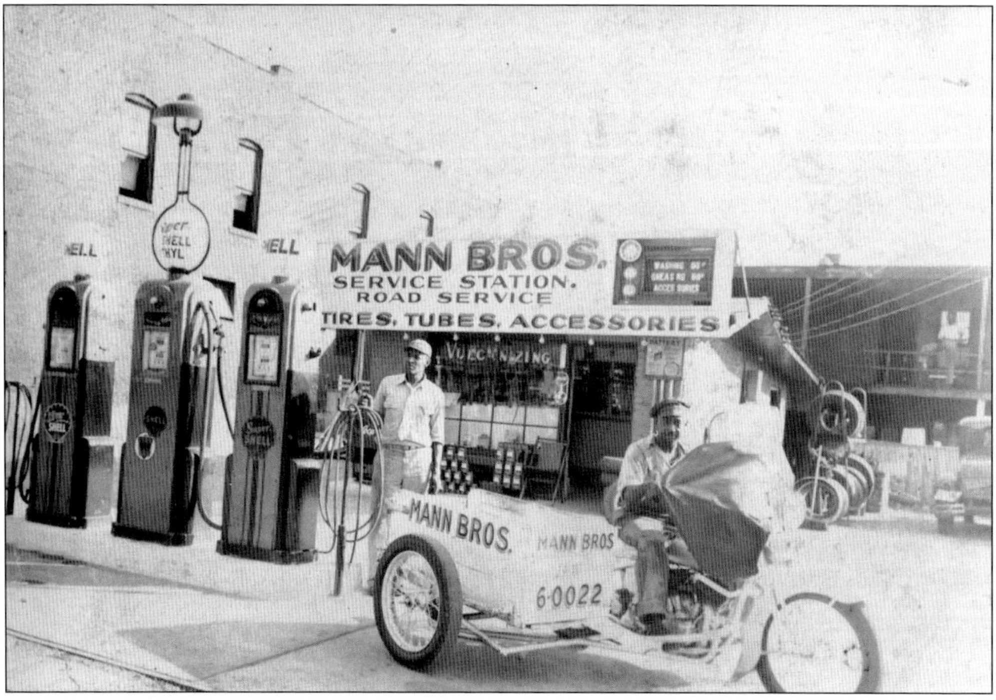

Mann Brothers Filling Station was located at 526 East Ninth Street. This business began in 1920. They had an up-to-date vulcanizing plant. Jim Mann, the proprietor, would boast they were second to none in service to Chattanooga.

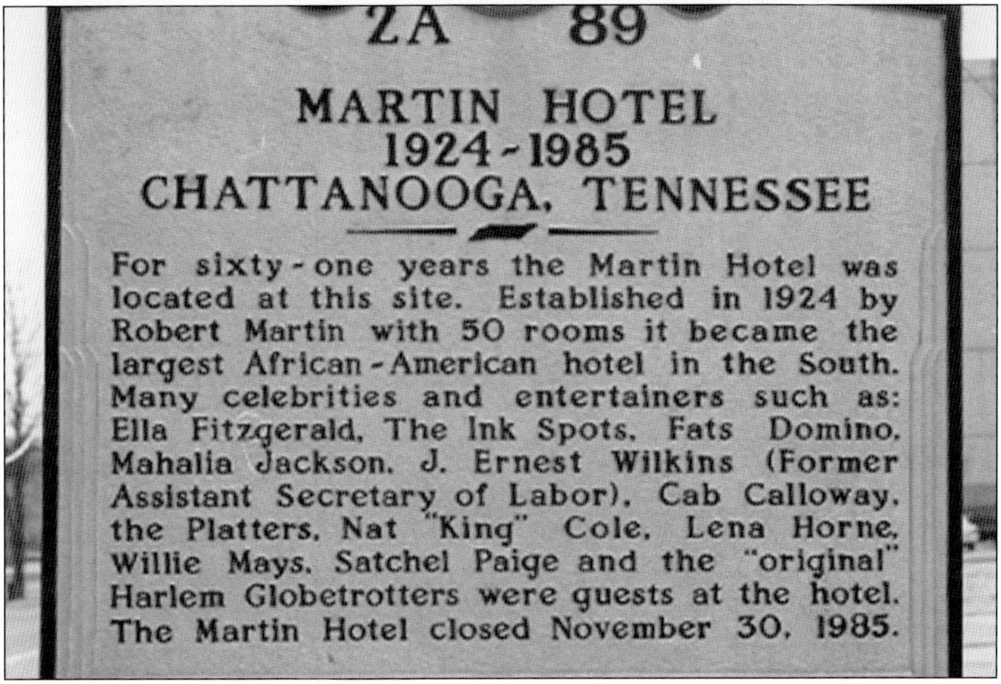

The site of what was once the South's largest African American hotel, the Martin, was honored with a historic marker. The Martin was in business for over 60 years on what was then Ninth Street (Martin Luther King Boulevard).

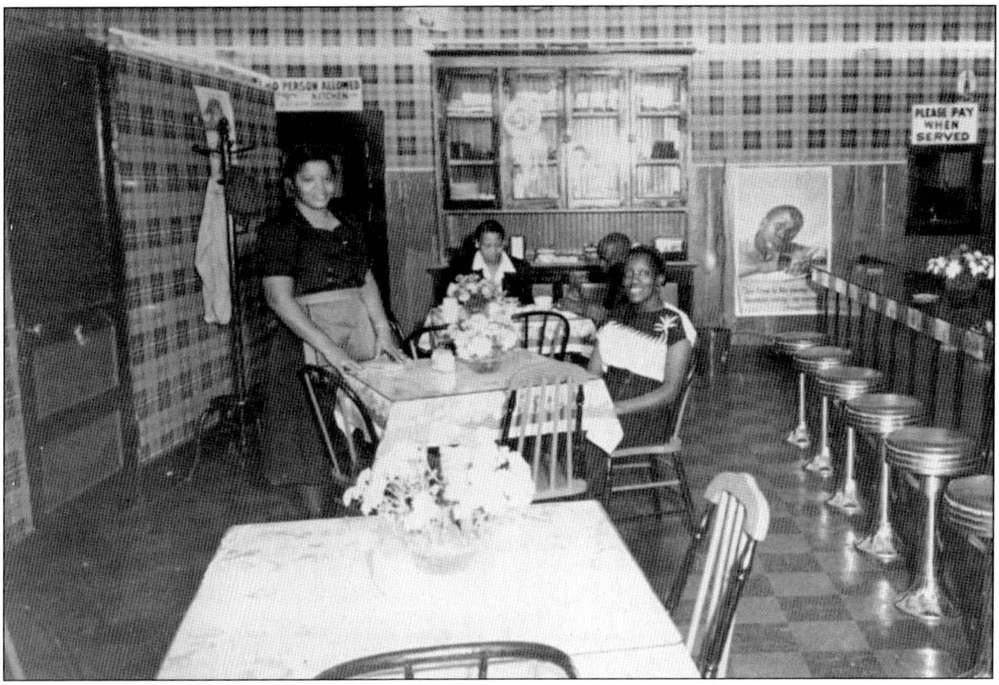

The Snack Shop, located inside the Martin Hotel, was managed by Mamie Martin. Mamie Martin was a schoolteacher in South Carolina who quit her job to come help her uncle Robert Martin run the Martin Hotel.

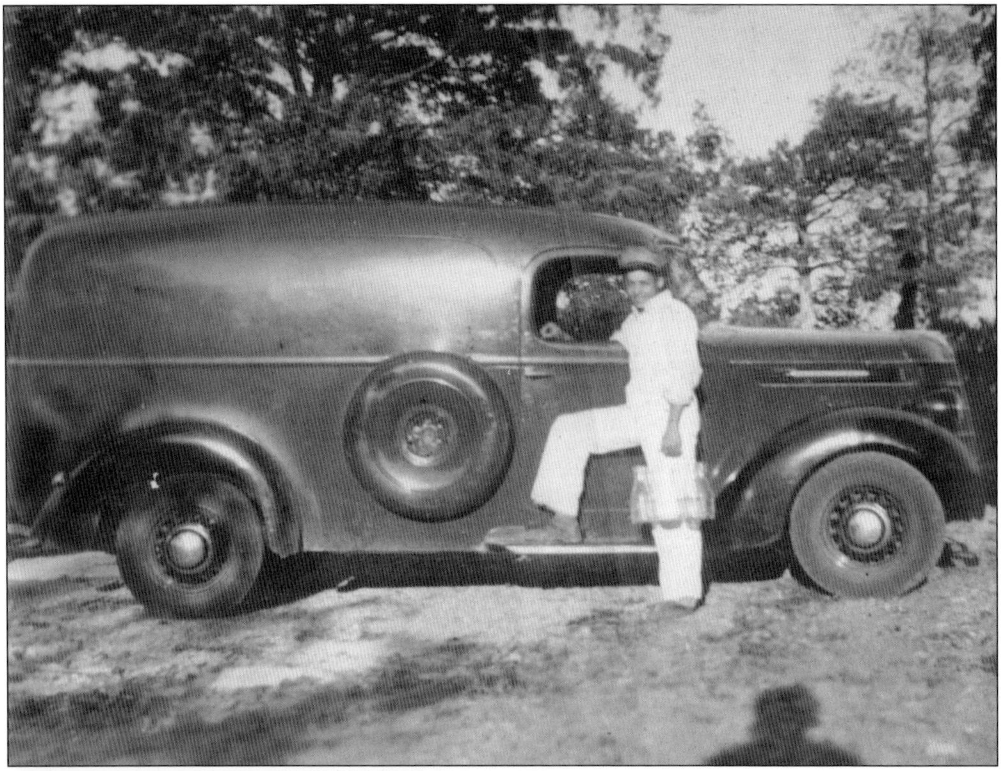

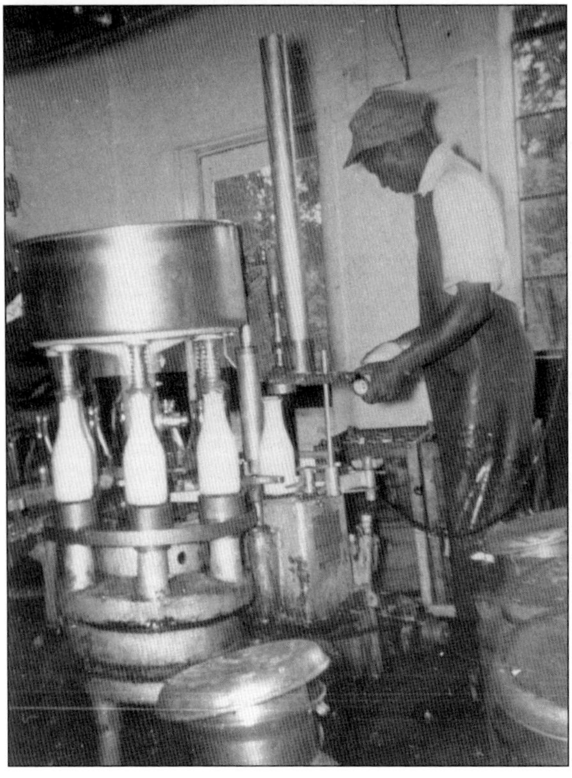

Shown here is a refrigerated dairy truck used for daily delivery for the Haselrig Dairy Plant. The Haselrig Dairy was the only one of its type in the South. The Haselrig Dairy was started by C. D. Haselrig in the late 1920s, selling cheese and produce. In 1949, the dairy started processing and delivering milk, making it the only black-owned dairy of its type in the South. The dairy closed in 1965.

The Haselrigs owned and operated the only African American dairy in town before 1960, and they delivered milk door-to-door throughout Chattanooga.

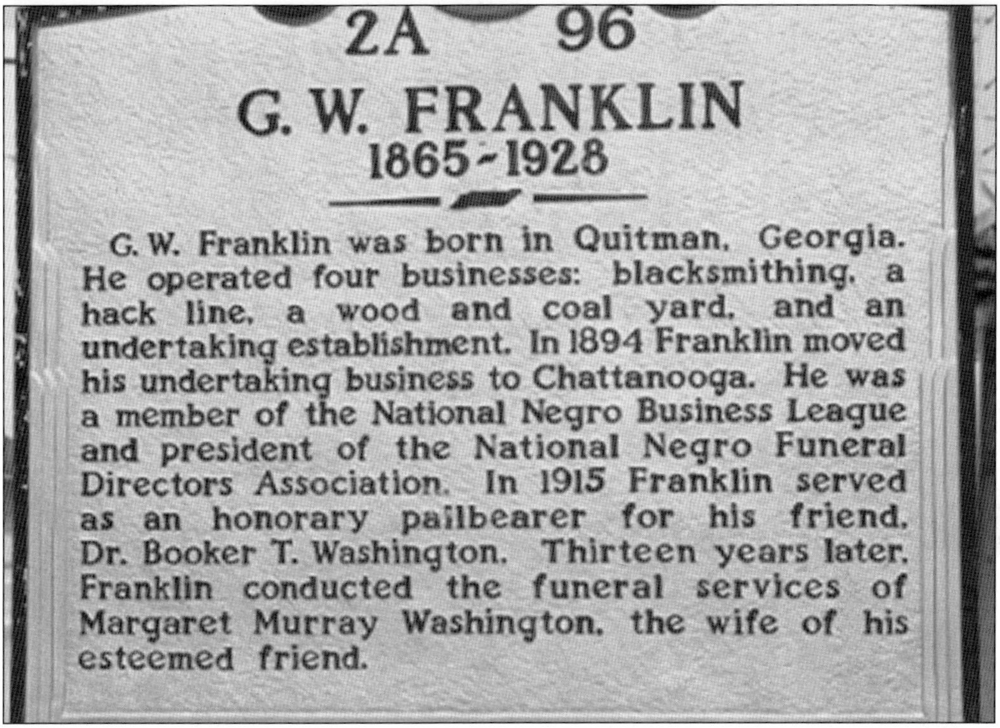

G. W. Franklin's historic marker is located on Chestnut Street, where the funeral-home business once stood. Franklin also owned real estate, two cemeteries, and a farm with 111 acres that contained coal, iron, ore, and some timber. Franklin attributed his success to the encouragement he received from his friend Booker T. Washington and the National Negro Business League.

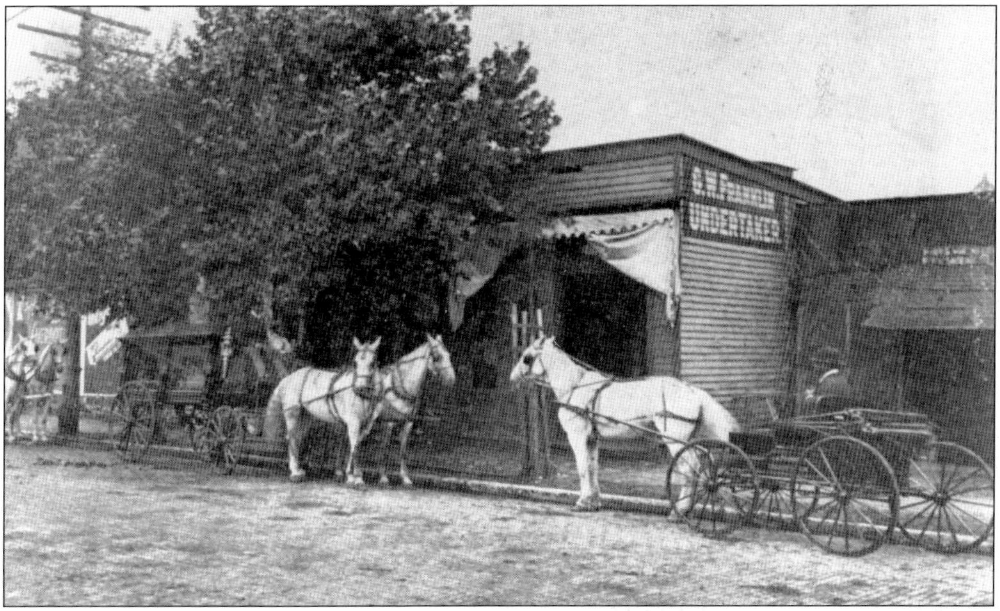

The G. W. Franklin Funeral Home was located on 610 Chestnut Street in 1896. He was a pioneer funeral director. The Franklin family is still in the funeral business, with multiple locations of Franklin-Strickland Funeral Home in Chattanooga.

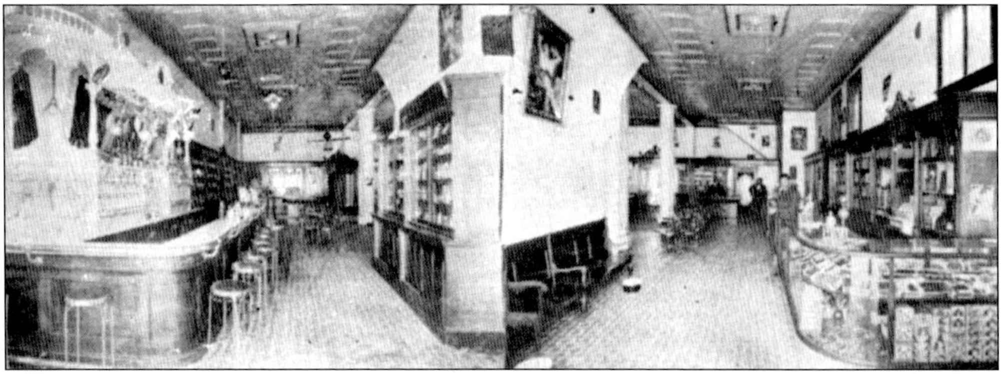

Above is an interior view of the East Side Pharmacy, located on East Ninth Street in the James Building. Owned by Mr. James and Mr. Allen, this was one of the finest black-owned drug stores in the United States.

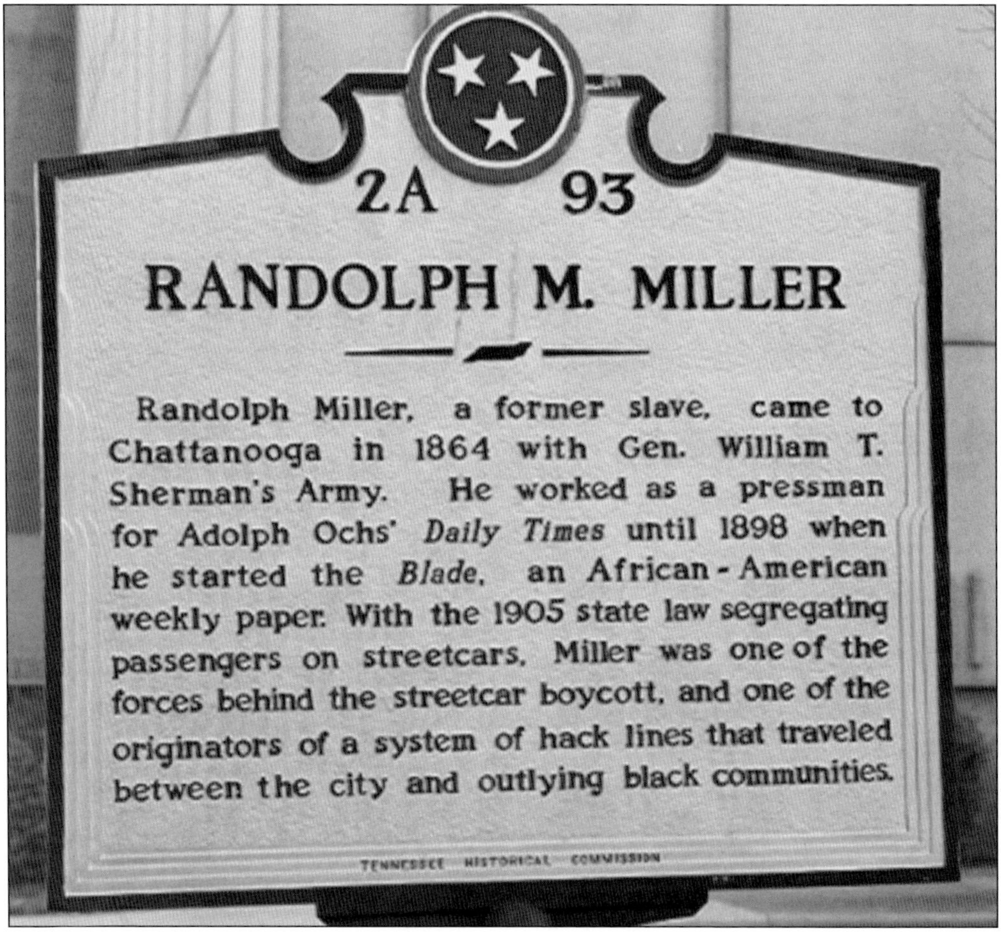

Randolph Miller was a former slave who came to Chattanooga with Gen. William T. Sherman's army. Miller was the only ex-slave to own, publish, and edit a newspaper in the United States (the *Blade*). He worked as a pressman for Adolph Ochs and the *Daily Times* until 1898, when he started the *Blade*. Miller boycotted the transit system and started the Hack line, a jitney taxi service that traveled between the city and the outlying black communities in 1905.

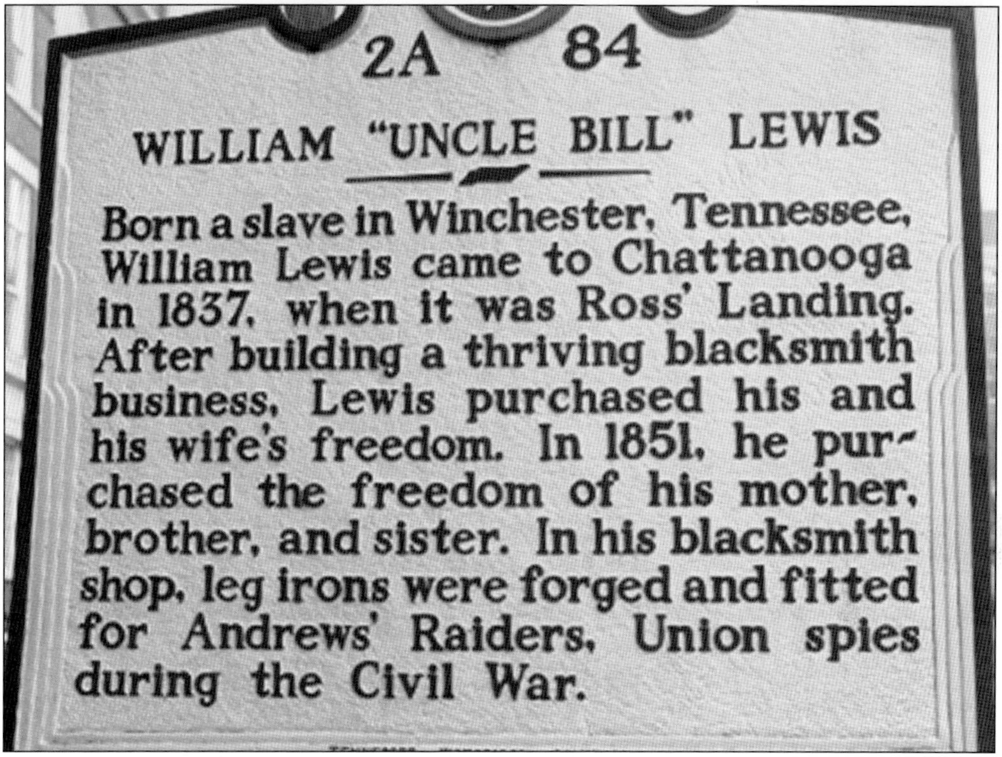

William Lewis was the first African American blacksmith and wagon-maker in Chattanooga. There is a historic marker at Seventh and Market Street, where his business was once located.

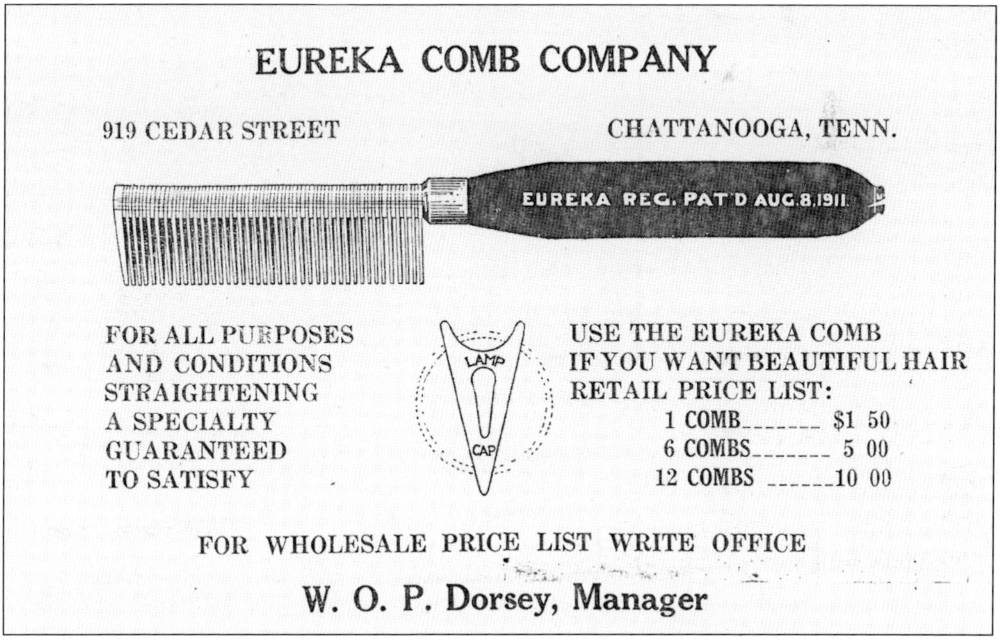

Eureka Comb Company was owned and operated by the Dorsey family on the west side of Chattanooga. This advertisement for a hot comb shows one of the many beauty products that they produced.

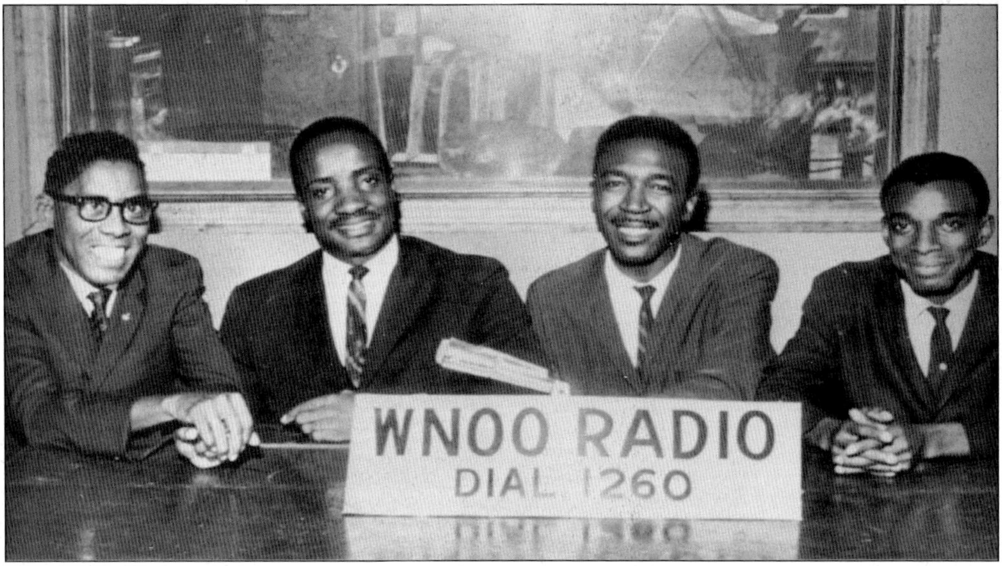

The white-owned WNOO radio station was operated by African Americans and provided infrastructure for the black community. WNOO, now known as "Your Heritage Station," still serves the community today.

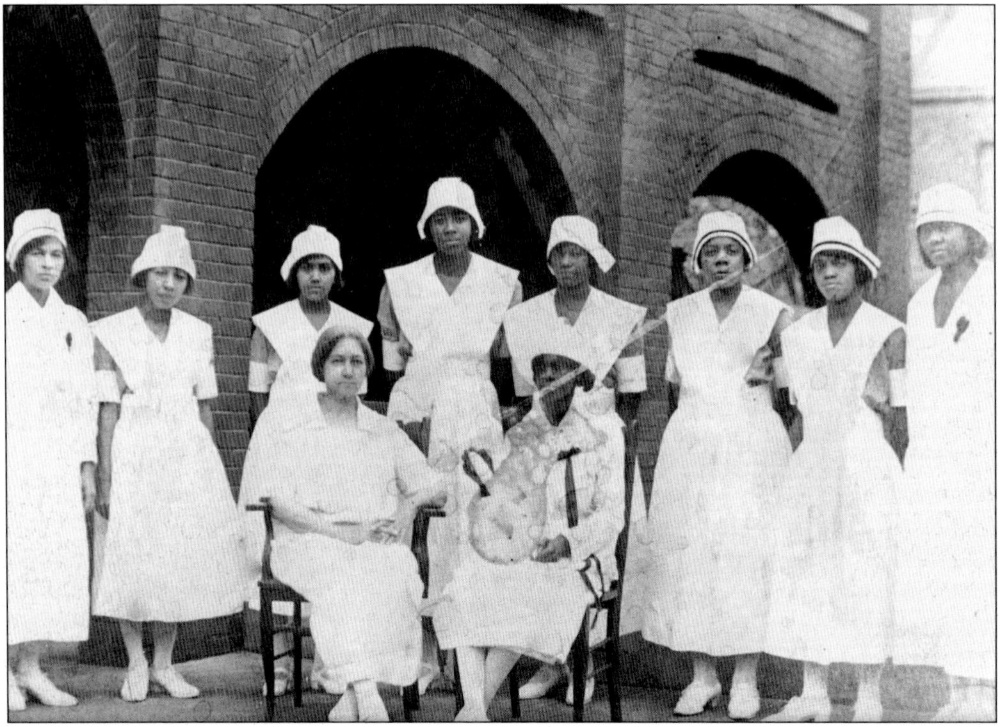

Owned and operated by blacks at the turn of the century, the Walden Hospital had an all-black staff and 19 black doctors. Founded in 1914 by Dr. Emma Wheeler and her husband, Dr. John Wheeler, the facility served the black community for over 35 years.

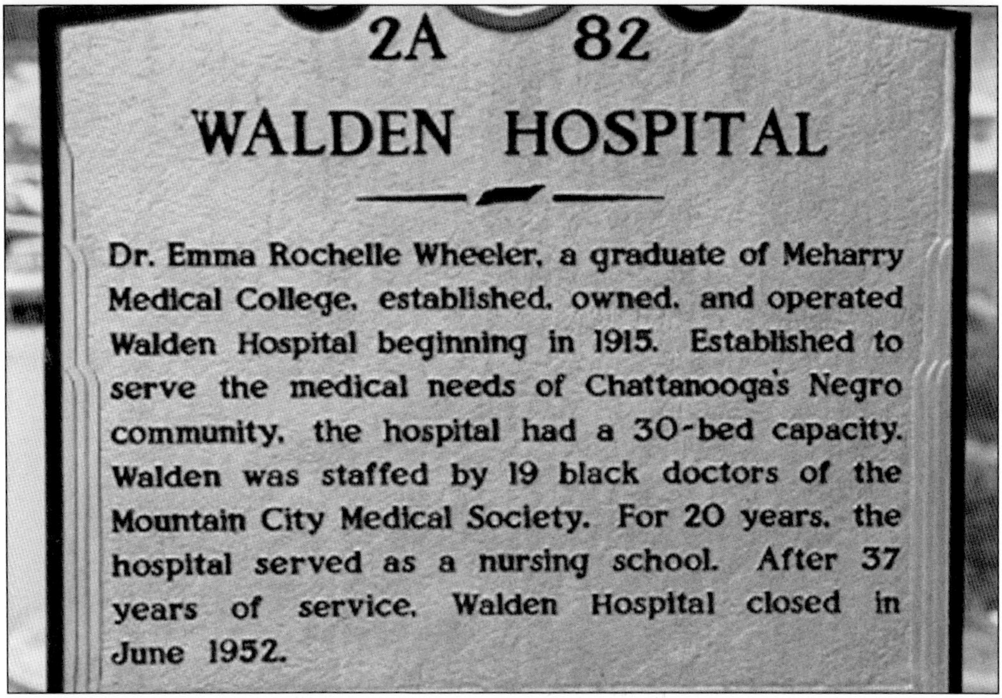

The historic marker for Walden Hospital is located at East Eighth Street, where the building still stands. The building now serves as an apartment complex for students of the University of Tennessee at Chattanooga.

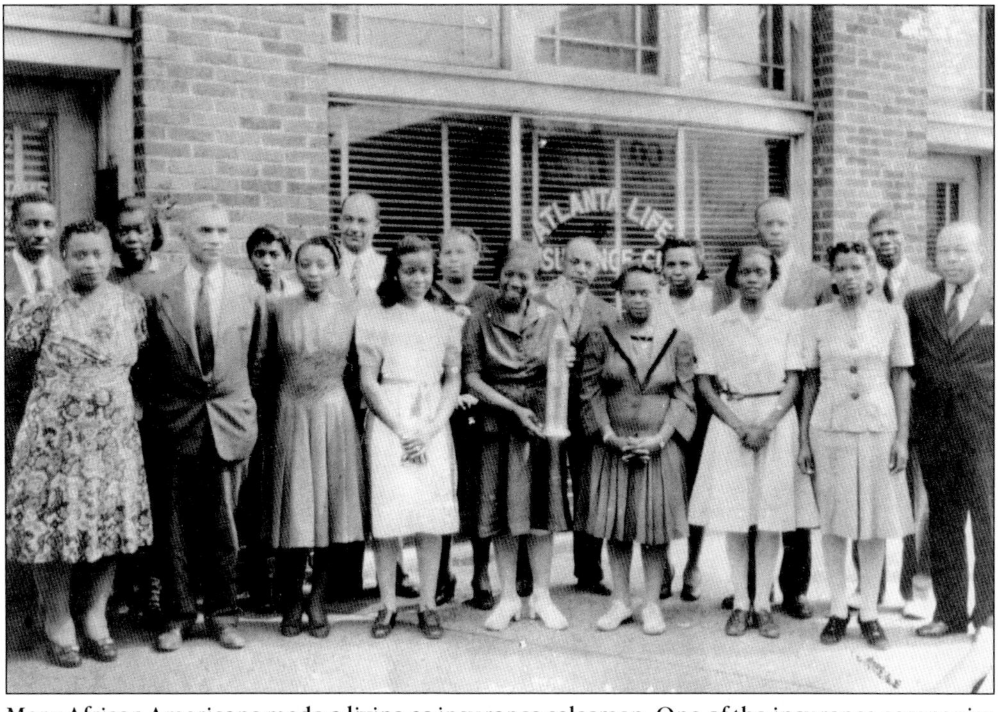

Many African Americans made a living as insurance salesmen. One of the insurance companies that blacks worked for in Chattanooga was Atlanta Life Insurance Company.

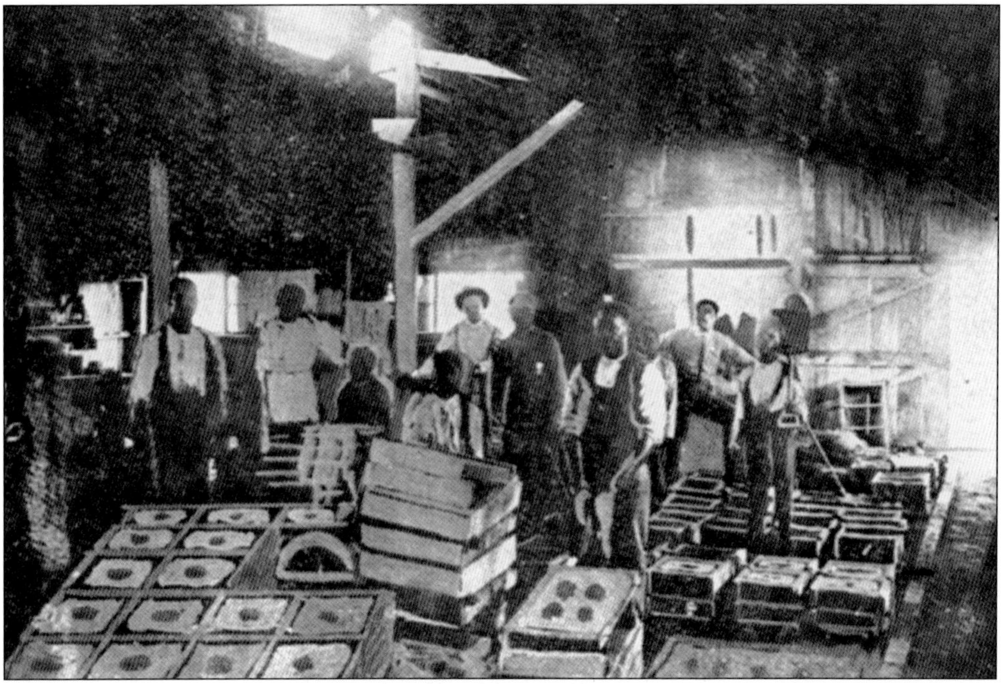

The Rising Sun Manufacturing Company was managed and operated by African Americans and was the only enterprise of its kind owned and controlled by African Americans in Tennessee. They made specialty stoves, grate baskets, fenders, fronts, stove repairing equipment, and hollowware.

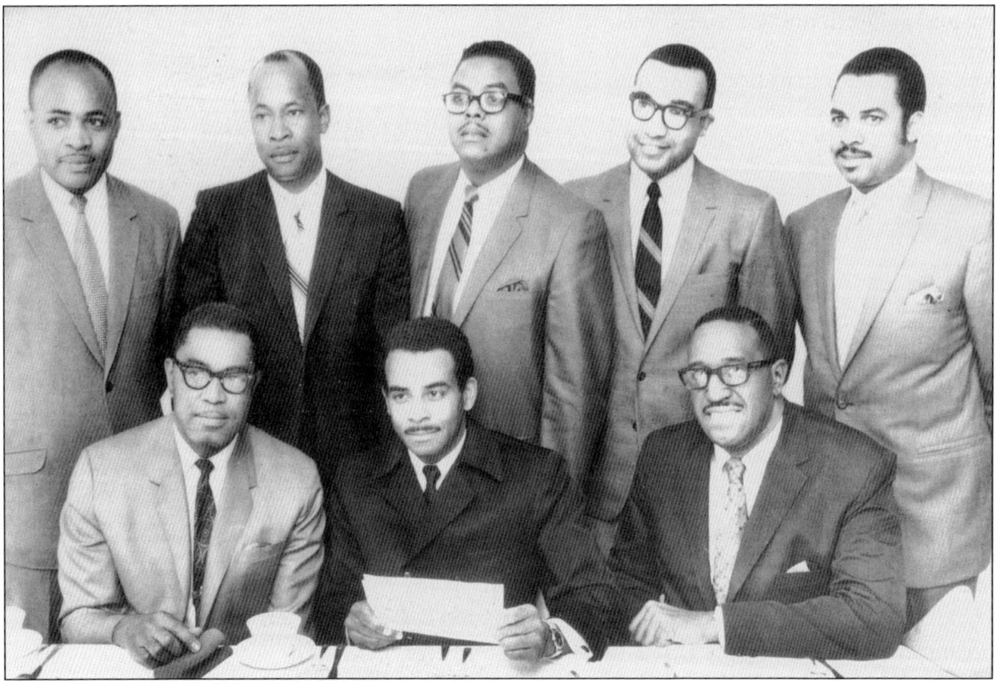

Security Federal Savings and Loan was the first African American savings and loan corporation in town, established in Chattanooga in 1971.

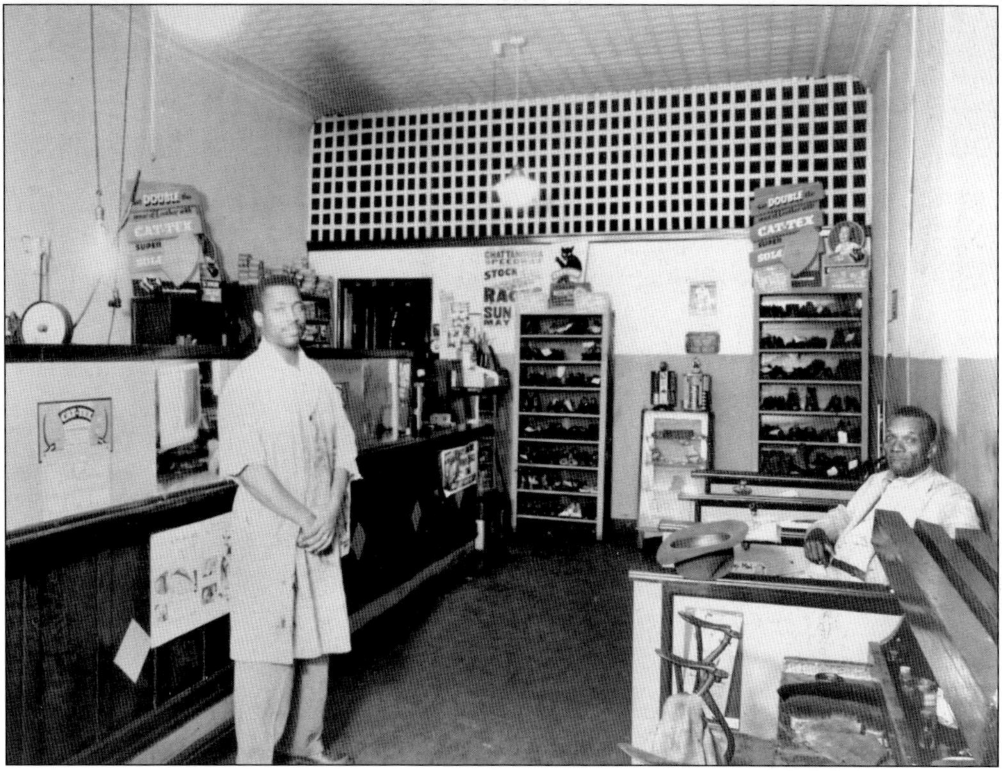

Jackson's Wood and Coal Yard, located at Tenth and E Streets, was owned by Mr. G. W. Jackson and was a striking illustration of African American accomplishment in the early 20th century in Chattanooga.

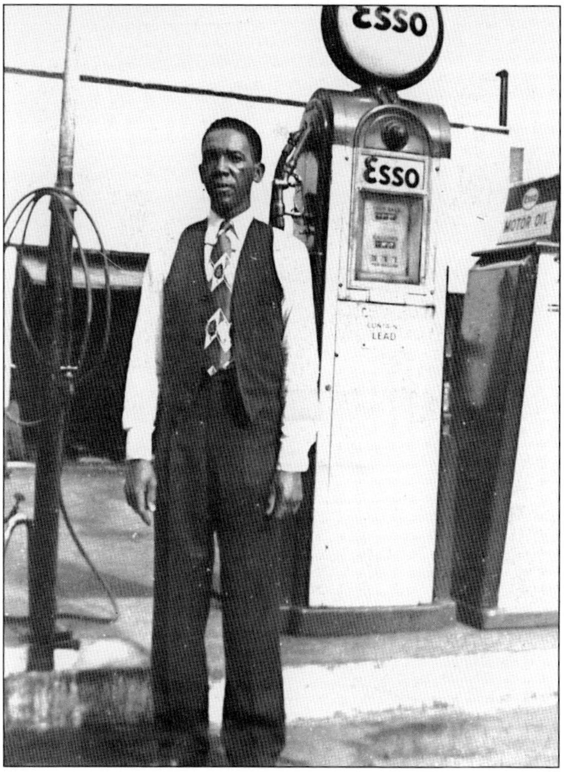

Martin Service Center, a family-owned business, was located at 3701 Alton Park Boulevard for over 40 years. Mr. Martin was involved in many organizations, including the Urban League, NAACP, Alton Park Chamber of Commerce, and the Chattanooga National Business League.

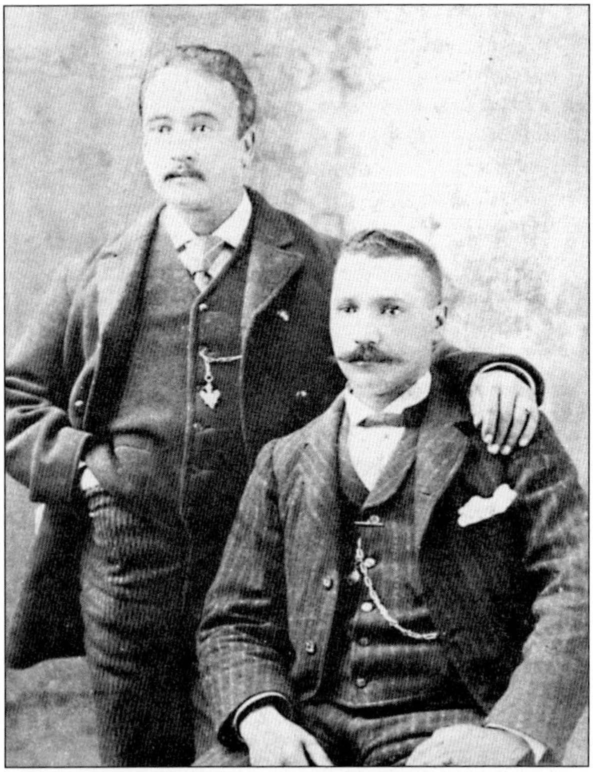

Edwin Horne was a teacher, publisher of a weekly paper called *Justice*, and grandfather of legendary performer Lena Horne. Mr. Horne was also co-owner of Perry and Company—"The Peoples Drug Store"—located on Ninth and B Streets in Chattanooga, Tennessee.

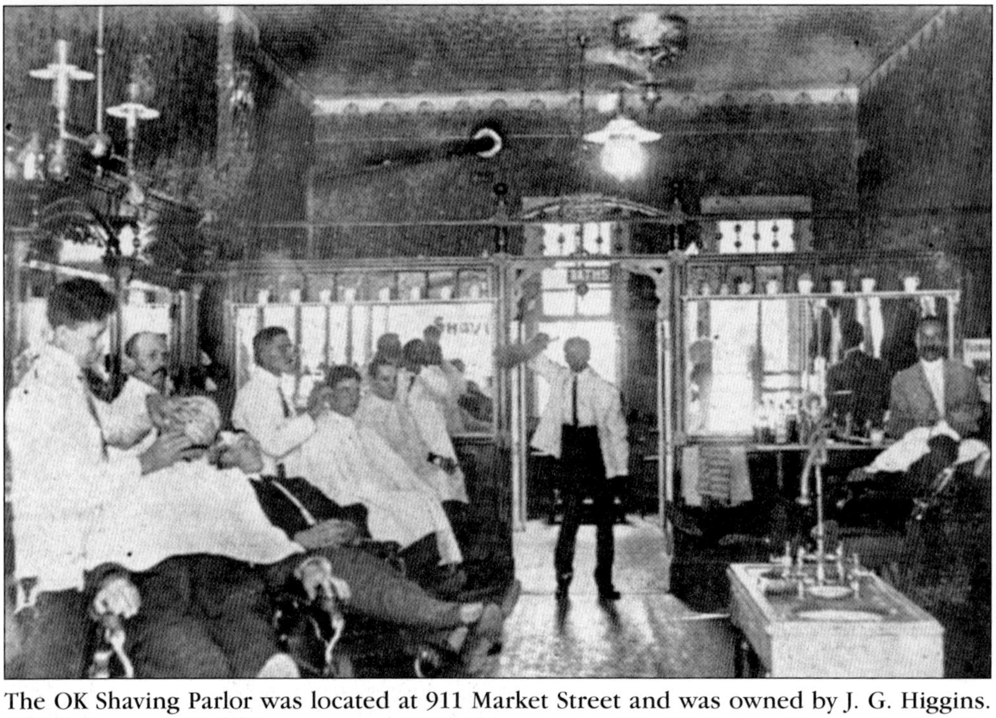

The OK Shaving Parlor was located at 911 Market Street and was owned by J. G. Higgins. Higgins owned 12 different successful businesses over his lifetime and was a barber for more than 40 years.

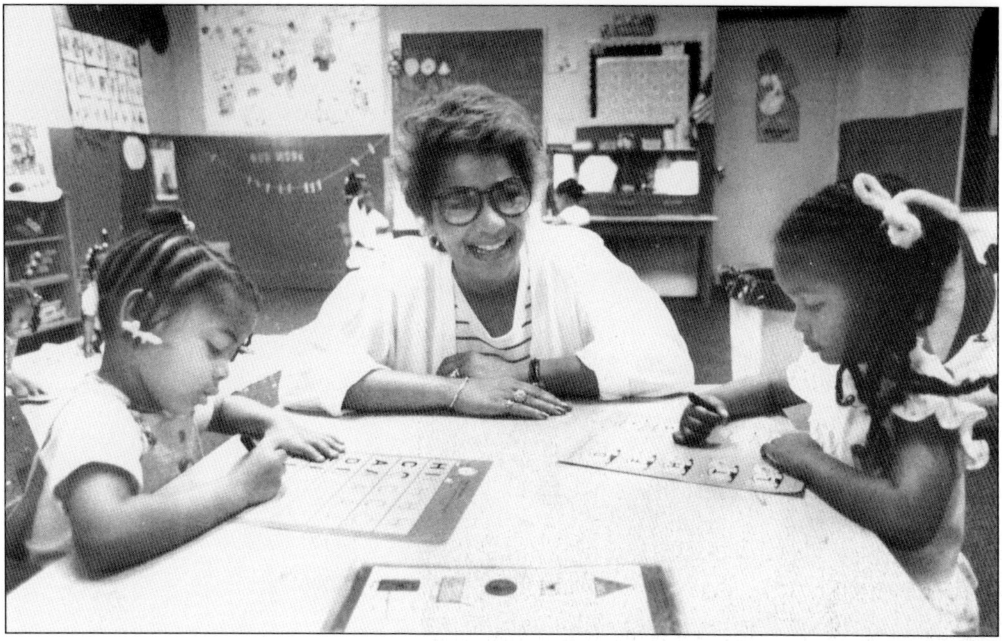

Kandy Kastle Daycare served the African American community for over 20 years. Pictured here is owner and community philanthropist Diane Mason with some of her students.

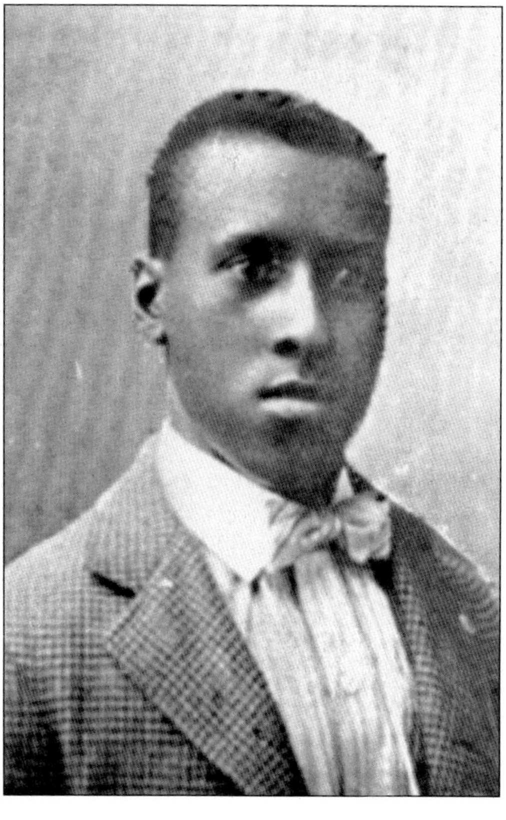

Mr. S. S. Wester obtained employment as a porter in grocery stores in the latter part of 1882. By close application, he became acquainted with the business. In 1897, he and his brother started Westers' Grocery Store and added a bakery as the business became successful.

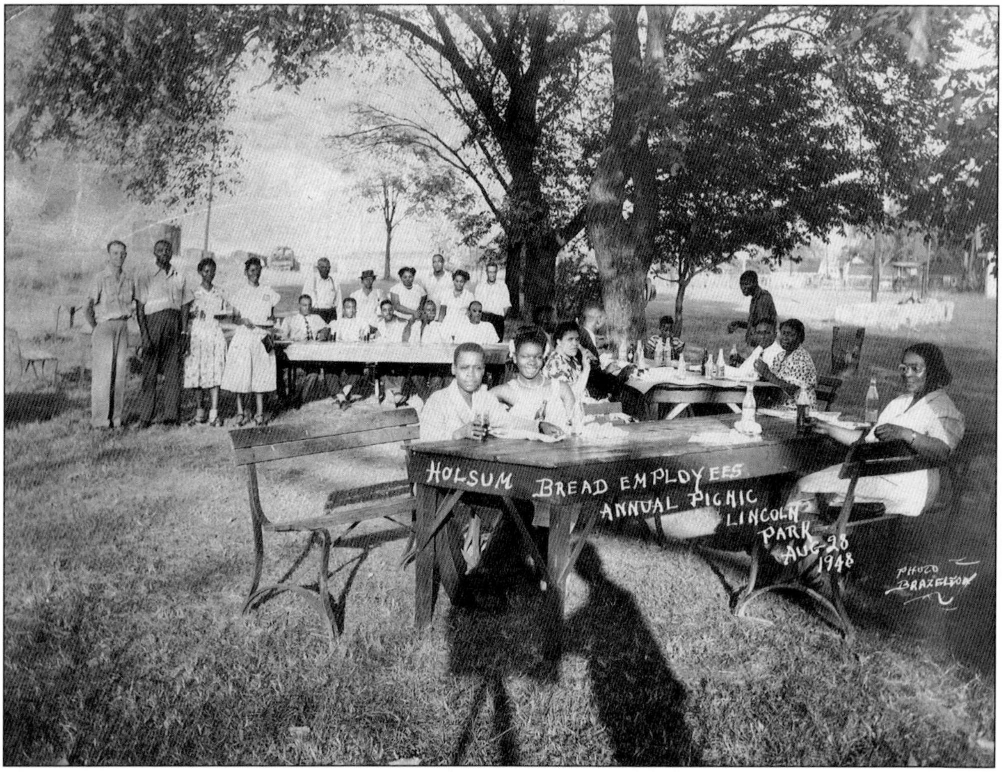

This is a company picnic held at Lincoln Park. Many companies held outings for their black employees in Lincoln Park. Pictured is the Holsum Bread Company's annual picnic for employees held on August 28, 1948.

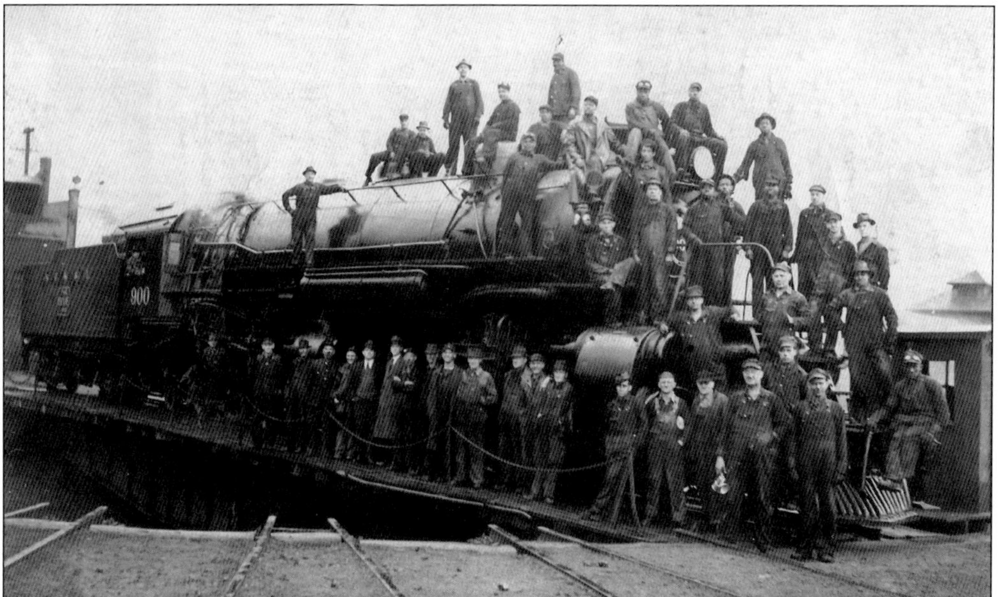

Chattanooga Railroad, a subsidiary of Louisville and Nashville Railroad, provided many jobs for blacks in Chattanooga.

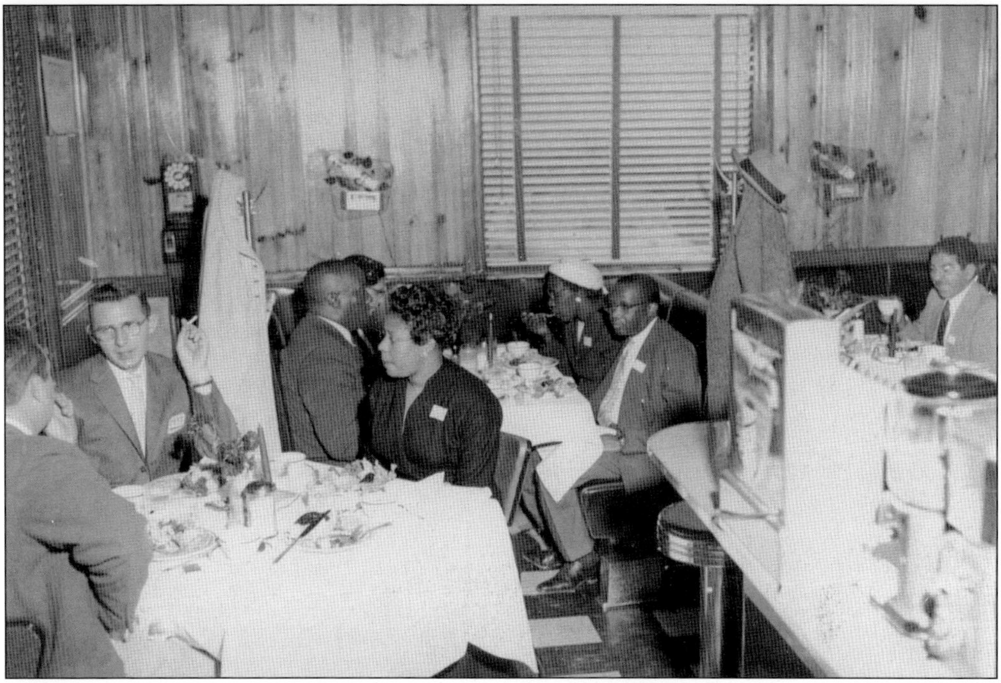

WNOO radio staff personalities Evelyn Cato and Fred Webb are pictured here at the famous Imperial Drive Inn on South Market Street. Evelyn Cato was the first black woman announcer in Chattanooga on WNOO, and Fred Webb was the manager of WNOO.

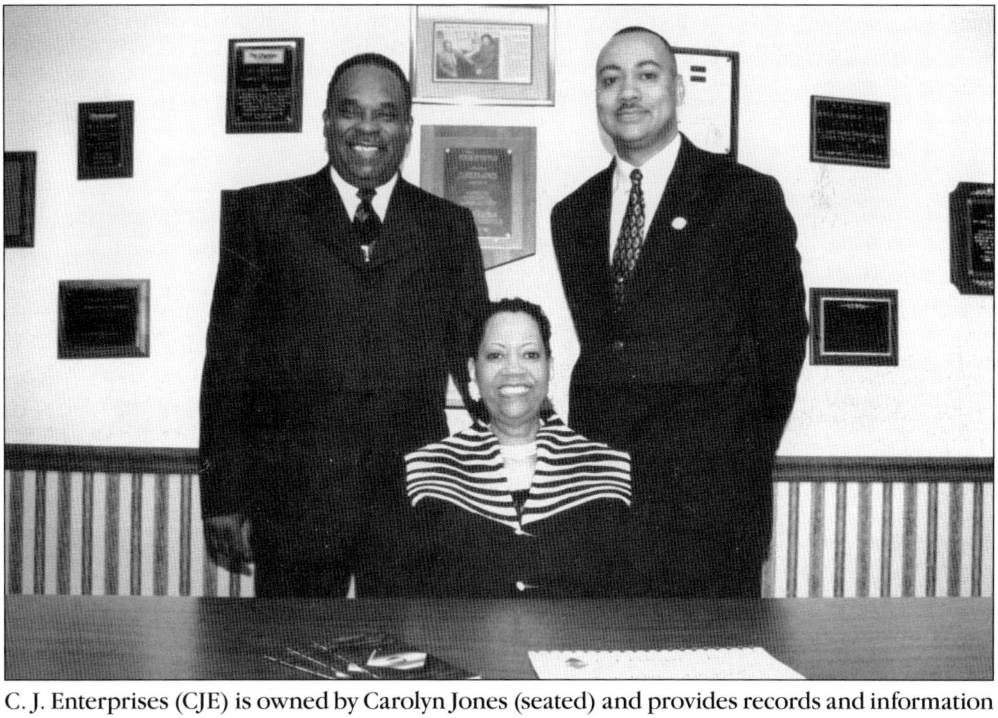

C. J. Enterprises (CJE) is owned by Carolyn Jones (seated) and provides records and information management, administrative management, technical assistance, and consulting services, as well as training for government agencies, health care facilities, and commercial businesses.

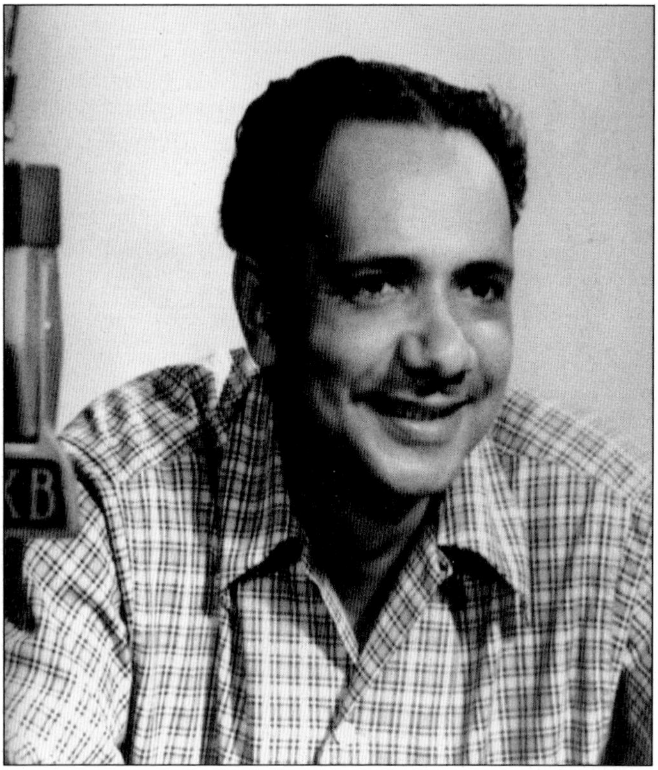

Ted Bryant, the first African American radio announcer in Chattanooga on WDXB, was also a successful entrepreneur who owned Ted Bryant Printing Company. He is pictured here in the 1940s.

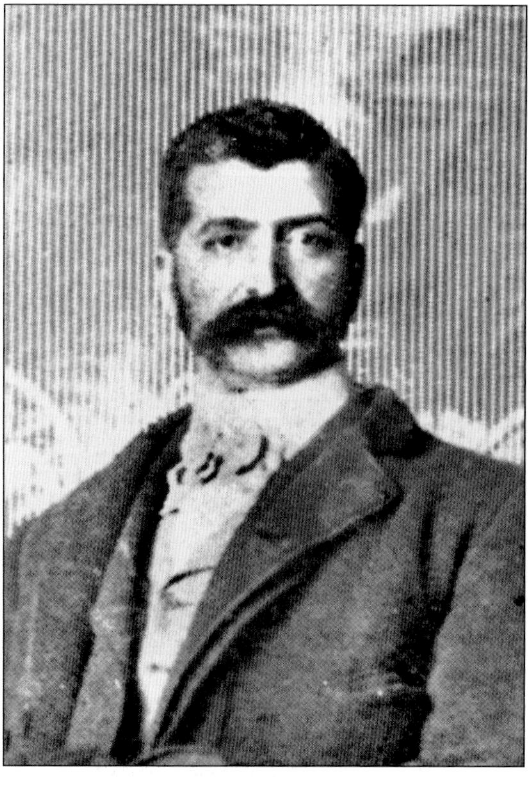

Henry Ferguson came to Chattanooga in 1885 as a contractor and builder, and he resided in the city until his death.

E. D. Wisdom came to Chattanooga in 1886. He went to work at once for Montague and Company and later for the Chattanooga Tannery. He was employed there for five years, after which he opened a grocery store located at 110 Ash Street. He was a successful businessman and had a wife and four children.

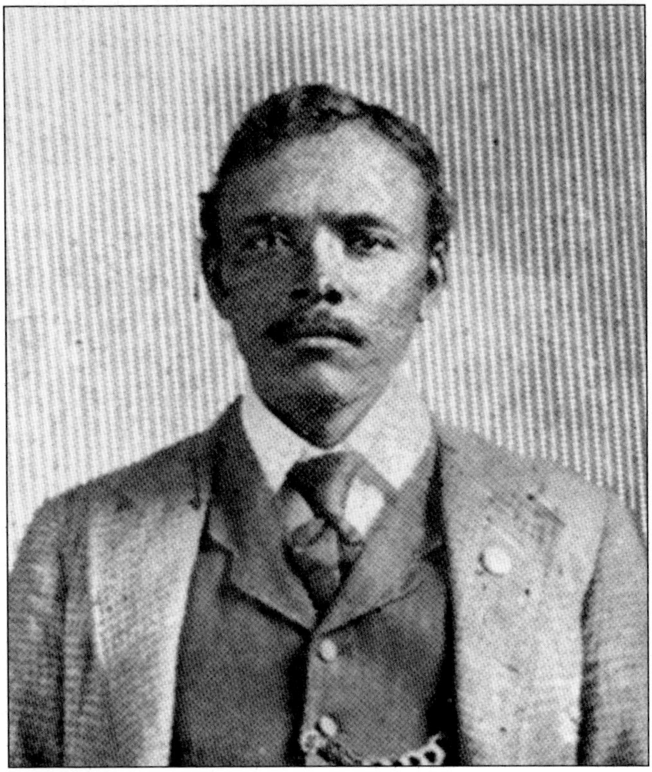

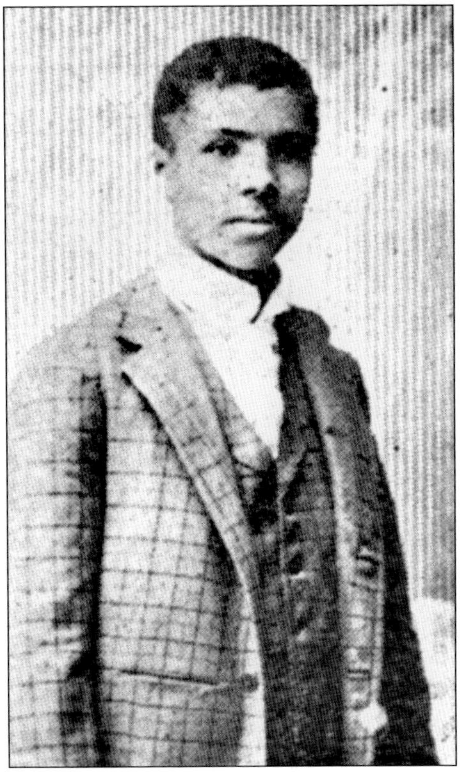

A. H. Henderson was born in Bradley County, Tennessee, and came to Chattanooga in 1882. He opened Henderson Café at 331 West Ninth Street in 1901. The café was said to have electric lights and fans and served the delicacies of the season at reasonable prices.

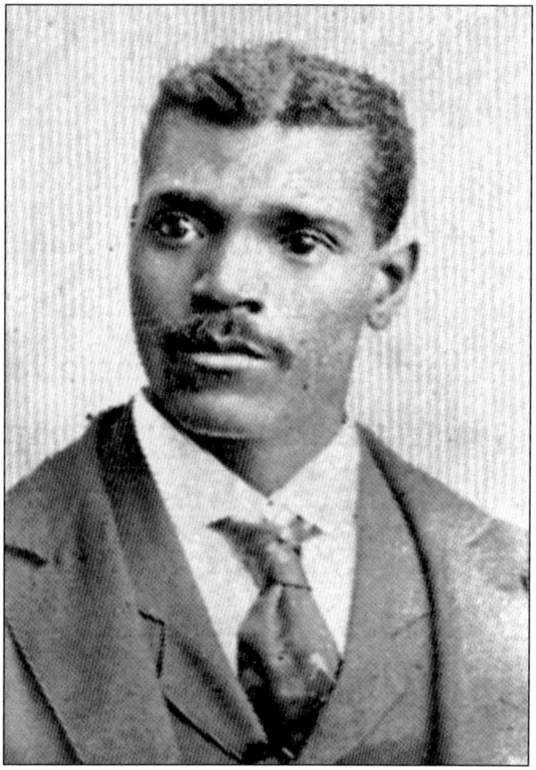

M. H. Miller came to Chattanooga in 1894 and was employed as a cook in some of the various hotels throughout the city. In 1898, he opened a confectionery business at 106 East Ninth Street, which was one of the most popular black-owned businesses in the city at that time.

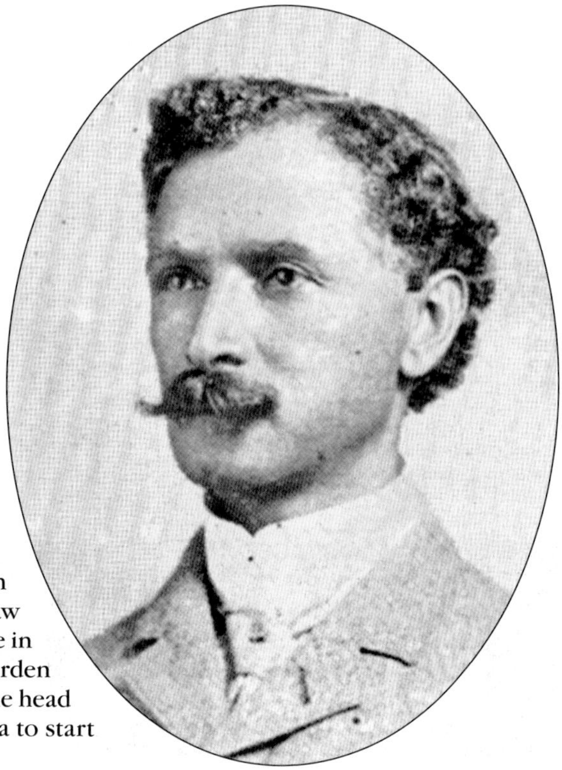

Noah W. Parden, LL.B., came to Chattanooga in 1884. He entered Howard High School in 1885, worked five years for his boards, and graduated in 1890. In the fall of 1890, he entered the law department of Central Tennessee College in Nashville, Tennessee, without a dollar. Parden graduated from the law department at the head of his class and returned to Chattanooga to start his own practice.

W. R. Hastie was born in Chattanooga, Tennessee, in 1873. He began at an early age to learn the moulder's trade, and he worked at the same for about 16 years. He was one of the young black men of the city who rapidly made their way to the front in the business world. He was in business for six years and enjoyed the respect and confidence of all who know him.

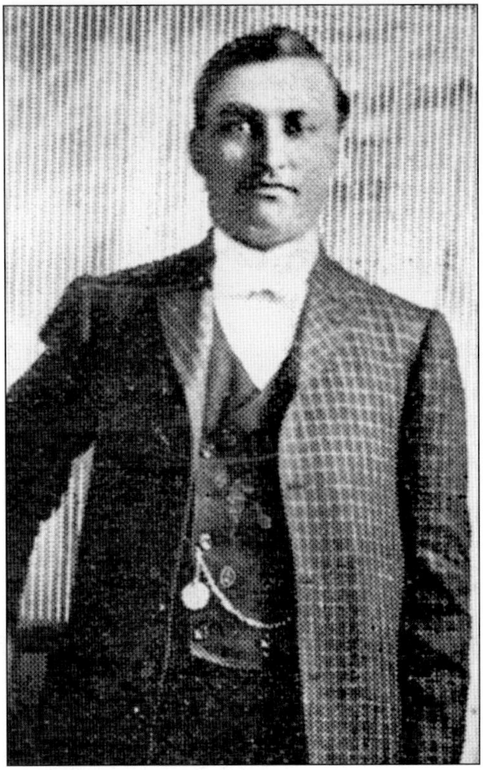

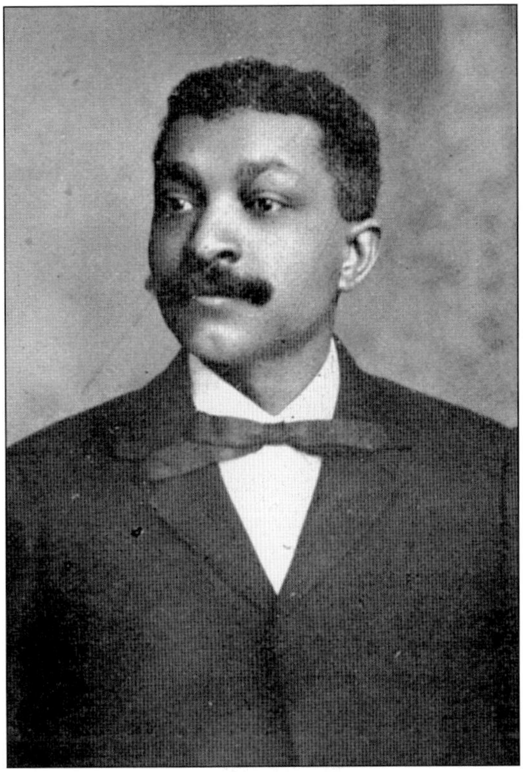

B. F. Johnson was born in Dalton, Georgia, on August 25, 1863, and came to Chattanooga in 1887. A boot- and shoemaker by trade, he was a member of Hill City Lodge No. 5 of the Knights of Pythias and the Mount Moriah Lodge No. 14 of the Masons.

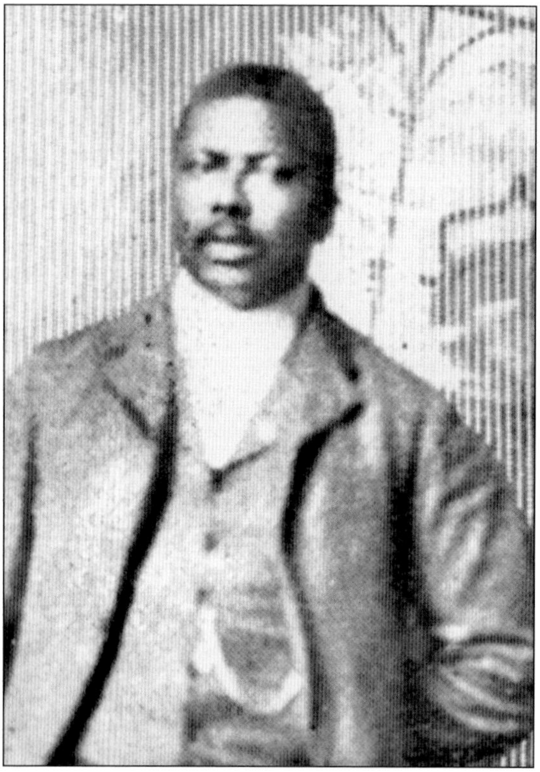

J. A. Strickland owned a grocery and general merchandise business at 826 Frank Street and was one of the most successful black men of Chattanooga. He was one of the promoters of the Rising Sun Manufacturing Company, and its existence was largely due to his efforts. He was president when the business opened in the early 19th century, and his greatest desire and hope was that the Rising Sun Manufacturing Company came to the front rank as a manufacturing enterprise.

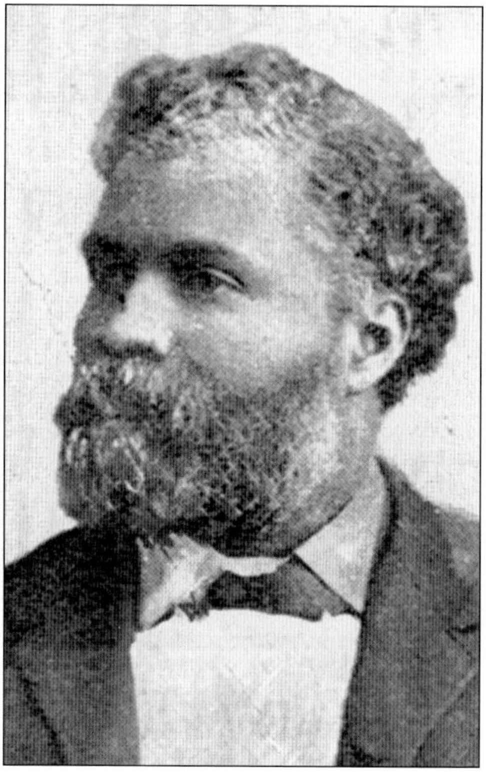

J. W. White was a teacher in the public schools of Chattanooga, teaching regularly for 15 years, after which he went into the banking business. He was the head of the Penny Savings Bank until its failure during the panic of 1902–1903. He has held various positions—as justice of the peace for 12 years, alderman of the city at large for one term, tax assessor for the 4th Ward, and a member of the City Board of Tax Assessors. White was the poor commissioner for nine years, and he later went into the practice of law with his son.

Seven

PUBLIC AND CIVIC SERVICE

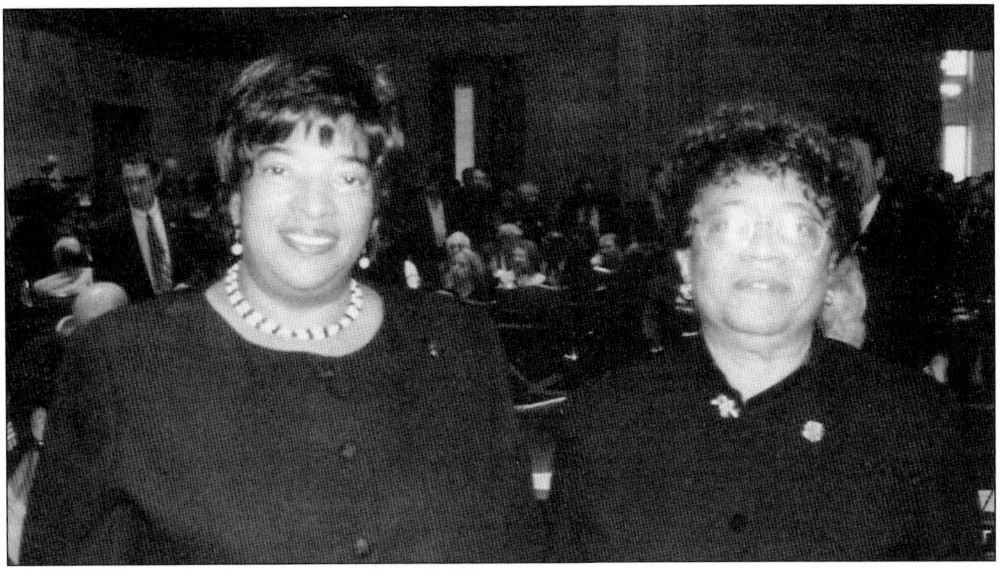

Tennessee state representatives Joanne Favors (left) and Tommie Brown (right) are lifelong residents of Chattanooga. Favors has been appointed to be assistant whip for the 104th General Assembly by Majority Whip Kathryn Bowers. Brown serves as chairwoman of the Legislative Black Caucus.

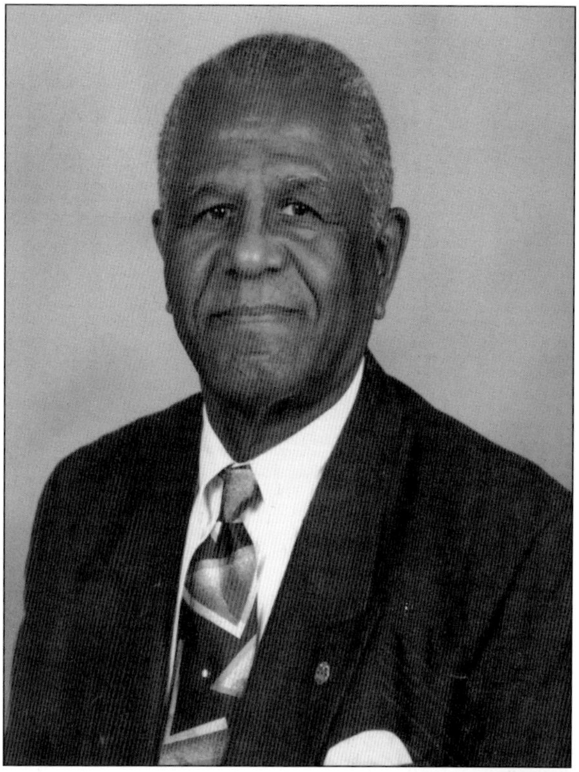

John P. Franklin is a longtime activist and businessman as co-owner of Franklin-Strickland Funeral Homes. In the 1980s, Franklin was the first African American to serve as vice mayor and education commissioner for the city of Chattanooga.

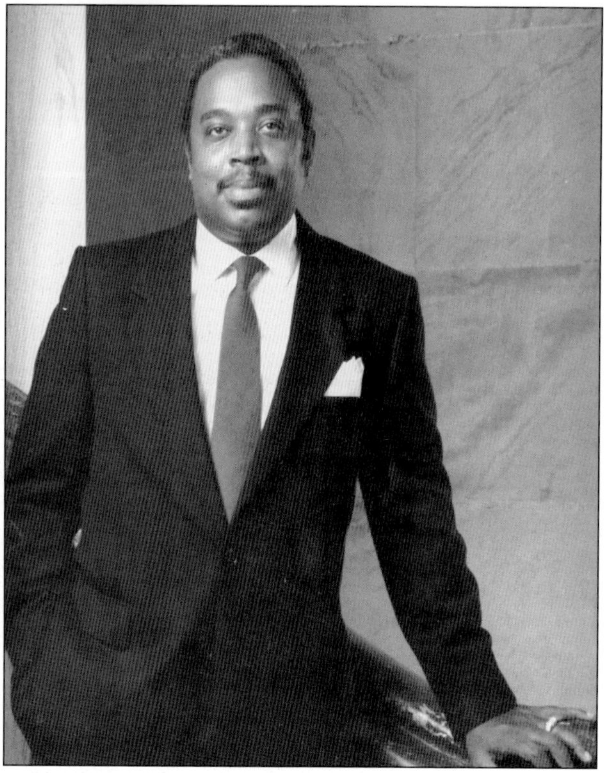

Rayburn Traughber was the first African American to serve as general services administrator in city government. Traughber has also served as commissioner of employment security for the State of Tennessee and Democratic Party chair.

Clarence B. Robinson was a nationally known educator and Tennessee state representative. Also known for establishing the Tennessee Black Caucus, the famous lawmaker and educator had the C. B. Robinson Bridge named in his honor.

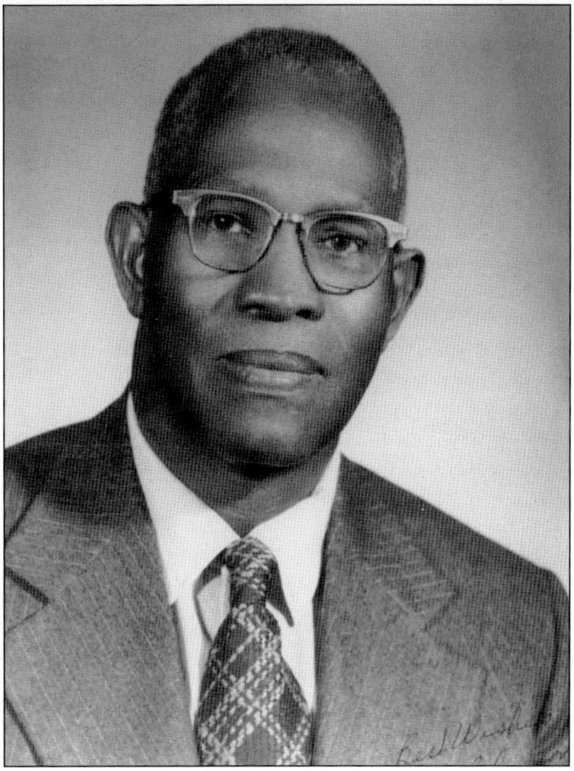

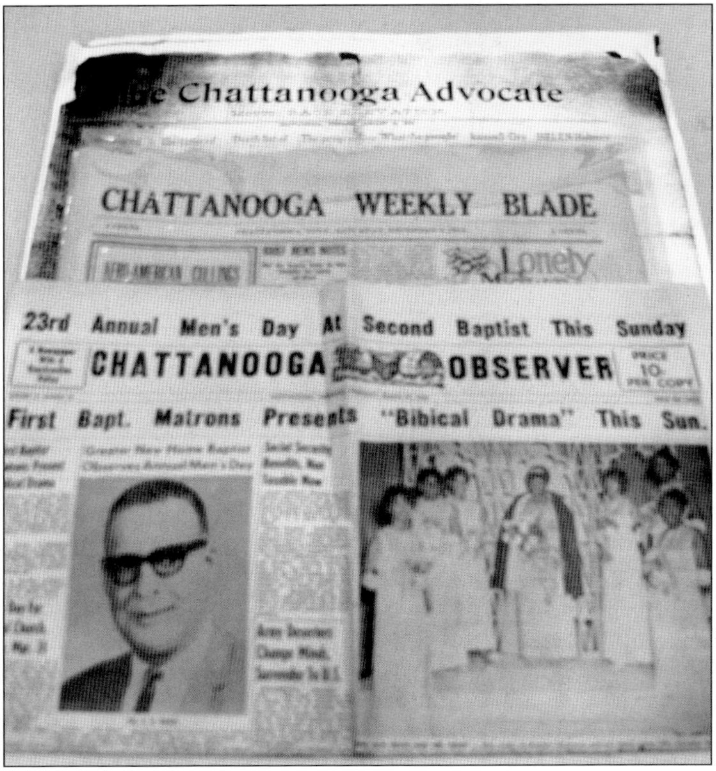

Local African American newspapers serve the community by keeping blacks informed. Some of the earlier papers were the *Chattanooga Observer*, *Chattanooga Weekly Blade*, and *The Chattanooga Advocate*.

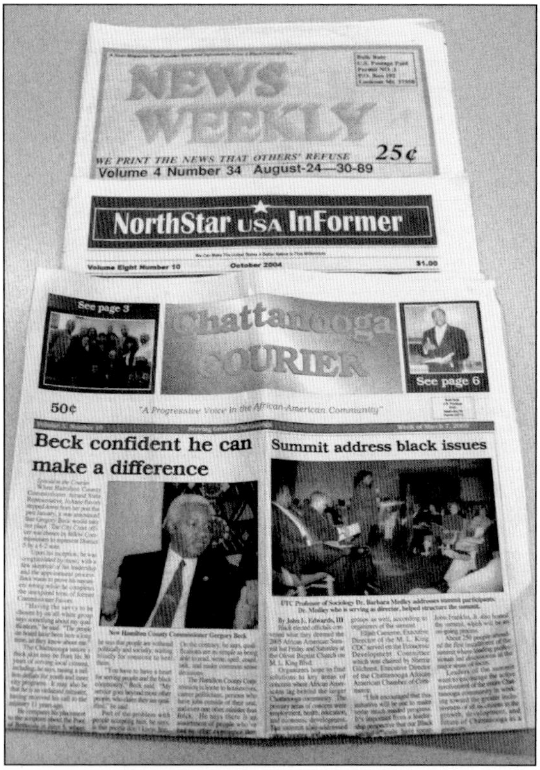

More recent black-owned and -operated papers are *The News Weekly* (no longer in circulation), *Northstar USA Informer*, and the *Chattanooga Courier*.

Members of the Chattanooga Police Department stop to pose for a picture after helping with the 1966 James A. Henry YMCA Branch membership drive. This YMCA branch was the site of many community dances and talent shows.

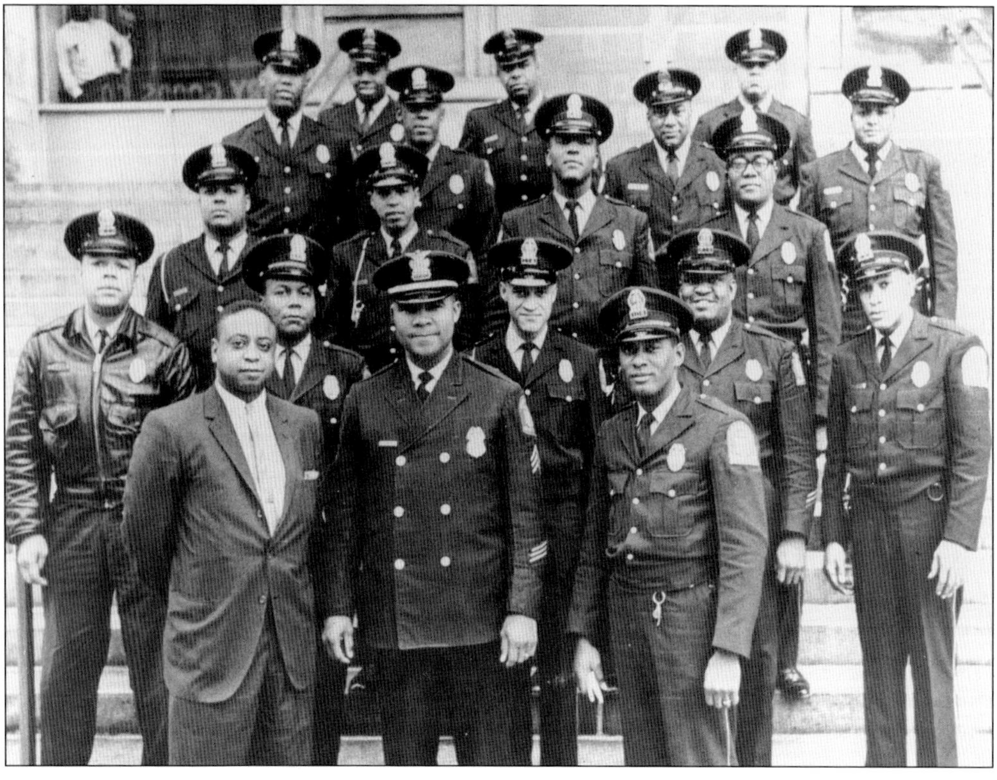

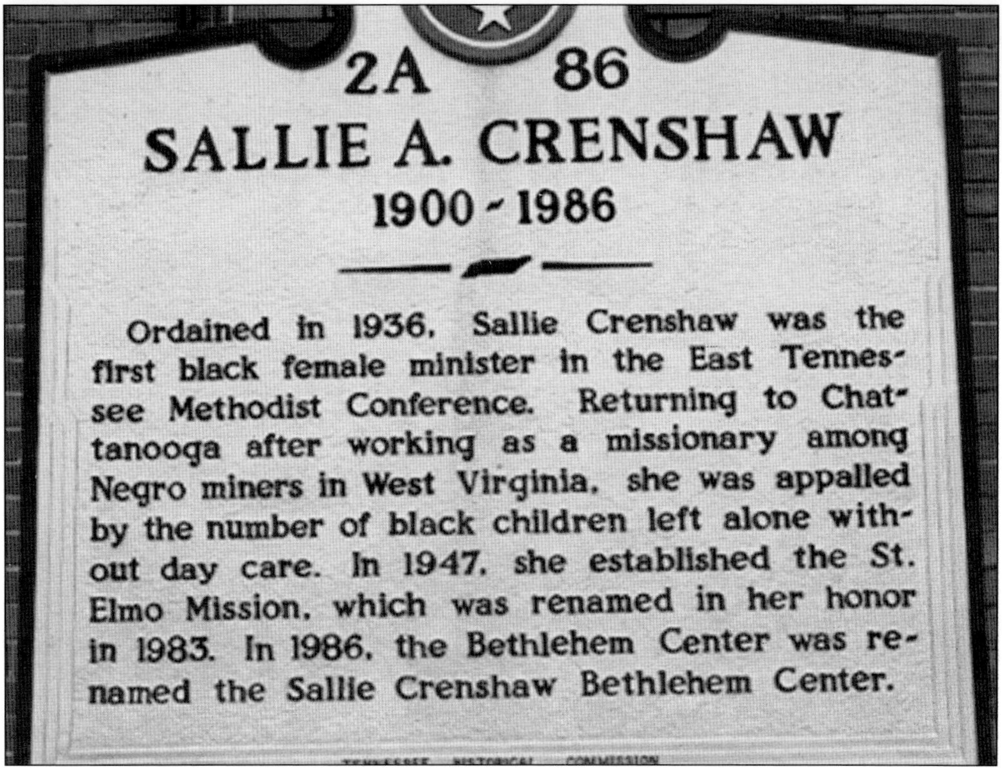

United Methodist minister Sallie Crenshaw was so appalled by the number of black children left without day care that she established the St. Elmo Mission in 1947. This historical marker is located on West Thirty-Eighth Street in her honor.

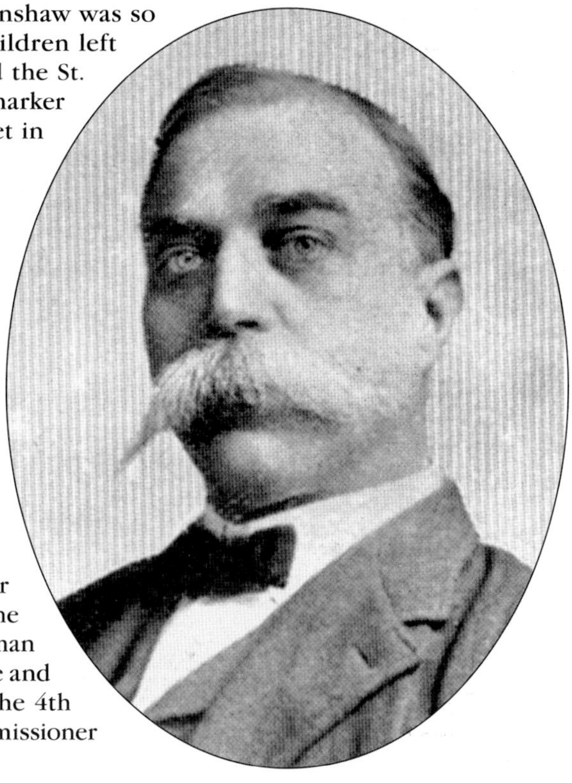

Hyram Tyree came to Chattanooga in 1867, secured employment on the Knoxville and Kentucky Railroad, and worked there for two years. After several years working as a night yardmaster then a general yardmaster, he retired after sustaining an injury on the job where he lost his leg. In 1898, he was elected chairman of the Republican Executive Committee and soon after was elected alderman of the 4th Ward. He also served as a school commissioner for 10 years.

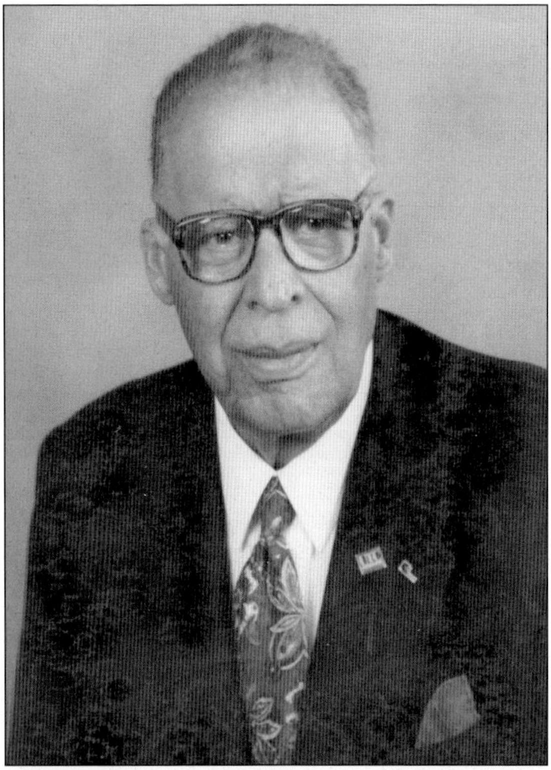

Dr. Claude C. Bond was an outstanding educator and the first African American assistant superintendent of Chattanooga City Schools, responsible for pupil personnel.

Mary Walker (standing) was born into slavery in 1848. In 1917, "Grandma" Walker moved to Chattanooga and, at the age of 117, learned to read and write. The Mary Walker Museum and Literacy Program have both been named in her honor.

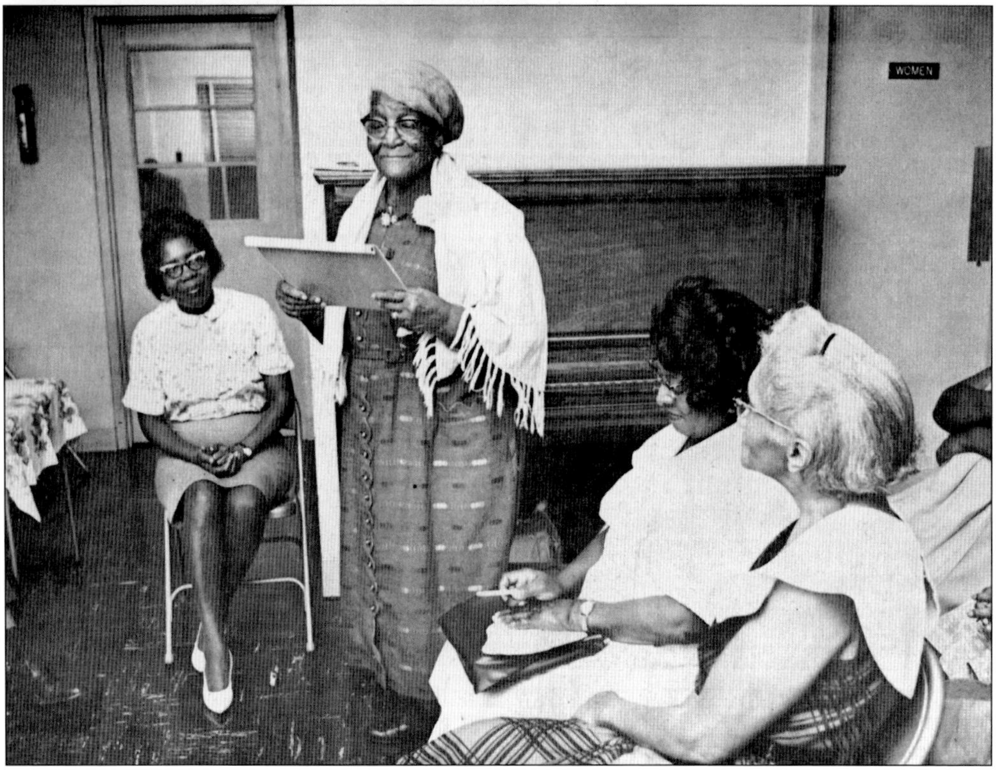

Benita Scruggs Owens is the first African American female lieutenant and the first African American female captain with the Chattanooga Fire Department, being promoted to captain on June 25, 2004.

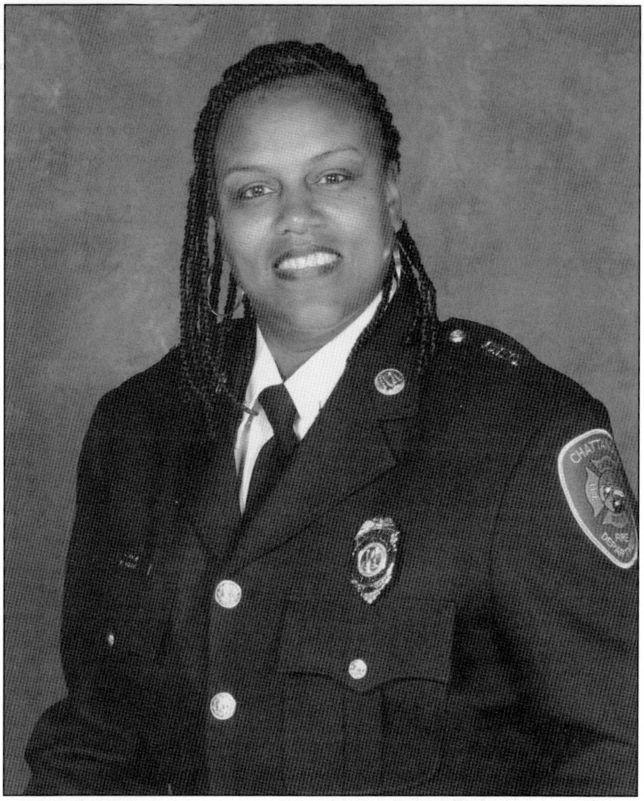

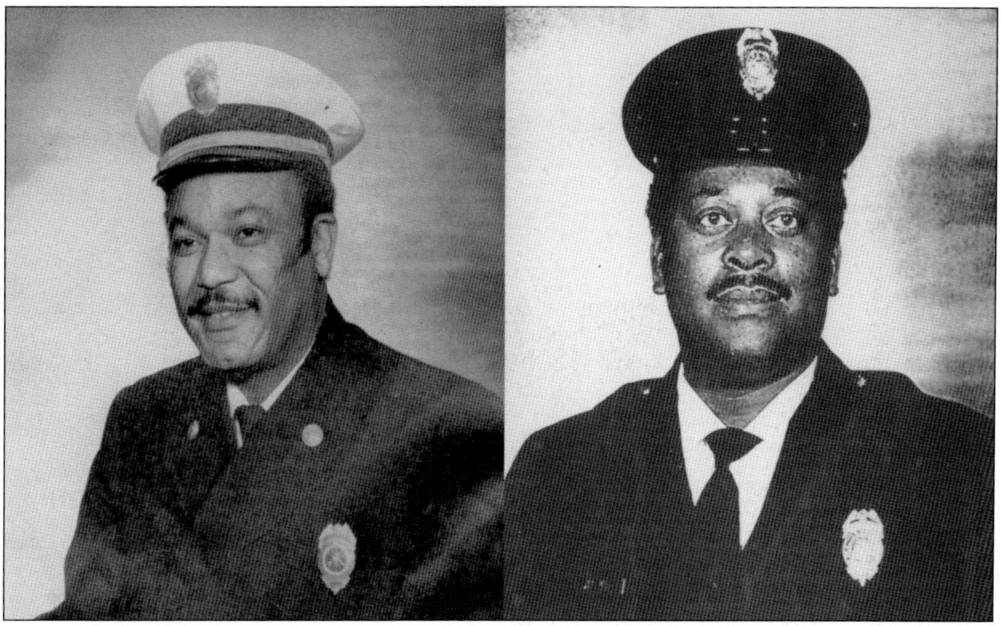

Jessie Sims and John Courtney were Chattanooga's first African American firefighters since Reconstruction. Sims and Courtney were hired within minutes of each other on August 16, 1964.

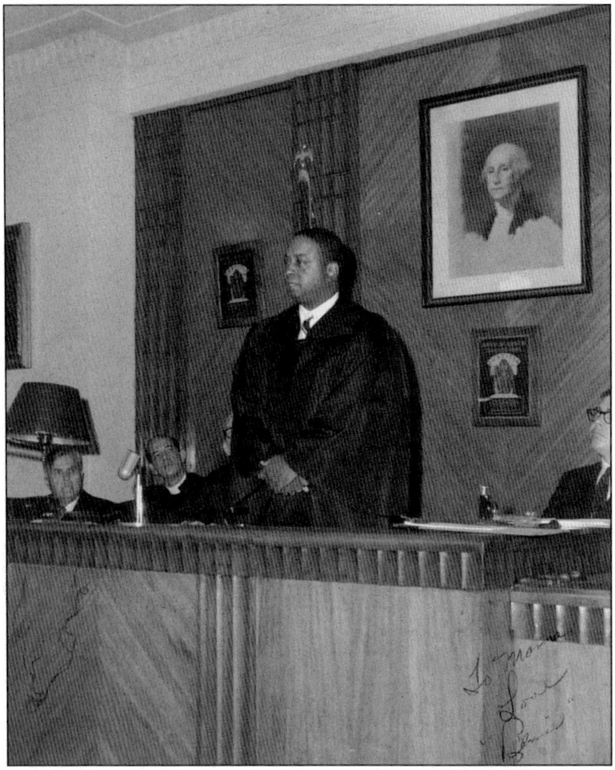

Bennie Harris served as the first African American judge after Reconstruction. He was sworn in as judge of the Second Division of the Municipal Court on July 1, 1969.

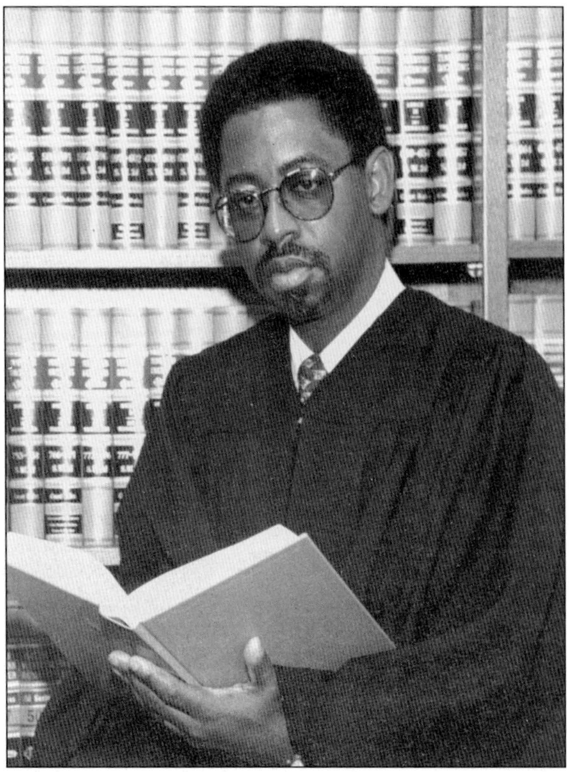

Retired judge Walter Williams now works in private practice. Williams is a graduate of Howard High School and Morehouse College and works with several organizations including 100 Black Men of Chattanooga and the alumni chapter of Alpha Phi Alpha Fraternity, Inc.

Napoleon "Donut" Williams was the first African American police officer to be promoted to detective in Chattanooga. Now retired, Williams is one of the key organizers of the Southside Family Reunion, he hosts a radio talk show on WNOO, and he heads security at Chattanooga State Community College.

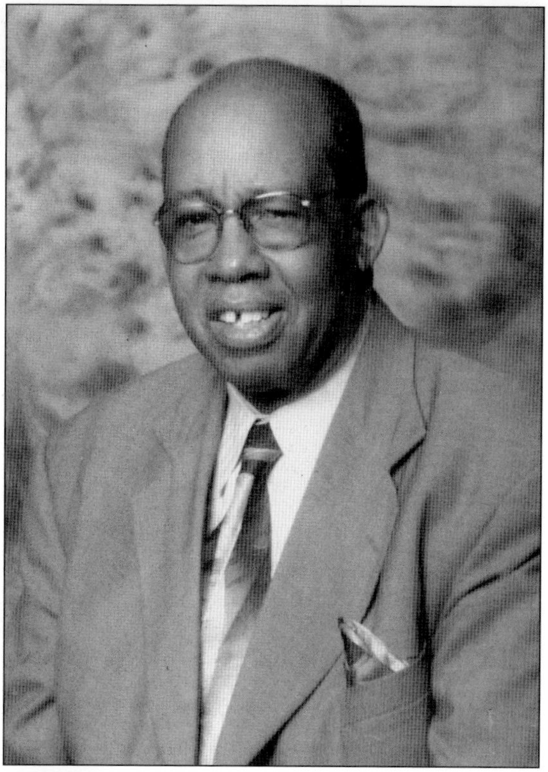

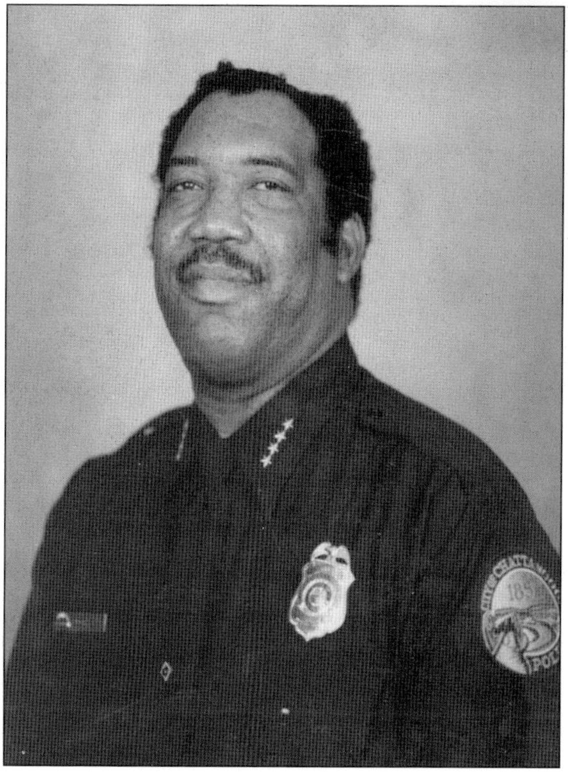

Ralph Henry Cothran joined the Chattanooga Police Department in 1964. In 1989, he was appointed chief of the Chattanooga Police Department, making him the first African American to hold that position.

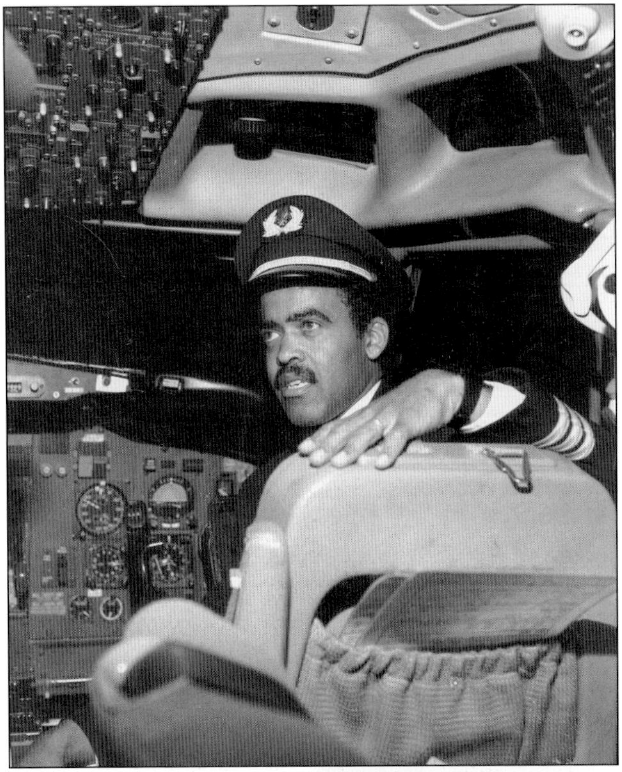

Rheubin Jones is the first African American commercial airline pilot with American Airlines. Mr. Jones started his career in the armed forces and still flies for commercial airlines.

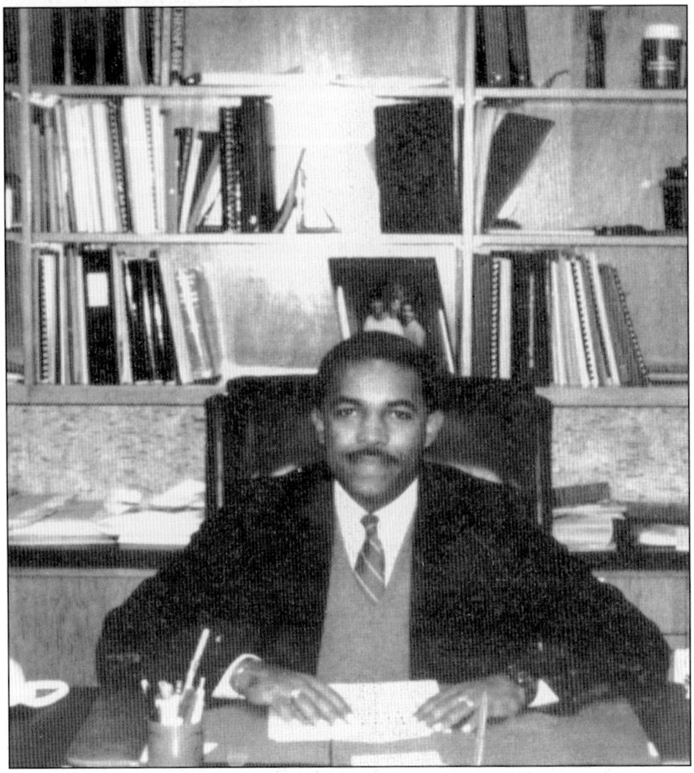

Howard W. Roddy Jr. became the first African American to head the Chattanooga/ Hamilton County Health Department in 1987. Mr. Roddy is now an executive at Memorial Health Services.

Irvin Overton is the first African American to serve as executive vice president of Erlanger Medical Center. Mr. Overton now serves as a consultant and is also a community activist.

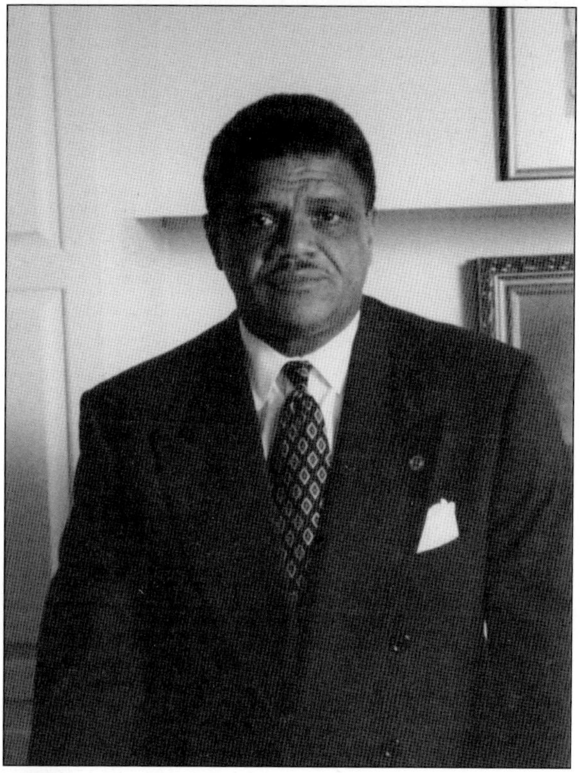

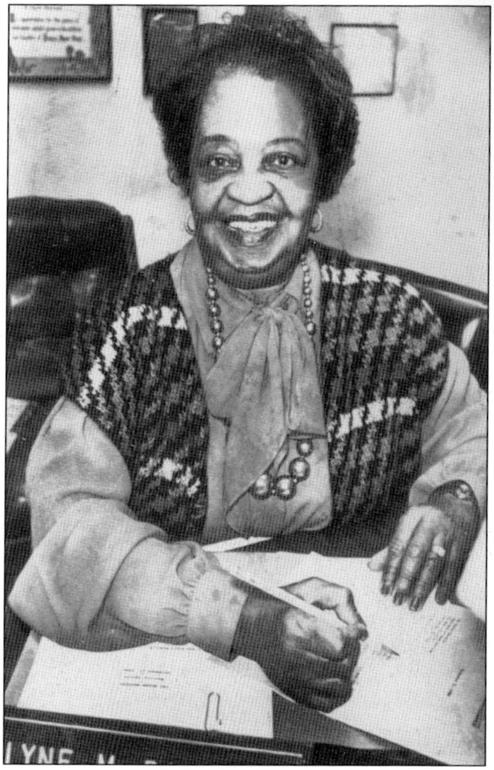

Civic and social activist Evelyne Barnett is the first African American to head the Chattanooga Department of Human Services.

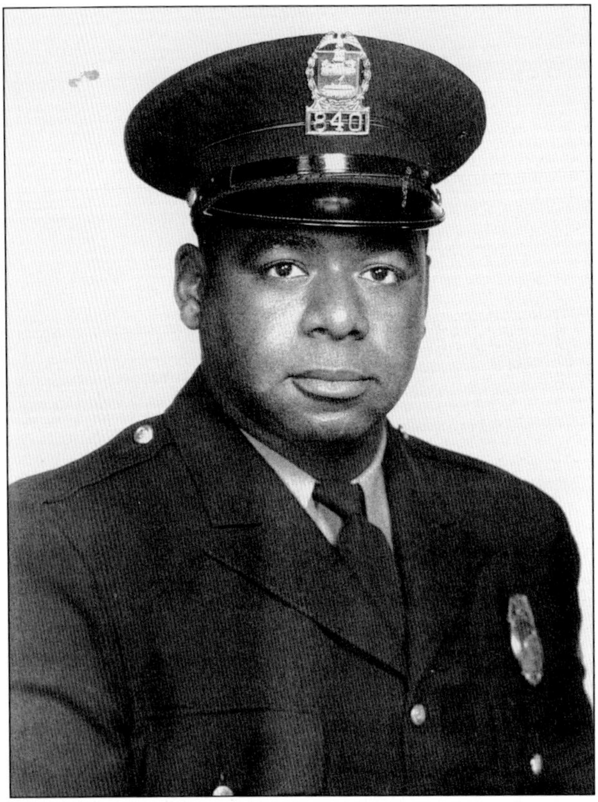

Randy Stargin started his career in the Chattanooga Police Department in 1955. Known as a local "Santa," Stargin would take his own money—usually award money from being named Policeman of the Month—to buy shoes and haircuts for local needy children. Stargin retired from the police department in 1981.

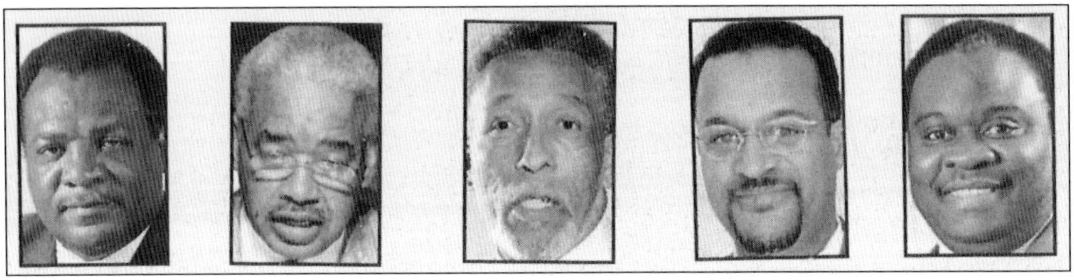

Chattanooga City and Hamilton County commissioners William Cotton Jr., Greg Beck, Leamon Pierce, John Franklin Jr., and Yusuf A. Hakeem are pictured here from left to right. All of these commissioners are still serving the community.

Eight

EDUCATION

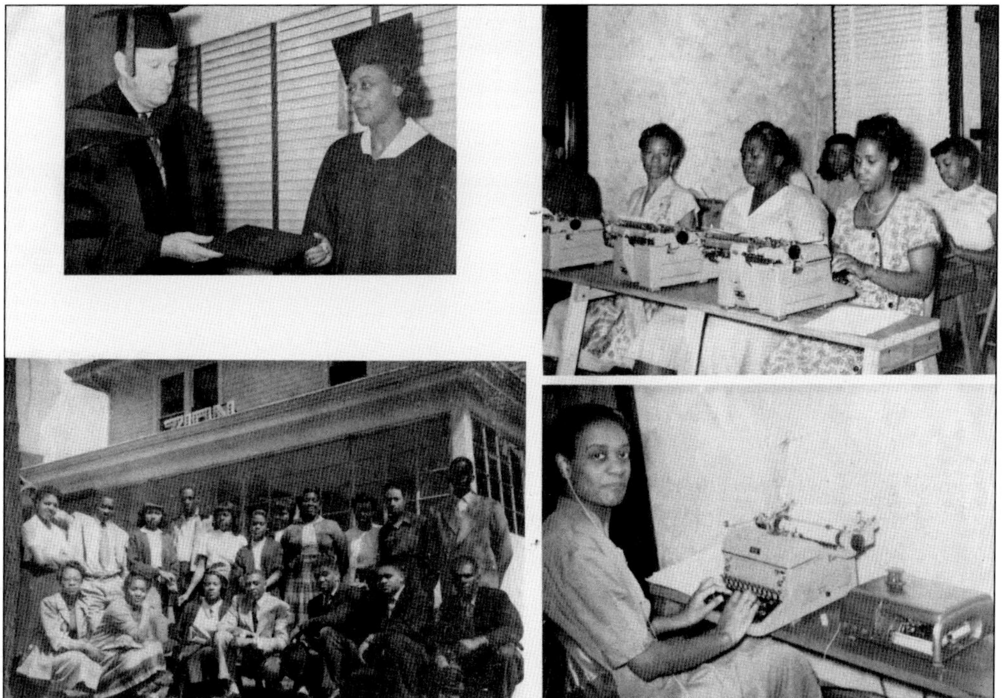

Largely due to the vision of Dr. Lee Robinson, Zion College was established in 1949. The first African American president of the college was Horace Traylor, who was appointed in 1949.

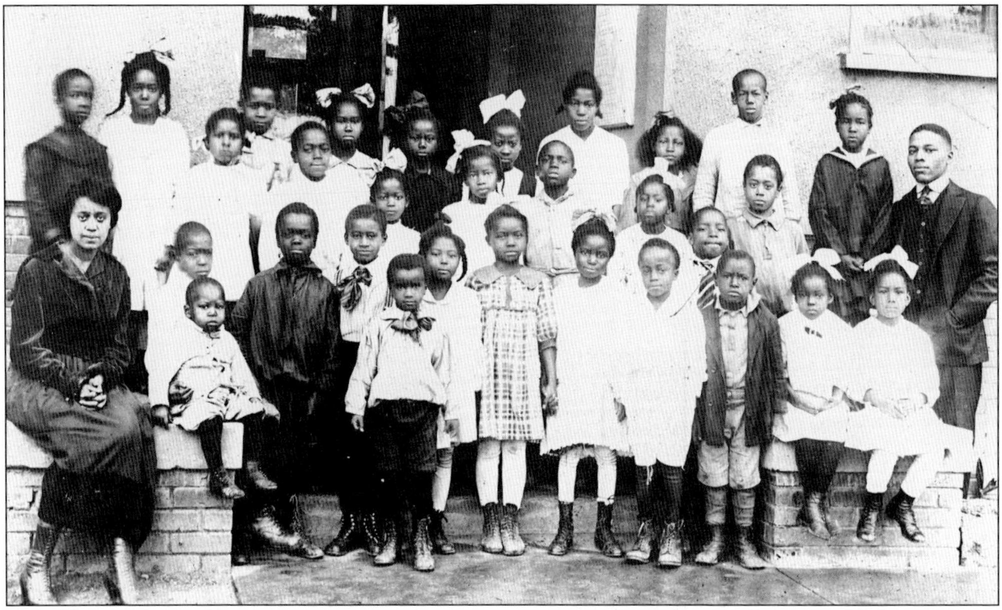

East Fifth Street School, established in 1904, served pupils in grades one through nine. Enrollment declined after integration, and the school needed repairs beyond its budget. The remaining students were sent to other surrounding schools, the school closed, and the property was donated to the University of Tennessee at Chattanooga.

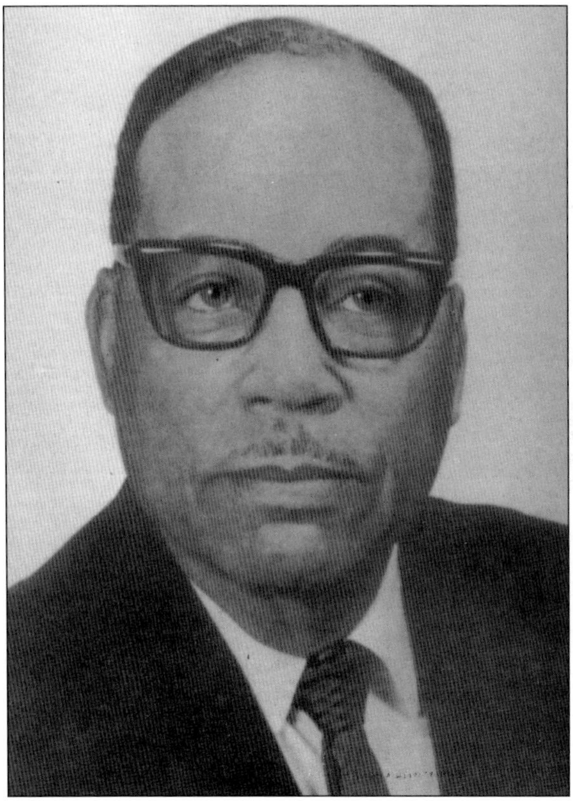

Theodore B. Kennedy was the first African American elected justice of the peace for Hamilton County, and he was an educator in the Chattanooga Public School System. He also served as a coach at the junior high school

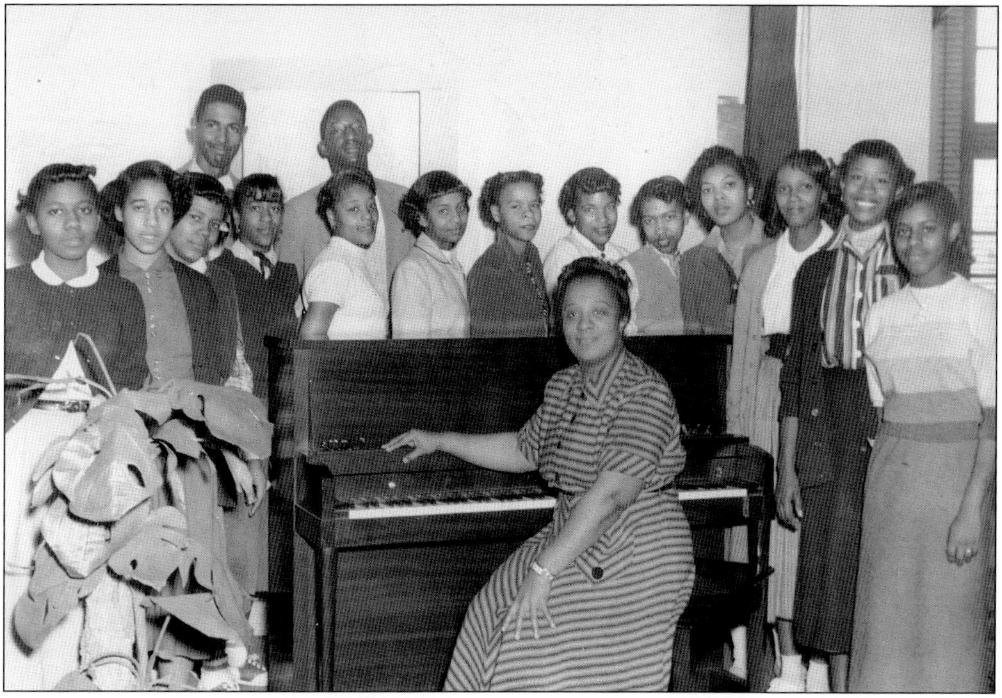

Edmonia Simmons was the music director at Howard High School for over 30 years. Some of her most noted students include Roland Carter, Russell Goode, and Joyce Mathis.

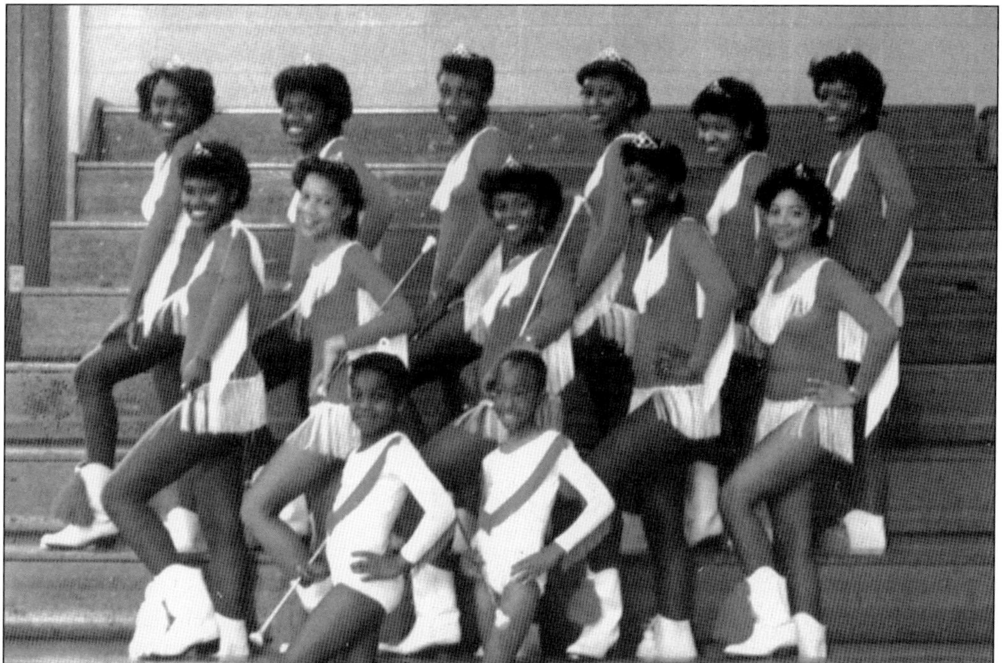

Alton Park Junior High School majorettes pose before a game. Alton Park Junior High School was established in the early 1950s and was later renamed John Franklin Middle School in honor of John P. Franklin.

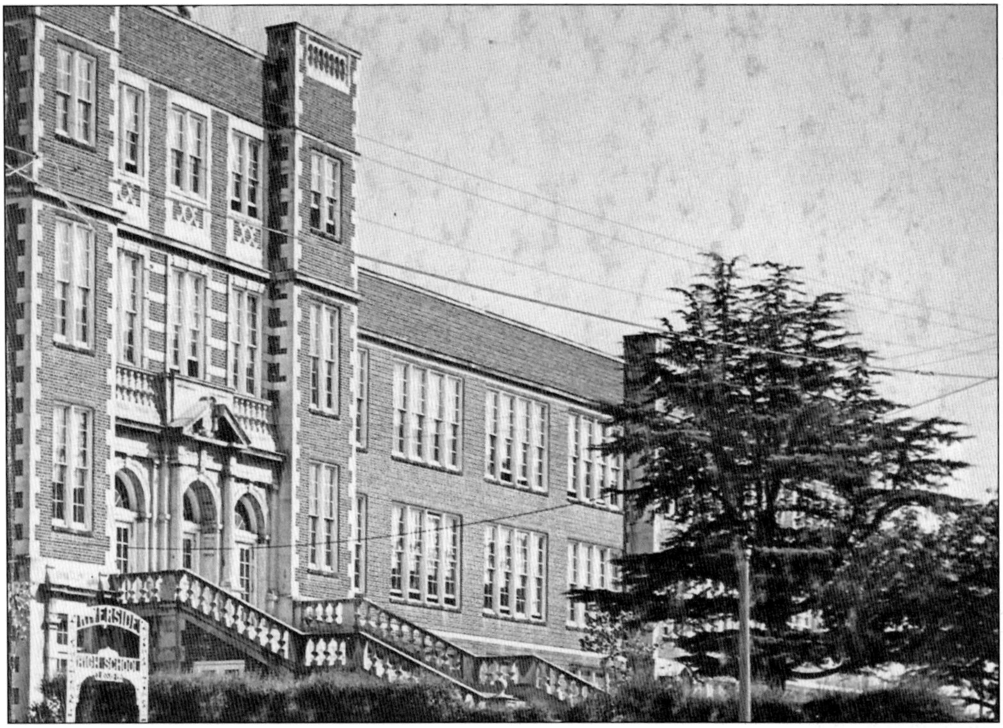

Due to the shifting of a large segment of the black population to the extreme eastern communities of Chattanooga, a hardship was placed on a large number of students who lived some distance from Howard, who had to travel by bus or walk across town to school because of segregation. Howard was overcrowded because it was the only school for African American students. Riverside High School was opened on August 31, 1963, to solve that crisis. It closed in June 1983.

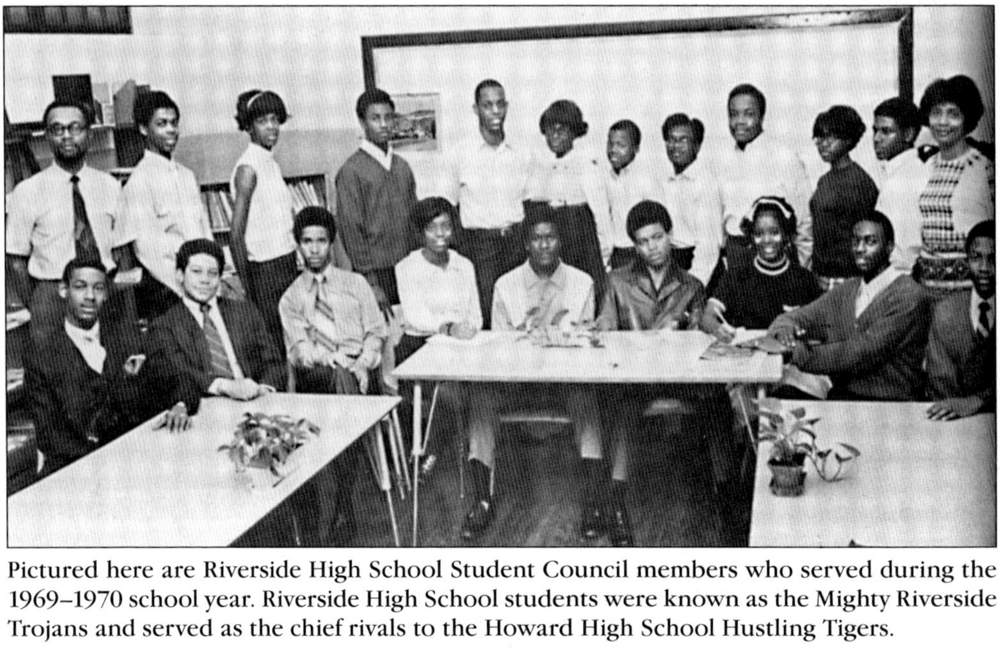

Pictured here are Riverside High School Student Council members who served during the 1969–1970 school year. Riverside High School students were known as the Mighty Riverside Trojans and served as the chief rivals to the Howard High School Hustling Tigers.

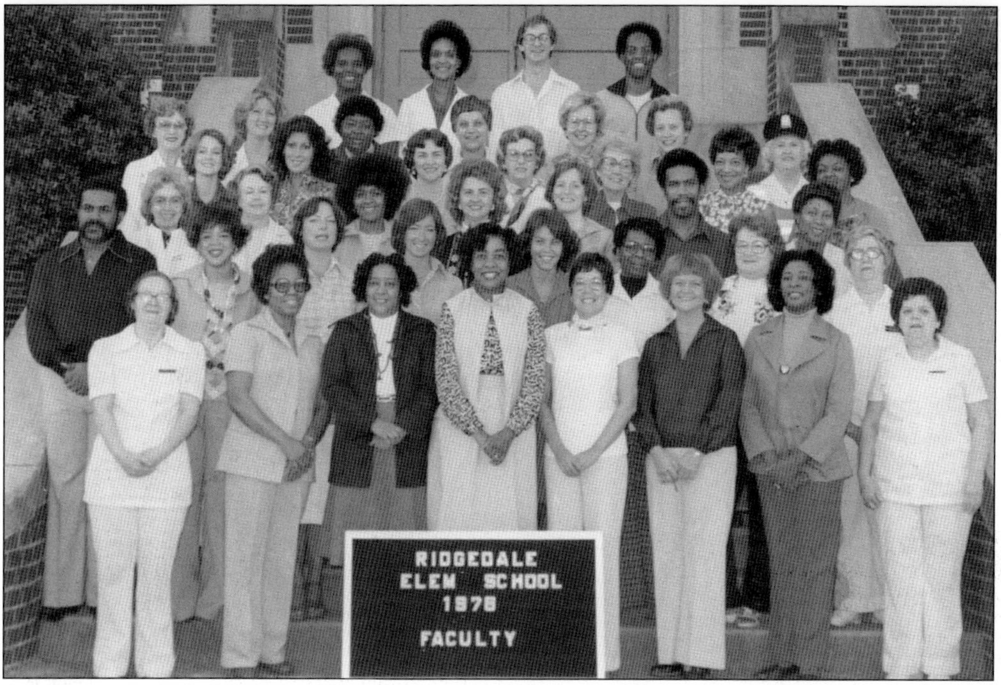

Janie Holder (front row center) was the first African American to principal an integrated school in the 1970s.

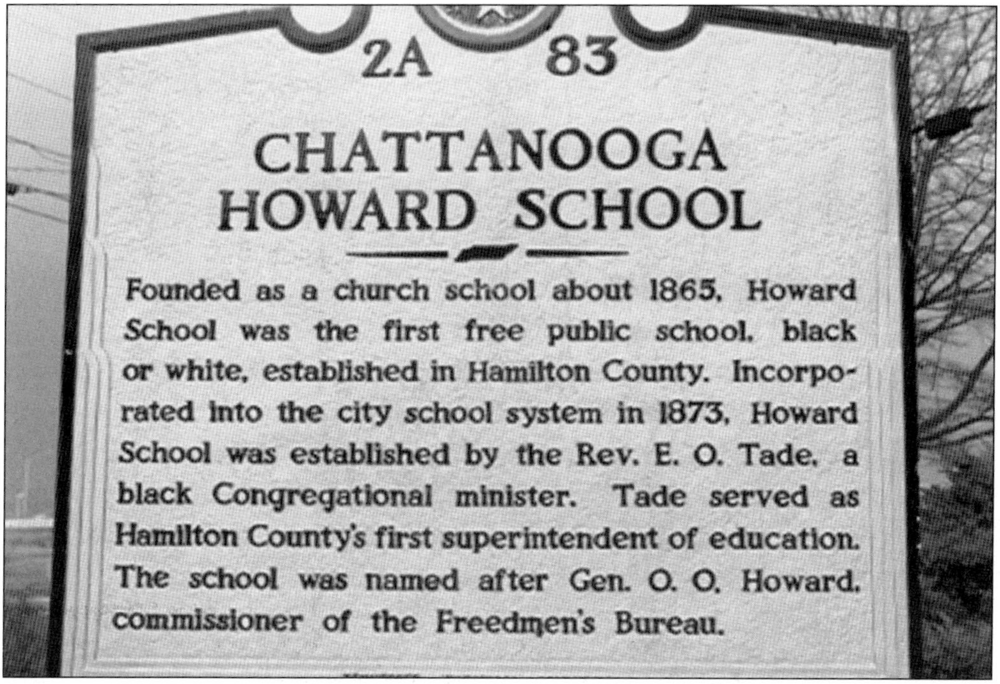

A historic marker acknowledges the historic location of Howard School. Rev. E. O. Tade, a Congregational minister, established Howard School, which was sponsored by the American Missionary Society, in 1865. Howard was the first free public school, black or white, established in Hamilton County.

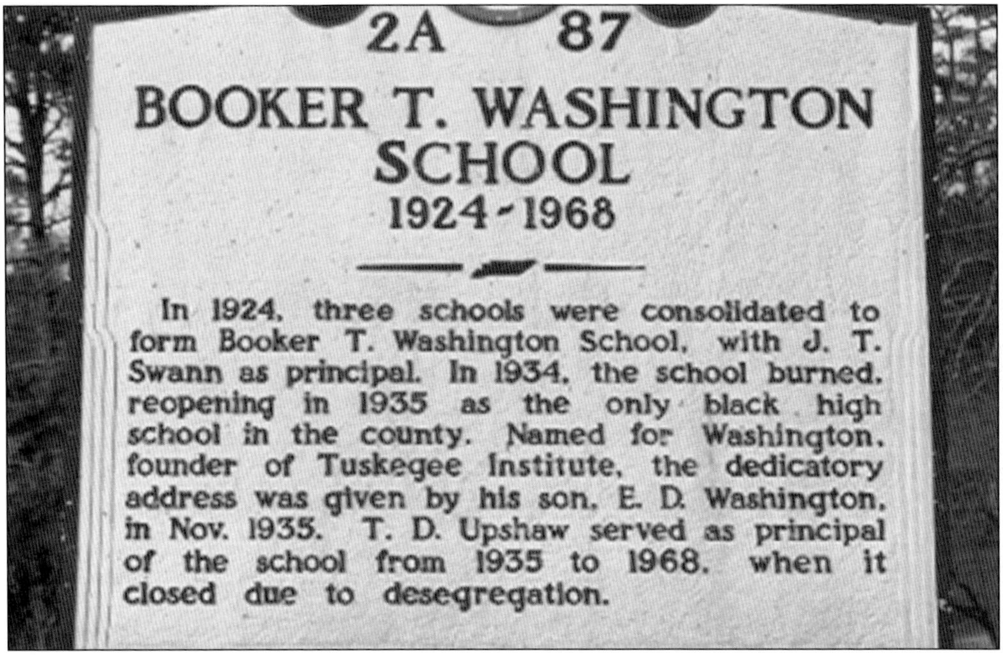

A historic marker acknowledges the historic location of Booker T. Washington School. The Booker T. Washington School was a consolidation of three schools in 1924 with J. T. Swann as principal. The school eventually closed because the U.S. Department of Health, Education, and Welfare ruled that the rate of integration in the communities was too slow and would be accelerated by the closing of the school.

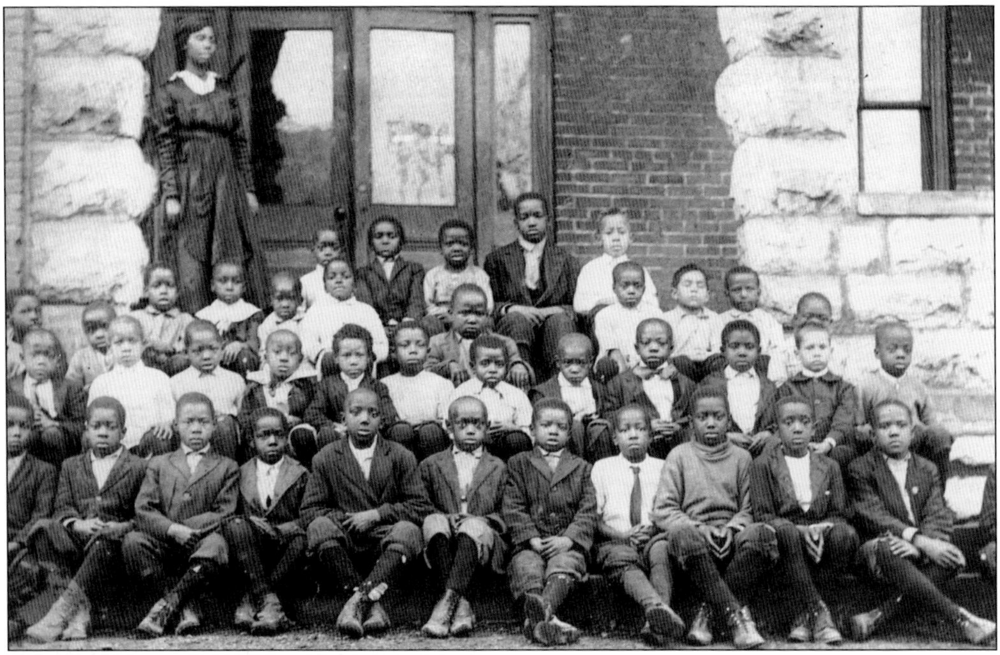

West Main Street School was a school that served the African American community for over 60 years, from 1900 to 1961. School reunions are still held annually to share fond memories of this school.

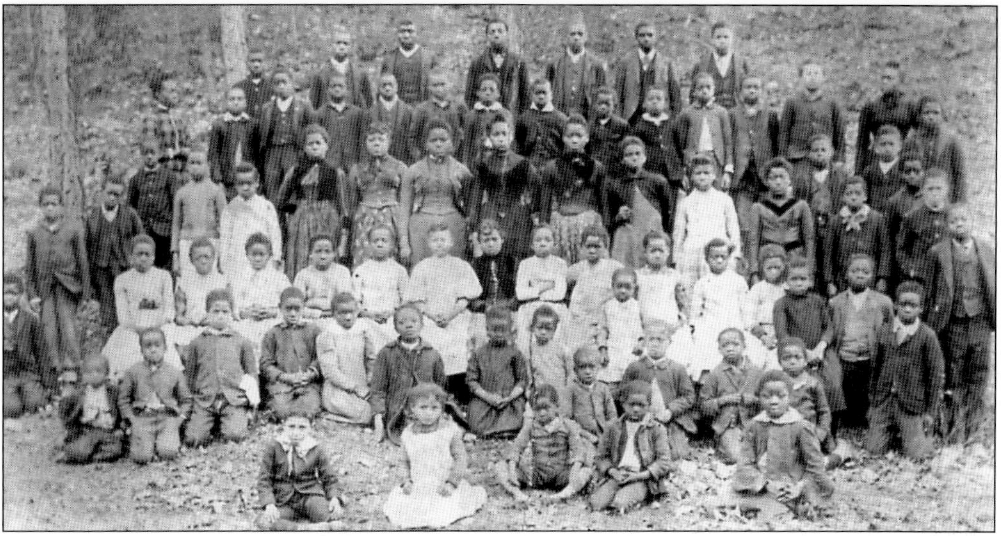

Hill City School was located in the historically African American community of Hill City (now North Chattanooga). The school opened in the early 19th century in a one-room schoolhouse. All grades were taught by two or three teachers.

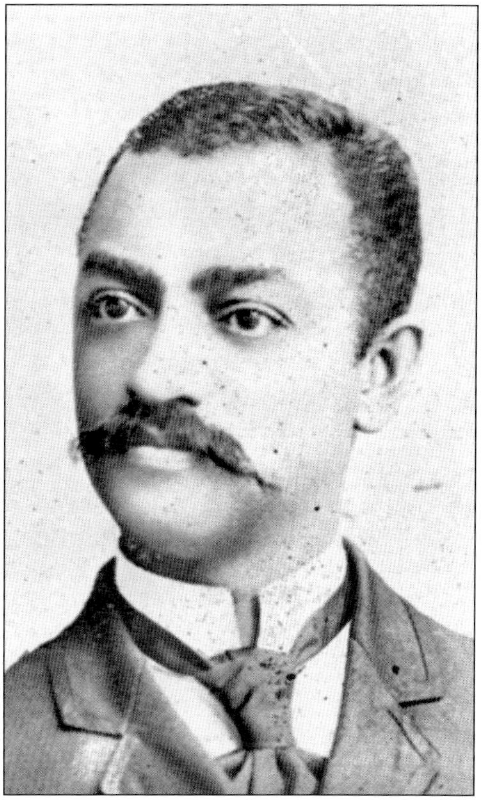

James A. Henry, an Atlanta University graduate, became the first black principal of Howard High School in 1884. He held that position until his death in 1914. Mr. Henry held memberships and offices in many civic and social organizations and traveled to lecture on improved methods for running a school. The Henry Branch of the YMCA is named in his honor.

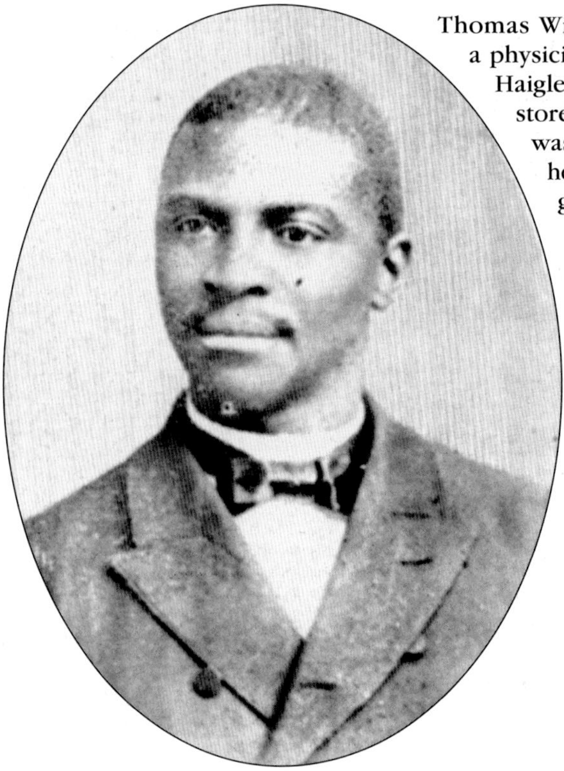

Thomas William Haigler first began practice as a physician and surgeon in 1878. In 1890, Dr. Haigler opened a drug store and operated the store until his death. His remedy for living was religion for the soul, education for the head, and money for the pocket—or grace, grit, and greenbacks.

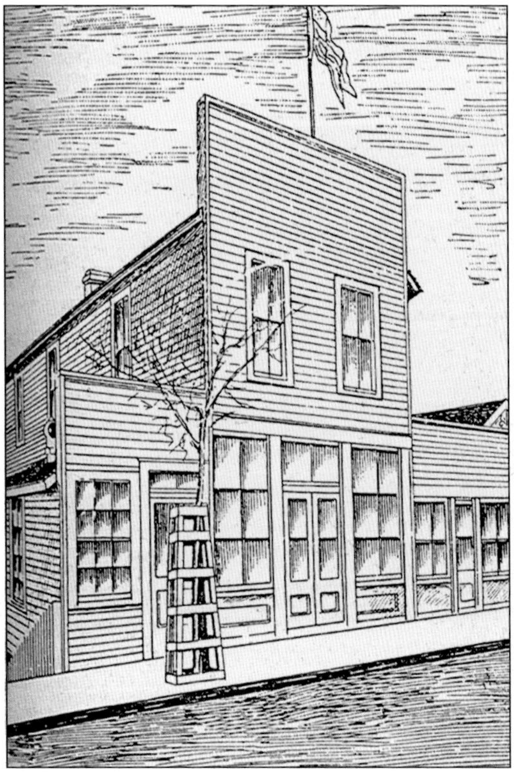

Dr. William Haigler organized the Chattanooga National Medical College on October 3, 1898, and chartered it June 1, 1899. Many doctors have gone forth from this college and succeeded admirably in their undertaking.